Escort Carriers and Aviation Support Ships of the US Navy

Escort Carriers
and Aviation Support Ships of the US Navy
Stefan Terzibaschitsch

The Rutledge Press
New York, New York

Original German edition,
Flugzeugträger der US Navy: Band 2: Geleitflugzeugträger
© 1979 Bernard & Graefe

First English language edition
© 1981 Conway Maritime Press Ltd

Published by The Rutledge Press, 112 Madison Avenue, New York, New York 10016

Distributed by W. H. Smith Publishers Inc., 112 Madison Avenue, New York, New York 10016

First Printing 1981.
Printed in the United Kingdom

Library of Congress Catalog No 81-40654
ISBN 0-8317-2979-1

Foreword

This volume should be considered as a direct continuation of *Aircraft Carriers of the US Navy*, which was published in Spring 1980. Although it is complete in itself, for reasons of conciseness we have not repeated much of the information that was presented in detail in the first volume.

The previous volume was devoted to Fleet Carriers ('. . . anything big and/or fast . . .'), a breed of ship which will remain a feature of the fleets of the major naval powers in the future, although perhaps in a different form. This volume, on the other hand, presents a complete, self-contained documentation of an historical epoch. Some readers expressed the wish to see the modern helicopter carriers (LHA and LPH) included in this volume, but we could not do this for the following reasons:
1) The extent of the material to be detailed, and the need to cover the aviation auxiliary ships in this volume, forced us to restrict ourselves to the ship types covered
2) Modern helicopter carriers are covered adequately in an overall study of modern American warships which is currently in preparation

This book is the first to provide extensive coverage of the escort carrier – a type of warship which played an important part in the naval operations of World War II, both in the Pacific and in the Atlantic. To this end all the known facts have been exhaustively researched. The remaining uncertainties – in particular the exact details of many camouflage measures and a few items of electronic equipment – will possibly be the subject of a special publication at a later date. There are at least three drawings accompanying each of the CVE classes, including the CVHA and AGMR conversions. Every one of the escort carriers completed is represented by at least one photograph; generally there are several, in which cases we have always attempted to select photographs from different periods of service. The 'Aviation Auxiliaries', which were so closely associated with the aircraft carriers and with naval aviation generally, are deliberately included in this volume, every class being represented by one or more photographs. The tables at the end of the book give construction details and the more important technical data concerning vessels described in the main text.

As with *Aircraft Carriers of the US Navy*, the *appearance* of the ships, their *equipment* and the *alterations* affecting the first two factors, are the focus of this book; design and construction can only be touched on.

All the drawings in this volume – reproduced to the standard scale of 1:1250 – were prepared by Herr Eberhard Kaiser, who has a profound understanding of US ships which transcends pure draftsmanship. This has made him an invaluable assistant to the author, and I wish to thank him for his help.

In obtaining the photographs for this book, new sources had to be tapped. The majority of the pictures are official US Navy photographs, from the author's collection, the Bibliothek für Zeitgeschichte (BfZ) in Stuttgart, the US Naval Institute in Annapolis, Maryland (including the former *Our Navy* collection), the 'International Naval Research Organization' (INRO) and the well-known American naval expert W A Davis. A small number of photographs were obtained from professional photographers, such as Real Photographs, Marius Bar, Anthony Pavia, Aldo Fraccaroli and Ted Stone. My special thanks go to: Mr Robert Heller from San Bruno, California, for providing some pictures from the late J A Casoly's collection; Mr Don McPherson, who provided some photos and information and whose untimely death in October 1978 was keenly felt; as always, the Chief of Naval Information, and the Military Sealift Command at the Navy Department in

Washington, for providing photographs; the Office of Naval Aviation History and Mr Jim Dresser from Ames, Iowa, for extra information regarding the aircraft groups employed; the Ingalls Yard in Pascagoula, Mississippi, which provided several photographs via its European press officer, Mr Dirk Koerber; also Herr Friedrich Villi from Maria Enzersdorf, who contributed photographs, and also Herr Gerhard Albrecht, Franz Mrva and Siegfried Breyer; Professor Dr Jürgen Rohwer for permission to use the photographs from the BfZ collection; CDR Erik B Mezger, USNR, for his critical view and professional help; and not least, the publishers who have promoted and supported the publication of this volume. Thanks to their efforts, this series of books will undoubtedly constitute the most extensive photographic documentation of American warship types that has ever existed.

The publishers and the author note with satisfaction and pleasure the success of the previous volume. The author has received many letters in this regard, for which he is grateful, and which he is trying to respond to as rapidly as possible. This correspondence has provided many positive suggestions, which will be accepted in so far as it is feasible.

Stefan Terzibaschitsch

Contents

Abbreviations

Ship Types

AC	Collier
AV	Seaplane Tender
AGMR	Major Communications Relay Ship
CC	Command Ship
CV	Aircraft Carrier
CVA	Attack Aircraft Carrier
CVAN/CVN	Attack Aircraft Carrier, nuclear powered
CVB	Large Aircraft Carrier
CVL	Small Aircraft Carrier
CVE	Escort Aircraft Carrier
CVS	ASW-Support Carrier
CVT	Training Aircraft Carrier
LHA	Multi-purpose Amphibious Assault Ship
LPH	Amphibious Assualt Ship
AVT	Auxiliary Aircraft Transport
IX	Unclassified Miscellaneous

Fleet Divisions

ASW Group	Anti-Submarine Warfare Group
CARDIV	Carrier Division
CARGRU	Carrier Group
CTF	Carrier Task Force
TF	Task Force
TG	Task Group
TU	Task Unit
HUK	Hunter/Killer Group

Carrier Squadrons

CVG/CAG/ CVBG/CVW/ CVLG/CVSG/ CVEG	Carrier Air Group/Wing (the various abbreviations apply to the relevant carrier category)
CVG(N)	Night Carrier Air Group
ATG	Air Task Group
Sqn	Squadron
VF	Fighting Sqn
VF(N)	Night Fighting Sqn
VB	Bombing Sqn
VS	Scouting Sqn
VS (later)	Air Anti-Submarine Sqn
VSB	Scouting/Bombing Sqn
VT	Torpedo Sqn
VT(later)	Training Sqn
VTB	Torpedo/Bombing Sqn
VC	Composite Sqn
VA	Attack Sqn
VAH	Heavy Attack Sqn
RVAH	Reconnaissance Attack Sqn
VAP	Heavy Photographic Sqn
VFP	Light Photographic Sqn
VAW	Carrier Early Warning Sqn
VAQ	Tactical Electronic Sqn
VQ	Fleet Air Reconnaissance Sqn
HS	Helicopter Anti-Submarine Sqn
HSL	Helicopter Sea Control Sqn
HU	Helicopter Utility Sqn
HC	Helicopter Combat Support Sqn
MAW	Marine Air Wing
MAG	Marine Air Group
VMF/VMFA	Marine Fighting Sqn
VMA	Marine Attack Sqn
VMA/AW	Marine All-Weather Attack Sqn
VMAQ	Marine Tactical Electronic Sqn
VMFP	Marine Light Photographic Sqn
VMCJ	Marine Composite Reconnaissance Sqn
VMC	Marine Composite Sqn
HMH	Marine Heavy Helicopter Sqn
HMM	Marine Medium Helicopter Sqn
HML	Marine Light Helicopter Sqn
HMA	Marine Attack Helicopter Sqn

Miscellaneous Abbreviations and Codes

BPDMS	Basic Point Defence Missile System
BU	Broken up

CHAFROC	Chaff Rocket	SCB	Ship Characteristic Board
CTOL	Conventional Take-off and Landing	SLEP	Service Life Extension Program
		SPN	Standard prefix for landing approach radar systems
COD	Carrier Onboard Delivery		
DCT	Depth-charge thrower	SPS	Standard prefix for search radar equipment (from about 1950)
DD	Drydock		
ESM	Electronic Support measures (passive countermeasures)	SPG	Standard prefix for missile fire control systems
ECM	Electronic Countermeasures (active)	SQS	Standard prefix for surface ship sonar systems
ECCM	Electronic Counter-Countermeasures	SRN	Standard prefix for satellite communications antennas
FRAM	Fleet Rehabilitation and Modernization Program	STOL	Short Take-off and Landing
		TACAN	Tactical Air Navigation Aid
IFF	Identification Friend or Foe	URN	Standard prefix for TACAN systems
Mk	Mark		
Mod	Model	USMC	United States Marine Corps
MSTS	Maritime Sea Transportation Service	USN	United States Navy
		USS	United States Ship
NRT	Naval Reserve Training Ship	USNS	United States Naval Ship
NTDS	Naval Tactical Data System	USAAF	United States Army Air Force
N Yd	Navy Yard	USAF	United States Air Force
SB	Shipbuilding or Shipbuilders	VTOL	Vertical Take-off and Landing

US Escort Carrier Names

The nomenclature is as colorful and many-sided as the history and service of the CVEs themselves. Basically, ships of the AVG/ACV/CVE categories were initially named after bays. Many of the ships retained these names to the end.

All the ships transferred to the Royal Navy were given their own British names before being transferred, and there were a few ships which were given British names without having had a US name previously. In one case, USS *Charger* (CVE-30), the ship received the name which it would have had if it had been transferred to the British. Many US ships were allotted names which were subsequently abandoned when they were transferred to the RN. Essentially however, all the ships up to and including CVE-119 were given the names of bays.

Beginning with the *Casablanca* class early in 1943, many CVE names were changed, and the new names were selected from important US naval and amphibious battles during World War II and earlier. These names included many islands and archipelagos as well as bays. Initially the CVEs were also named after great naval and aerial battles of World War II, but this was soon discontinued; the names *Midway* and *Coral Sea* were retained for large Fleet Carriers.

From CVE-120 onwards, bay names were no longer used. The eight units in the 1944 budget were immediately given names of battle sites. Only two of these ships – *Mindoro* and *Palau* – carried these names until their decommissioning in the mid-1950s. The helicopter carriers (LPH) introduced later continued this tradition of naming, and *Tripoli*, *Guadalcanal* and *Okinawa* (among others) can be found today.

The four ships of the *Sangamon* class are an exception, in that they retained the river names they had had as Navy oilers when converted to CVEs. The main section of this book (which follows) details the individual names which each ship carried.

US Escort Carriers

Classification and Codes

There were a large number of changes in the classification of American escort aircraft carriers during their wide variety of service. The code AVG = Aircraft Escort Vessel, was introduced on 31 March 1941, and the initial A indicates that this was a category of auxiliary ship. As early as 20 August 1942 this was changed to ACV = Auxiliary Aircraft Carrier. The next reclassification, to CVE = Escort Aircraft Carrier, took effect on 15 July 1943, and bestowed the status of warship ('Combatant Ships') on this category of vessel. Up to hull number 55 these ships were ordered as AVG, and from hull number 56 as ACV, as can be gleaned from the titles to the individual ships' service careers. Usually the title also includes the code with which the ship was laid down. As far as is known, only a small number of escort carriers actually operated under the code AVG. Further reclassifications of individual ships are shown in the tables at the end of the book. After the end of World War II the CVEs came under various commands. During the War six CVEs were lost, and there were others which were so worn out from constant service and damage that they were retired and scrapped soon after the War. A few more were converted into merchant ships. Seven ships, all of them belonging to the CVE-105 class, remained in active service after the War, and another seven were reactivated after a short period in reserve, thereafter serving for several years until being withdrawn from service again. Eleven more CVEs were reactivated in turn from around 1950 to 1965, for transportation tasks, carrying a civilian MSTS crew. The remainder were withdrawn from service between 1946 and 1948, and 'mothballed'.

In the 1950s, when advanced jet aircraft technology more or less precluded the operation of aircraft from a CVE, and when the helicopter had become an important factor in ship-based aviation, it became clear that the CVEs would best be able to serve as aircraft transports or as helicopter platforms if they were activated. Hence from 12 May 1955, a few CVEs were reclassified as CVUs = Utility Aircraft Carriers, or CVHE = Escort Helicopter Carriers. The code CVHA = Assault Helicopter Aircraft Carrier, was introduced on 17 December 1954 for the future category of helicopter carriers. Only one ship, *Thetis Bay*, carried this code, and it was changed again to LPH = Amphibious Assault Ship, on 27 October 1955. The initial letter L (for 'landing') indicates that these ships were intended specifically to be part of the amphibious assault forces. The converted *Gilbert Islands* was a special case, being reclassified as AGMR-1. Finally 36 former CVUs and CVHEs were reclassified as AKVs on 7 May 1959 (see under 'Aviation Support Ships'). The last active ships and the remaining 'mothballed' units of the former CVE category were stricken, and all these codes are now finally extinct, with the exception of the LPH.

Weapons

The escort carriers' armament was, understandably, much weaker than that of CVs, which were much larger, and were priority targets in combat. However, CVEs carried the same 5in, 40mm and 20mm guns, although in much smaller numbers. The use of the 5in/51 and the 3in/50 gun on USS *Charger* (CVE-30) was exceptional. Almost every class had one or two 5in/38 guns on board. These were, without exception, in open mounts, located on the fantail. The *Bogue*, *Sangamon* and *Commencement Bay* classes also carried quadruple 40mm, while the *Casablanca* class only had twin mounts, more of which were added in the course of the War. The 20mm AA gun was part of the fixed equipment of all CVEs in the War, while no CVE ever carried the 1.1.in AA machine gun, which had been superseded by the time escort carriers were beginning to appear. USS *Gilbert Islands* (CVE-107) was the sole former CVE to be fitted with four twin mounts of the 3in/50 caliber after being reclassified as AGMR-1 (USS *Annapolis*).

Radar

During World War II radar was the principal form of electronic equipment installed on escort carriers. Each ship usually carried only three antennas because of the ships' small size and displacement:

1) one navigation and surface search radar antenna
2) One longer range air search radar antenna
3) One aircraft navigational antenna — the 'homing beacon'

The inventory of antennas on the CVE is a reflection of wartime radar development. In this connection, the reader is referred to the relevant section in *Aircraft Carriers of the US Navy* (page 17), which enumerates the individual radar systems.

Nearly all escort carriers carried the YE aircraft homing beacon antenna, usually at the highest point of the mast. This was replaced by TACAN in the 1950s on those CVEs which remained in service after World War II. The SG surface search radar antenna is also found on virtually every escort carrier. The only differences in equipment occur in the longer range air search radar antennas. On early CVEs the almost square SC antenna can still be seen, and a few ships featured the rectangular SC-2 antenna, which was introduced in large numbers on the Fleet Carriers as a counterpart to the SK. The majority of the *Bogue* and *Casablanca* classes were fitted with the large, square SK search radar antenna. We have not been able to establish that these ships were converted to SK-2; in fact, some ships such as USS *Windham Bay* (CVE-92) and USS *Cape Esperance* (CVE-88), carried their SK antenna right into the 1950s, by which time they no longer had Navy crews, but civilian personnel of the MSTS. From CVE-98, the systematic fitting of the circular SK-2 antenna began. This continued in sequence on the ships of the *Commencement Bay* class. Ships of this last CVE class were also fitted with the supplemental SG-6 radar antenna from 1946 on; this was later designated the SPS-4.

The CVEs reactivated in the 1960s which had an MSTS crew relinquished their SK antennas and usually only carried an oblong Decca navigation antenna. The new CVEs, on the other hand, were fitted with SPS-6, and some SP after the War. A slightly larger parabolic antenna, which can be seen on USS *Saipan* (CVE-48) and — after the War — on USS *Bairoko* (CVE-115), has never been named. It was only fitted to a small number of ships. In the early 1950s a few barely perceptible ECM antennas can be made out on the CVEs still active at that time. The photographs at this period show that there were numerous other sensors, whose designations and abbreviations in many cases give clues to their use. Identification of the electronic equipment is complicated by the fact that many of the units pictured here were still not covered by the uniform system of abbreviation introduced jointly by the Navy and the Army. This system is still in use at present, and the table below gives the relevant abbreviations for naval usage. The correct designation of the devices covered by this system should always begin with the prefix AN-(Army/Navy), which indicates that the unit belongs to the standard series. In practice, however, only the three letters behind the oblique stroke are quoted, and these combinations are used with a sequence of numbers to designate the series of devices which often followed, for example:

AN/SPS	for search radar systems
SPN	for landing approach radar systems
SPG, SPQ, SPW	for fire control systems for guns and missiles
SRN, WSC	for satellite reception systems
SQS	for sonar systems
SQA	for VDS system components, which are used in conjunction with other sonar systems
BQQ, BQS	for submarine sonar systems
SLQ, WLR	for ECM and ECCM systems
UPX	for IFF systems
URN	for TACAN systems
SPY	combined radar and fire control systems

Right: The narrow island of USS *Copahee* (AKV-12), photographed in August 1942, showing the open bridge, one searchlight in front of it, and the short lattice mast, which carries the sparce electronics of the early CVE period: SG radar on the forward mast platform, the SC antenna higher up behind it, and the aircraft homing beacon YE on the masthead.
USN (BfZ collection)

Bottom right: USS *Windham Bay* (CVE-92) was under the control of the MSTS when this picture of the island was taken on 25 January 1954. The electronic equipment shows similarity to that of USS *Cape Esperance*. Note the slightly different shape of the SG-1b antenna, compared with the SG.
USN (BfZ collection)

Below: Five years after being reactivated for the MSTS: USS *Cape Esperance* (CVE-88) with her white code number on the side of the island; this was not used on later MSTS ships. The short lattice mast features the radar antenna SK from World War II, here without its IFF supplement BT-5, in addition to smaller, more recent units. The approach control antenna SPN-5 has replaced YE on the masthead. The picture was taken on 15 October 1954 in San Francisco Navy Yard.
USN (BfZ collection).

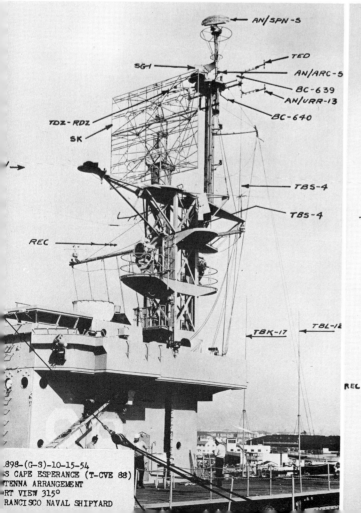

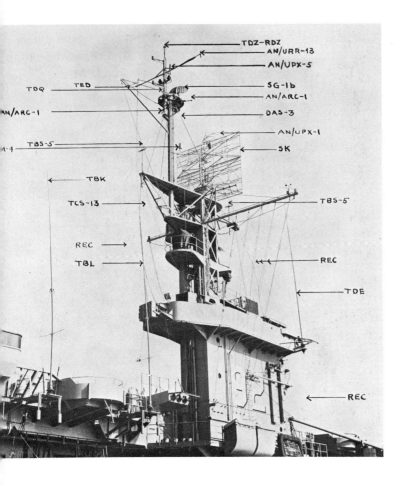

The starboard side of USS *Windham Bay*'s island, showing
the code number with shadow effect, in contrast to that on
the other side. On the far left of the picture is a stack.
(USN BfZ collection)

Fire Control

At no time did escort carriers mount fire control
directors as large as the Mk 37. Even the 5in guns
were optically trained – in all probability by Mk
51 directors in most cases, as were the 40mm AA
guns. No official information is available on the use
of particular types of director on CVEs and only
the study of photographs provides evidence of the
use of radar-aided directors (types Mk 51 Mod 3,
Mk 57 or Mk 63). It is certain, however, that the
20mm AA guns were equipped with the usual opti-
cal Mk 14 devices.

Designations of Electronics

The abbreviation AN before the oblique stroke is
uniform for all equipment of this series. The three
letters following the oblique stroke have the
following meaning:

First Letter: Location

A	Airborne
B	Underwater mobile, submarine
D	Pilotless carrier
F	Fixed
G	Ground, general ground use
K	Amphibious
M	Ground, mobile
P	Pack, portable
S	Water surface craft
T	Ground, transportable
U	General utility
V	Vehicular, ground
W	Waterborne, underwater

Second Letter: Type

A	Invisible light, heat radiation
F	Photographic
G	Telegraph, teletype
K	Telematic
L	Countermeasures
M	Meteorological
N	Sound in air
P	Radar
Q	Sonar and underwater sound
R	Radio
S	Special types, magnetic or combination of types
T	Telephone (wire)
W	Armament

Third Letter: Purpose

A	Auxiliary assemblies
C	Communications
G	Fire Control
N	Navigational aids
Q	Fire Control
S	Detecting, range and bearing
W	Control
X	Identification and recognition
Y	Special

DAU

UHF bay #1
UHF bay #2

YE-3
DBF
UHF bay #5
APX
UHF Bay #7
TDQ #1
TDQ #3

AN/ARC-1 #2
UHF Boy #9
AN/ARC-1 #3
UHF Bay #10

AN/CPN-6
UHF Bay #3
TDQ #2
TDQ #4
UHF Bay #4
SG-1b
IDS #1
ABK (Removed)
Long wires
#8 #9 #10
& DBE

SP
BQ,BM

AN/ARC-1 #1
Long wire #4
long wire #5
long wire #6
long wire #7

AN/SPS-6b

ECM Cone #1
ECM Stub #1
ECM stub #2

UPX

TDE #1

PBM (High fre...
DBM (Low fre...

ECM Open waveguide

ECM Stub #...

Long wire #11
DBE
Long wire #10
Long wire #9
Long wire #8

On 26 October 1953, the service life of USS *Sicily* (CVE-118) approaches its end. The upper bridge is now completely enclosed, and the following radar antennas can be seen — from top to bottom — YE, SG-1b, SP and SPS-6b. In place of the lattice mast a conical tubular mast is fitted with a longer pole mast on top. As can be seen, some of the devices already feature the AN/– system of designation. At the time of this photograph the ECM antennas were still very small.

Coloring and Camouflage

For general information on color schemes and camouflage the reader is referred to the detailed account on Page 19 of *Aircraft Carriers of the US Navy*. That information applies equally to the camouflage designs and colors of escort carriers. During their period of service in World War II, a large number of CVEs were given camouflage designs as well as camouflage color measures. With a few exceptions, the camouflage measures corresponded to those of the Fleet Carriers, but there were, understandably, separate camouflage designs, as explained below.

Although virtually complete information is available on the camouflage measures and designs for Fleet Carriers, similar research on escort carriers has not yet been published, nor even completed. When this research is finished, the author intends to undertake an overall study of the camouflage of American aircraft carriers and battleships.

The present study of camouflage schemes used on the escort carriers is based on two sources:
1) The partial results of research into camouflage measures and the designs associated with them which have already been published
2) Evaluation of photographs

It must be realized that many escort carriers had two or more camouflage schemes during their periods of service. As far as the information is known, camouflage schemes are detailed in the notes on individual ships. Without anticipating the later, definitive results of research, we have tried to give an overall view of the present state of knowledge on this subject, bearing in mind the inadequacy and uncertainty which still prevails.

It is especially difficult to evaluate the photographs of single-color, dark camouflage schemes. As far as it is known, the CVEs carried such schemes in 1942-43, and then again around 1944-45, after a period in which the 'dazzle pattern' was preferred. There are no comprehensive official publications on this subject, and distinguishing the schemes from black and white photographs, which were taken under the widest possible variety of lighting conditions, is very difficult. In theory, the Sea Blue of Measure 11 might occur, but it seems that the Ocean Gray of Measure 14 and the Navy Blue of Measure 21 are the most common colors. Although one cannot be certain of this, it seems that Measure 14 was used principally in the early period of the War mentioned above, and Measure 21 towards the end. In the photographs, it is more

or less impossible to distinguish between these two schemes. Photographic research until now has established that at least 24 CVEs carried one of these schemes, many of them perhaps twice. Where it is known with *certainty* that *one* of these two schemes was used, this is mentioned in the notes on the individual ships.

There are fewer identification problems in respect of the two-color camouflage measures. There is the theoretical possibility that one or more ship(s) featured the later version of Measure 12 (without color patches) instead of Measure 22; however Measure 22 is the usual one here. Photographic research has shown that at least 11 ships carried a two-color camouflage scheme, although the real number is undoubtedly higher.

The partial results of research into multi-color camouflage measures has allowed us to establish the following facts:

Measure/Design	Number of Ships	Known Ships CVE-
17	1	29
32/9a	1	1
32/4a	5	9, 11, 13, 67, 69
32/2a	1	16
32/12a	3	55, 57, 87
32/15a	7	63, 73, 77, 79, 81, 83, 85
32/16a	4	91, 101, 105, 115
33/10a	5	65, 66, 76, 80, 84
33/18a	3	94, 96, 106
unknown	12	12, 20, 31, 58, 59, 60, 62, 72, 82, 93, 97, 102

This means that at least 30 ships were camouflaged with Measures 17, 32 or 33, ie with 'dazzle patterns'.

At one time USS *Santee* (CVE-29) is supposed to have carried Measure 17, the essential feature of which was that the patterns were identical to port and starboard. The four colors of this measure were probably Navy Blue, Light Gray, Haze Gray and Ocean Gray. *Santee* carried this camouflage scheme when commissioned in September 1942. Only about three more ships are said to have featured this measure. Photographic evaluation has shown that at least a further 12 escort carriers had a multi-color camouflage scheme at some time during the War. At present, however, we cannot attempt to identify these camouflage schemes.

In the course of the early post-war years, the CVEs remaining in service were given a Haze Gray scheme, the standard Peacetime Gray which is still carried today by most surface ships. This corresponded to Measure 13 of that time — in so far as the ships were painted completely in Haze Gray.

War Service, Damage and Total Losses

The war service of the escort carrier varied enormously. When it is considered that the type was originally conceived for transporting aircraft and for anti-submarine warfare in the Atlantic, it is astonishing how many other types of combat operations the large numbers of CVEs took part in. The service careers of the ships give ample evidence, backed up by the amount of damage and number of losses suffered in the course of the War. Of the first three classes USS *Charger* (CVE-30) took no part at all in hostilities, being employed as a training ship. USS *Long Island* (CVE-1) similarly played little part, as did USS *Copahee* (CVE-12), which carried out mainly ferry duties. Many other ships took part in combat operations and the four units of the *Sangamon* class saw particularly heavy action in the Atlantic and, later, in the Pacific.

The name ship of the *Casablanca* class functioned primarily as a training ship and transport, and it was the numerous succeeding vessels which bore the brunt of the War action. Five of the six ships written off as total losses were in this class,

and this class also suffered the most damage, although the figures are exaggerated because the class included more vessels than any other. Of the later ships of the *Casablanca* class, there were several which took no direct part in combat operations, their task being transportation.

Of the *Commencement Bay* class units which were delivered shortly before the end of the War, CVE-106, -107, -109 and -111 saw a small amount of active service in the Pacific. A few ships of this class (CVE-107, -108, -110, -112, -114, -115, -116, -118 and -119) were reactivated around 1950-51. Of these, CVE-114, -115, -116, -118 and -119 took part in combat operations off the Korean coast.

Six escort carriers were lost in the course of World War II as a result of enemy action, two of them in the legendary battle off Samar, in Leyte Gulf, on 25 October 1944, in which Task Unit 77.4.3 (codenamed 'Taffy 3') was subjected to heavy gunfire and aircraft attacks from superior Japanese surface forces. Six more of the total of 16 CVEs of Task Group 77.4 were damaged. Two total losses were attributed to submarine torpedoes, and the last two CVEs were lost to Kamikaze hits early in 1945. In the course of World War II the following escort carriers were lost:

Hull number	Name	Date	Location and cause of loss
CVE-21	Block Island	29 May 1944	Near the Canary Islands; submarine torpedo
CVE-56	Liscome Bay	24 November 1943	Near the Gilbert Islands; submarine torpedo
CVE-63	St Lo	25 October 1944	In the battle off Samar; Kamikaze
CVE-73	Gambier Bay	25 October 1944	In the battle off Samar; gunfire
CVE-79	Ommaney Bay	4 January 1945	Near the Philippines; Kamikaze
CVE-95	Bismarck Sea	21 February 1945	Near Iwo Jima; Kamikaze

The sole American escort carrier to be sunk by a German submarine in the Atlantic: USS *Block Island* (CVE-21). The camouflage is that of Measure 22. *USN official*

As far as is known, there was only one case of a CVE suffering damage in the Korean War which was not a result of enemy action. In contrast, a large number of CVEs were damaged during World War II, not through direct enemy action, but through collisions, operating accidents and typhoons, as can be seen from the following table:

Hull number	Name	Date	Cause of Damage
CVE-11	Card	2 May 1964	Mined at Saigon
CVE-18	Altamaha	18 December 1944	Typhoon
CVE-26	Sangamon	19 October 1944	Aircraft bombs
CVE-26	Sangamon	25 October 1944	Kamikaze
CVE-26	Sangamon	4 May 1945	Kamikaze
CVE-27	Suwannee	25 October 1945	Dive bombers
CVE-27	Suwannee	26 October 1945	Dive bombers
CVE-27	Suwannee	24 May 1945	Internal explosion
CVE-28	Chenango	9 April 1945	Crash of own aircraft
CVE-29	Santee	25 October 1944	Submarine and aircraft torpedoes
CVE-29	Santee	July 1945	Aircraft operating accident
CVE-61	Manila Bay	5 January 1945	Kamikaze
CVE-62	Natoma Bay	7 June 1945	Kamikaze
CVE-65	Wake Island	3 April 1945	Kamikaze
CVE-66	White Plains	25 October 1944	Kamikaze and gunfire
CVE-68	Kalinin Bay	25 October 1944	Kamikaze and gunfire
CVE-70	Fanshaw Bay	25 October 1944	Gunfire
CVE-71	Kitkun Bay	25 October 1944	Kamikaze
CVE-71	Kitkun Bay	8 January 1945	Kamikaze
CVE-74	Nehenta Bay	18 December 1944	Typhoon
CVE-74	Nehenta Bay	17 January 1945	Typhoon
CVE-75	Hoggatt Bay	15 January 1945	Internal explosion
CVE-76	Kadashan Bay	8 January 1945	Kamikaze
CVE-77	Marcus Island	18 December 1944	Typhoon
CVE-78	Savo Island	5 January 1945	Kamikaze
CVE-83	Sargent Bay	3 January 1945	Collision
CVE-85	Shipley Bay	16 May 1945	Collision
CVE-87	Steamer Bay	25 April 1945	Collision
CVE-87	Steamer Bay	16 June 1945	Aircraft accident
CVE-88	Cape Esperance	18 December 1944	Typhoon
CVE-92	Windham Bay	5 June 1945	Typhoon
CVE-94	Lunga Point	21 February 1945	Kamikaze
CVE-96	Salamaua	13 January 1945	Kamikaze
CVE-96	Salamaua	5 June 1945	Typhoon
CVE-98	Kwajalein	18 December 1944	Typhoon
CVE-100	Bougainville	5 June 1945	Typhoon
CVE-102	Attu	5 June 1945	Typhoon
CVE-115	Bairoko	9 May 1951	Explosion off Korea

Shipboard Aircraft and their Organization

The escort carriers were relatively small, light ships. Although the flight deck extended the entire length of the ship in most classes, they were still so short that only small, light aircraft could take off and land safely – provided there was an adequate headwind.

When USS *Long Island* (AVG-1) was first put into service, Scouting Squadron 201 still used the F2A Buffalo fighter, and the SOC Seagull light reconnaissance aircraft. The SOC was the last biplane made by the Curtiss company: it had a take-off weight of 2.5 tons, a speed of 165mph, and was also supplied in a float-equipped version. This was already obsolescent, and was very soon retired from CVEs but, in other roles, flew until the end of the War. The SBD Dauntless was tried initially on *Long Island*, but this aircraft was only employed on the four *Sangamon*s. The standard equipment of the CVEs during the War consisted of the FM-2 fighter, a version of the F4F Wildcat made by General Motors, and the Avenger torpedo aircraft in its TBF and TBM versions. The F6F Hellcat appeared occasionally later on, and not only on the *Sangamon* class. During the Korean War the F4U Corsair fighter was used, especially in the Marine Corps squadrons. In their capacity as aircraft transports, the carriers did, of course, carry every possible type of aircraft.

The ships' aircraft on the escort carriers were divided in two ways:
1) Those on ships of the *Sangamon* and *Commencement Bay* classes at 'Air Group' level for certain periods
2) Those on ships of the other classes at 'Squadron' level

The few air groups used on CVEs were named 'Escort Carrier Air Groups' (CVEG), and initially they were composed of one VGF and one VGS squadron. Nominally at least, there was a total of 22 CVEGs, although only CVEG-24, -25, -26, -27, -28, -33, -35, -36, -37, -40 and -60 logged extensive periods of service during World War II.

The subsequent standard arrangement of a CVEG comprised one VF squadron of 12 F6Fs, and one VC squadron of 9 SBDs and 10 TBFs/TBMs, giving a total of about 30 aircraft. Here too there were extreme variations, according to the task in hand, for example: one VF squadron of 22 F6Fs and one VT squadron of 9 TMFs/TBMs; or (especially early on) four squadrons, two VGFs and two VGSs, in which one of the VGS squadrons included F4F, and the other TBF/TBM aircraft. In mid-1945 there were also a few groups with the designation MCVEG, such as that on CVE-110, consisting of Marine Corps squadrons.

Normally, however, larger 'Composite Squadrons' were employed, abbreviated VC. Before these were introduced, a few VGF and VGS squadrons existed for a time, but they were all reclassified as VC squadrons by mid-1943. The nominal total of VC squadrons was 84, some of which saw service for only a short period, before being converted into some other sort of squadron, such as VG, VB, VT etc. The VF squadrons were specially tailored to suit the particular task in prospect, as far as circumstances made this possible. Usually they comprised 19 to 24 aircraft (on the *Bogue* class), of which 9 to 12 were fighters, and 12 to 15 torpedo aircraft. Here too the variations were great, for example 3 FM-2 and 16 TBF/TBM aircraft. Ships of the *Casablanca* class normally carried about 24 aircraft, but occasionally as many as 32, of which slightly more than half were fighters. VOC-1, a special squadron on CVE-65 had as many as 35 aircraft on board in early 1945, as did many other squadrons.

A summary of all the known CVEGs and VCs can be found in the tabular section at the end of the book, and the individual ships' notes include the CVEGs and VCs stationed on them. The reader is referred to the appropriate summary in the tabular section of *Aircraft Carriers of the US Navy* for the chief characteristics of the aircraft mentioned here.

Origins and Development of US Escort Carriers

'The story of the escort carriers is like a story with a surprise ending. When the United States began to build them, there was a definite purpose in view – fighting off submarines and escorting convoys. But as the War progressed, the small carrier demonstrated surprising versatility. It became a great deal more than its name implies. From a purely defensive measure, the escort carrier emerged as an offensive weapon.' – Fleet Admiral Chester W Nimitz, 1945

The efforts of the US Navy to expand its very young ship-borne aviation element, and to extend its sphere of influence, manifested themselves in three parallel lines of development:
1) The expansion of the carrier fleet within the limitations set by the fleet treaties
2) Attempts to develop new, smaller, types of ship which were also capable of carrying aircraft
3) The employment of light reconnaissance aircraft on cruisers and battleships

The development of the Fleet Aircraft Carrier was covered in a previous volume, and this account concentrates on the known projects and ideas aimed at obtaining smaller carriers. Two separate lines of thought emerged:
1) The 1920s and 1930s concept of 'flying deck cruisers', which never materialized
2) The idea of creating auxiliary aircraft carriers – and later escort aircraft carriers – by converting commercial ships; this idea originated in the late 1930s

The Flying Deck Cruiser

Right at the start of the aircraft carrier era – and long before the arrival of what became known as escort carriers – the US Navy considered the idea of developing 'light aircraft carriers'. In May 1927 a study was completed which compared the creation of 'light aircraft carriers' with, on the one hand, the experience with the CVs *Lexington* and *Saratoga*, which were over-large for their time, and with the development and use of the light cruisers of the day, of which ten units (the *Omaha* class) had just been completed. The intention was to build smaller, carrier-type ships, which were to be as fast as cruisers. Their tasks were outlined as follows:
1) Bombing attacks on 'capital ships' by aircraft
2) Support of Fleet operations
3) Anti-submarine warfare
4) Reconnaissance and ship identification
5) Attacking enemy land bases

At first sight, these tasks show barely any differences from the tasks of the aircraft which operated from Fleet Carriers. However, as will be established later, the 'light aircraft carriers' planned at that time were intended to be units of the reconnaissance forces, in respect of their limitations as well as their advantages, and therefore only some of their original tasks remained.

How did the idea of developing lighter and faster carriers progress? Every idea depends on the circumstances in which it can be brought to fruition and the historical context has to be understood, at least in broad terms. The main factors were:
1) The outcome of the 1921 Washington Fleet Conference (the 'Five Power Treaty') set a limit of 135,000 tons on the USA for total aircraft carrier tonnage, and the individual carrier was to be no larger than 27,000 tons standard. Permission to complete *Lexington* and *Saratoga* as aircraft carriers of 33,000 (later 36,000) tons each, after they had been begun as battlecruisers, was a special concession
2) The London Fleet Conference of 1930 imposed a further limitation on battleship building by the three great powers (Great Britain, USA and

Japan), and also set tonnage limits for cruisers, destroyers and submarines

3) The US Navy – finally convinced of the necessity for shipboard aviation – sought early on for ways and means of overcoming the limitations of the Fleet treaties, and to push forward the expansion of the carrier force

In further discussions of the methods for achieving this goal, two articles of the Washington agreement were seen as the desired 'back door'. Article 3 of the first section contained the statement: 'Cruisers and other surface ships with a flight deck are not to count as aircraft carriers as long as they are not employed exclusively as such.' As a result their displacement was not counted in the total limit on carrier tonnage. Curiously, this paragraph referred to a category of ship which did not even exist at that time; we can therefore assume that skilful American negotiators introduced this clause into the treaty *in order* to leave a back door open. In this connection, article 16 of the third part of the agreement conceded that 25 per cent of the permitted cruiser tonnage could be converted to ships which had a flight deck. This clause coincided exactly with the type of ship projects which the US Navy was considering.

Of course, these projects had been under discussion long before the study mentioned earlier. At the end of 1920, when it had been decided to convert a collier into an aircraft carrier – later USS *Langley* (CV-1) – the 'General Board of the Navy' in the Navy Department considered the feasibility of converting one of ten *Omaha* class scout cruisers, then under construction, to include a flight deck. Apart from *Langley*, a second useable ocean-going aircraft platform was needed as quickly as possible, and it seemed to be most economical to convert an existing ship for the purpose. This plan foundered after further discussion in which it was agreed that it would not be wise to set aside one urgently needed cruiser, when its small displacement (just over 7000 tons standard) offered little hope that the ship could be transformed into a passable carrier. Admiral W S Sims, one of the most outstanding flag officers of the Navy, was of the opposite opinion; he believed that the extra aircraft capacity was well worth the loss of a conventional light cruiser. In his opinion two flying deck cruisers would have doubled the reconnaissance capacity of the entire cruiser fleet.

Despite the General Board's rejection, the discussions on additional carriers continued. The difference of opinion repeated itself when the building of eight heavy cruisers was authorized in 1924, and several officers demanded again that at least one such ship should be equipped with a flight deck. However, by the end of 1925, Congress had authorized only two of these eight ships, and they were considered to be more important than the acquisition of further carriers. Nevertheless, *Lexington* and *Saratoga* were already under conversion at this time.

One must bear in mind that all the discussions from 1920 on centered on the feasibility of a total rebuild of existing ships: a full-size cruiser was to be converted into a self-contained, small, high-speed carrier. Around 1925 a new element was introduced into the discussion, when somebody suggested that one could share the priorities in such a conversion – or even in a new design – and produce a hybrid type that would be half-cruiser and half-carrier. This concept became known as the 'hybrid vessel'. The General Board argued that past experience with dual-purpose ships militated against them, evidently citing the unsatisfactory results of the British with similar conversions.

In 1930, at the time of the London Fleet Conference, the Navy was desperately looking for ways of increasing the effectiveness of its Fleet at the lowest possible cost. One year earlier, in 1929, Congress passed a recently approved building program, which sanctioned the building of one more aircraft carrier as well as 15 cruisers, although nobody could say whether the necessary funds could be guaranteed. The economic crisis dictated the amount of money authorized for new warship building, despite the fact that at the time the Japanese fleet – particularly in the area of cruisers and submarines – had shown substantial expansion. During this period the US Navy was willing to attempt experiments, in an effort to obtain more cruisers and also more carriers in spite of all the limitations and disadvantages. One final point should be mentioned in order to complete the picture: the President of the time, Herbert Hoover, was by no means sympathetic to the Navy, and during his presidency not one new warship was contracted for. The Chief of the Bureau of Aeronautics at that time, Rear Admiral W E Moffett, who was fatally injured in April 1933 in the crash of the airship *Akron*, explained later that American demands at the London Fleet Conference were aimed at the 135,000 tons allowed by the Treaty being used entirely for the larger Fleet Carriers, while the smaller ones would have had to be built from part of the cruiser tonnage.

With article 16 in mind, as mentioned above, the Bureau of Construction and Repair produced the preliminary design for a 'flying deck cruiser' only a few months after the London Conference ended. This was to displace no more than the 10,000 tons negotiated in Washington. This preliminary design came at a time when there was widespread discussion on the ideal minimum size for Fleet Carriers – bearing in mind the permitted maximum total tonnage. At this time, the generally agreed figure was around 14,000 tons. The choice of this size was dictated more by the tonnage restrictions than by any understanding of the technical requirements. In fact, USS *Ranger* (CV-4), displacing 14,000 tons, proved later to be too small to provide a stable aircraft platform in heavy seas. In the general uncertainty, the Navy authorities showed a preference for questionable and imperfect solutions, represented by the cruiser/carrier hybrid, just to get more aircraft to sea. By the end of 1930, the 'flying deck cruiser' project was well under way – a concept which had been put forward seven years earlier. One factor here was the idea that an expansion of the aerial component of the Navy was needed; developments in aircraft technology also helped, as modern aircraft were by then able to operate from smaller platforms. With the preliminary design completed in October 1930, the General Board demanded the building of the first flying deck cruiser in the budget of 1932 (the fiscal year 1932 began on 1 July 1931). In this budget, the following ships were demanded: one aircraft carrier, two light cruisers, one destroyer leader, ten destroyers and four submarines. One of the two light cruisers was to be built with a flight deck. In the Congress hearings on this new design, Admirals W V Pratt and W E Moffett argued passionately for the new ship. Moffett even disclosed that in London in 1930 the Americans had sought permission to convert all their cruiser tonnage into flying deck cruisers. The figure of 25 per cent which resulted was just a compromise.

Nevertheless, the Admirals' efforts in Congress were unsuccessful. By the end of the session for the 1932 budget, no action had been decided on. The Navy repeated its demands, and placed the flying deck cruiser on the list of the ships required from the budget of 1933. *At that time the Navy wanted this ship at all costs!* Meanwhile naval architects continued to work on the preliminary design of the flying deck cruiser. For a 10,000 ton ship, it had a lot to incorporate:

1) Adequate flight deck and hangar surface area to accommodate a reasonable number of aircraft
2) On the other hand, adequate armament and armor, so that the ship could also carry out the full duties of a light cruiser
3) For both rôles high speed was essential – to guarantee safe take-offs and landings for the aircraft, and to enable the ship in its rôle as light cruiser to maintain an adequate distance from the very fast heavy cruisers of a potential enemy (at that time only Japan came into this category)

The first preliminary design was presented to the General Board early in 1931: it amounted to a masterpiece in the utilization of the limited resources permitted. As can be seen from the design sketch, this ship had a relatively low hull of about 650ft overall length. The forward half was occupied by the cruiser component: three triple 6in turrets, and a further six 5in guns – evidently for AA fire – on the side decks, projecting slightly over the sides of the hull. A 350ft long flight deck, angled slightly to port, was set over the aft half of the hull, and an aircraft elevator was located at its forward end. This connected to the hangar below, which was to accommodate 24 light bombers or scouts. Forward of the flight deck, but one deck lower and offset to starboard, was the bridge. A wide, flat stack and a tripod mast also occupied the starboard edge of the hull, as did the islands of conventional aircraft carriers later. The planned speed was 32kts, with a range of 10,000 miles at the most economical speed. It is noteworthy that this design included an

The probable appearance of the 'flying deck cruiser', which failed to get past the planning stage, as shown in a preliminary design sketch of 1931.

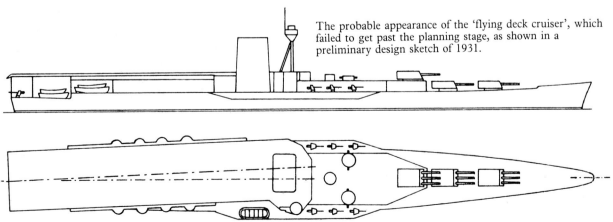

angled flight deck fully 25 years before the British finally exploited the advantages of this feature. In the history of shipbuilding there has only been one design of comparable appearance: the conversions of the *Hyuga* class battleships which the Japanese carried out early in 1944; here the after one-third became a hangar and flight deck, although no wheel-equipped aircraft ever took off from this flight deck. However, the forward two-thirds remained a very impressive battleship. Certain similarities to the flying deck cruiser design can also be found in the converted British cruisers *Blake* and *Tiger*, after these ships were rebuilt into helicopter cruisers in the late 1960s, although dimensionally there was no comparison. There are no real similarities with what the British now call 'through deck cruisers', the first of which entered service in 1981 as a platform for vertical take-off aircraft. This new type of ship is basically a conventional light aircraft carrier, but specialized for VTOL technology.

The flying deck cruiser project foundered on the effects of the economic crisis of the time. The first request failed in the 1932 budget, and was presented again in 1933. Once more, the financial means for this project were not available. The critical nature of the financial situation can be judged by the fact that in 1932 a bill was placed before Congress which called for the entire US battleship fleet to be withdrawn from active service. The great struggle at that time was not to acquire new ships, but to retain the existing combat strength of the fleet. The turning point for the Navy came with the Presidential elections, in which Franklin Delano Roosevelt was victorious over Herbert Hoover. The hopes placed in Roosevelt were justified: the former Secretary of the Navy could be expected to be sympathetic to the demands of the Navy. By mid-1933 Roosevelt's 'New Deal' proved beneficial to the Navy. The fight against unemployment was coupled with the Navy's need for new ships, and a program started to get under way. On 16 June 1933 President Roosevelt made $238 million available to the Navy Department for the construction of new ships. With this money, the United States began to regain its position as one of the great Naval powers once more. At the same time the intensive program of shipbuilding was one method of decreasing unemployment.

Now the Navy was again in a position to bring its plans to final fruition, after having them postponed for years – and yet the flying deck cruiser was no longer among them. This is easily understood: the flying deck cruiser was always looked upon as an emergency solution, designed for times of austerity. The restrictions were now at an end, and there were plentiful resources to be drawn on. Who would consider unlikely hybrids when the money was available for 'real' aircraft carriers, within the tonnage limits permitted? The Navy used the $238 millions to finance the building of two aircraft carriers (*Yorktown* and *Enterprise*), one heavy and three light cruisers, twenty destroyers and four submarines. In later consultations in Congress on the Navy's requests from the 1936 budget, some Senators asked why the flying deck cruisers, so urgently needed only a few years earlier, no longer featured on the list of requirements. The laconic answer from the Navy was that 'there are increasing doubts on the value of this design'.

But the flying deck cruiser was not yet completely dead. Many officers believed that, although this was not a type of ship which should be built in large numbers, they would nevertheless have liked to see a prototype with which to accumulate experience, in case the necessity should arise of converting existing cruisers at some later time. As late as Autumn 1938, the Chief of Naval Operations was asked to demand the funds for a flying deck cruiser, the purpose of which was as before: a 'scout cruiser' was to be produced, which would operate with the cruisers instead of with the Fleet. However, preliminary planning proceeded in fits and starts, and it was about two years before the planned characteristics of this initial design – now freed from the restrictions of the expired Fleet Treaties – crystallized: approximately 12,000 tons displacement, 640ft waterline length, 33kts, flight deck covering the after two-thirds of the hull, two 6in triple turrets (one forward of the flight deck, the other aft, below the flight deck).

This improved design gave obvious priority to the carrier section over the cruiser section. In spite of all these improvements, the decision was taken in 1940 to suspend all efforts in this direction, with the option of resuming work later. This never happened. One year later the Japanese attacked Pearl Harbor, and the Navy was forced to relinquish all unproductive experimental work in favor of a larger number of ships of proven design. However, the transition from the idea of the flying deck cruiser to the auxiliary aircraft carrier and what became known later as the escort carrier had been taking place at roughly the same time.

New Priorities: Escort Carriers

In March 1939, the Captain of USS *Ranger* (CV-4) – later to become famous as Admiral John S McCain – took the initiative and wrote to the Secretary of the Navy demanding the construction of at least eight 'pocket size' carriers *with the speed of cruisers*. They were by no means to replace the larger CVs, but rather to complement them in those operations where it would be wasteful to use the urgently needed aircraft of the CV. Meanwhile, by 1939 the Bureau of Construction and Repair was conscientiously working on design considerations concerned with the feasibility of converting merchant ships with a top speed of 20kts into auxiliary aircraft carriers. This work was abruptly halted in November 1940 by the Chief of Naval Operations; he blamed a very negative letter from the Secretary of the Navy to the head of the Maritime Commission, in which he expressed the opinion that the characteristics of the aircraft of the time had altered so much that they could no longer be operated satisfactorily from converted merchant ships. Thus it seemed that all activity aimed at obtaining smaller auxiliary aircraft carriers had ceased.

As sometimes happens in hopeless situations, help arrived from an unexpected quarter. No lesser person than the President of the United States, Franklin D Roosevelt, who had great understanding of Naval matters and was devoted to the Navy, became the real initiator of what was later to become the CVE. He personally joined in the debate, although initially from a different standpoint. Even before the USA entered World War II, the United States delivered large numbers of aircraft to Great Britain, which was struggling to counter German air superiority at that time. Thus there was a great need for ships which could transport completely assembled aircraft, ready for action. A similar requirement arose for the transport of US Army aircraft to the American bases in the Pacific. Rear Admiral, later Fleet Admiral, W F Halsey made it clear in February 1941 that he was worried that his Fleet Carriers *Enterprise* and *Saratoga* were being used to convey 80 aircraft each to Hawaii, during which time they were unable to carry out their real duties. In this he disagreed with his Commander-in-Chief.

Yet even before this difficulty, in October 1940, the CNO had received a memorandum from President Roosevelt's Naval Aide in which he was instructed to acquire a merchant ship and have it converted to enable 8 to 12 helicopters or aircraft to take off and land in a confined space (despite the fact that no helicopters had yet been introduced into the Navy!). The possible uses of these aircraft were outlined as follows:
1) Aerial surveillance of convoys
2) Location of submarines
3) Dropping smoke bombs to mark the position of submarines discovered

At the start of January 1941, a conference was called on the matter by the CNO, Admiral H R Stark, and it was rapidly established that the use of helicopters was not feasible. The lightweight helicopters of the time could hardly carry a greater load than a few smoke bombs. All further debate thus concentrated on the use of smaller aircraft of an offensive nature. Eventually agreement was reached on a ship with a full length flight deck. Diesel propulsion was considered, as this would not require large stacks. Immediately after this the CNO was informed that two diesel-powered ships of the standard C3 type, the *Mormacmail* and the *Mormacland*, were available for conversion. The whole business acquired a new urgency when President Roosevelt demanded that a single conversion should take no longer than three months, otherwise it was out of the question.

The *Mormacmail* was acquired on 6 March 1941, and the conversion was completed on 2 June, almost exactly within the three-month limit. This conversion produced the US Navy's first escort carrier, USS *Long Island* (AVG-1). Originally a 300ft long flight deck was planned, but safe operation of the proposed SOC Seagull aircraft called for a longer deck, and the final length was 360ft. *Long Island* had one aircraft elevator, had a top speed of 17.6kts, could accommodate 16 aircraft, 190 officers and 780 men. At the same time *Mormacland* was converted to a similar specification, and was transferred to the Royal Navy in November 1941 as HMS *Archer* (BAVG-1).

At this point it should be mentioned that the Royal Navy had put its first escort carrier into service in late Summer 1941, to protect convoys on the Gibraltar route. This was HMS *Audacity*, which was the result of a conversion of the captured German passenger ship *Hannover* in 1940-41. This carrier displaced a mere 6000 tons, and could carry only 6 aircraft. Its purpose was above all to disturb the operation of the German Focke Wulf 200 aircraft, which were employed to find British convoys and maintain contact until submarines could be brought to the area to do battle. Experience with *Audacity* may have had scarcely any influence on the construction of the American escort carrier, but the British were very pleased with her performance, and made even greater efforts to acquire more CVEs built in the USA, efforts which were redoubled when *Audacity* was sunk by submarine torpedo in December 1941.

After completion, USS *Long Island* (AVG-1) operated as an experimental and training ship, as had the first US aircraft carrier USS *Langley* (CV-1) in its time. Its chief purpose was to provide practical experience as a basis for further merchant ship conversions. The result of experience with *Long Island* was that the following improvements were regarded as absolutely essential:
1) Two aircraft elevators instead of one
2) A longer flight deck
3) Stronger AA armament
On 26 December 1941 the Secretary of the Navy signed contracts for the conversion of 24 merchant ship hulls, as part of the 1942 budget provisions. Somewhat later came the parallel order to convert nine cruiser hulls, then already under construction, into light aircraft carriers (CVL). This meant that the demands of the Navy Study of 1927 were finally met in full after 15 years, although the circumstances were completely different by this time.

As will be seen in the descriptions of the individual classes which follow, at first 20 C3 hulls were available for immediate conversion. Ten of them were for the use of the US Navy, and ten for the British. These ships later formed the *Bogue* class, named after the first ship to be completed for the US Navy. The actual lead ship was, however, HMS *Tracker* (BAVG-6). The main differences from *Long Island* were the 438ft by 79ft flight deck, steam propulsion instead of diesel, and substantially more hangar space.

Owing to the lack of further C3 hulls, four completed naval oilers were then converted, forming the *Sangamon* class. This class showed one important advance in that the flight deck was 503ft long and 85ft wide, and consequently two aircraft squadrons could be accommodated. The conversion of these ships was accelerated greatly during the Summer of 1942, because they were urgently needed for the invasion of North Africa, which was planned for Autumn 1942. With a speed of 18.3kts, these ships had a crew of 120 officers and 960 men. Gun armament consisted of two 5in/38 guns, two 40mm quadruple and ten twin mounts. The ships

also had a hydraulic catapult on the forward end of the flight deck. How soon these ships were completed before their employment off North Africa can be judged from the fact that the fitting-out of the last ship, the *Santee*, had to be carried out in great haste. There were still shipyard workers on board during sea trials, and the aircraft squadrons taken on board at the end of September 1942 had no more than a single day for practice take-offs and landings before undertaking operations. The same was true of firing practice and calibration of the brand new guns.

Nevertheless, these ships were ideally suited to their rôle. If the Navy had had more than just these four oilers available at the time, and if the need for oil tankers had not been equally great, this design would undoubtedly have become *the* standard design for escort carriers. The versatility of these ships during the North Africa operations can be judged from the example of the USS *Chenango*. On passage to the area, she carried USAAF fighter aircraft; whilst anchored at Casablanca she functioned as an oiler for other ships; and during the return cruise the ship took on board a borrowed squadron, and carried out flight operations with these aircraft in the Atlantic. During this time, TBF Avengers, F4F Wildcats and SBD Dauntlesses from her three sister ships joined in the support of land forces in the invasion of North Africa, as part of Task Force 34.

One real handicap in flight operations even at that time was the ships' low top speed, and this was especially true after the War when the heavier F4U Corsairs of the Marine Corps operated from CVEs. As is still true today, landings could only be carried out if a 30kt headwind was blowing along the flight deck. In the Mediterranean there was often complete calm, or such a light wind that landings had to be carried out at the dangerously low speed of only 22kts. If there was no headwind at all, flight operations had to be stopped, as the carriers were simply too slow, with their average speed of 18kts. The CVLs, with their cruiser propulsion, were much better off in this respect, and the large CVs suffered no such problem. Later on it will be seen that the problem of low speed was especially disadvantageous during escort duties in convoys.

In the early years of the War German submarines destroyed numerous Allied merchant ships in convoy. There was a pressing need for aircraft to spot the lurking submarines from the air, and, if possible, before they had a chance to make direct contact with a convoy. Initially long-range aircraft were employed for this task, based in Iceland, New-foundland and Northern Ireland. To make good the limitations of the surveillance program, and also to make it possible to combat submarines when spotted from the air, the Royal Navy intended to equip convoys with escort carriers – not least as a result of their experiences with HMS *Audacity*. The over-extended British shipbuilding industry had to rely on the assistance of their mighty US allies, who had joined the War by that time. The extent and chronological sequence of the supply of American BAVGs/AVGs to the Royal Navy is des-cribed in detail later. The first ship – HMS *Archer* (BAVG-1) – was transferred on 17 November 1941. By mid-1942 three more ships had followed. One might have thought that these ships would have gone into action as quickly as possible, but in fact the British considered the American ships to be exceptionally poorly fitted and incomplete, and sent all of them into shipyards for about six months, to bring them up to British standard specifications. This led to violent controversy between the two navies. One matter concerned the differing views on the layout of the fuel system, and the other was ballast compensation. The British added up to 2000 tons of ballast to each ship, as they disliked compensating for consumed fuel with sea water, as was American practice. According to American reports, there were *de facto* delays of 24 to 30 weeks between delivery from the USA and initial use by the British. The Americans re-proached the British for making extremely poor use of the carriers they had supplied. The commanders of the British ships were, however, surface navy personnel, and not aviators as in the American case. In addition, the crew of the Swordfish aircraft were too exposed to the elements for their rôle as submarine hunters. Finally, the British ships had far smaller maintenance crews – because of the shortage of men – than the Americans. For this reason air operations had to be carried out at a much lower frequency.

Because of all these delays, and also because the British CVEs which were ready for action were urgently needed for the invasion of North Africa, their utilization for the escort of convoys in the North Atlantic was postponed further. The result was that CVEs were not used on the North Atlantic route until March 1943, and even then the ship concerned was not a British escort carrier, but the USS *Bogue* (ACV-9).

In connection with the first two convoy assign-ments, it seems useful to know what the Air Squad-ron Commander on the *Bogue* was required to report on the tactical use of his ship. In March 1943 the ship steamed in the middle of a convoy, surrounded by the columns of merchant ships which were to be protected, while the other escort vessels took up their positions around the convoy. Take-off of the lightweight aircraft of the time was by means of catapults, for which the very low speed of the convoy – about 9kts – was insufficient, unless a very strong headwind prevailed. If this was not the case, it was necessary to turn the CVE into the wind – especially when the aircraft were due to land. This not only incurred risks in the relatively closely spaced convoy, but also took the carrier away from the convoy. This in turn meant that the carrier itself had to be protected, as it was a priority target. Although these tactics had already succeeded against submarines, they were princi-pally defensive. The ship's aircraft usually found the submarines cruising on the surface long after the submarines had made contact with the convoy, when they were attempting to stalk their quarry.

Later on, another tactic was developed, which proved to be much more effective. One escort carrier and several escort vessels would form a self-contained group, known as an 'Escort Group'. This unit would sail outside the convoy, mostly in such a position that it could 'service' two convoys simultaneously, travelling in opposite directions. It would spot the submarines, before they had made direct contact with the convoys, and hinder their search activities and further progress. This also had the advantage that the take-off and landing opera-tions of the CVE could be carried out free of the restrictions within the closely packed, slow-moving convoy.

Up to May 1943, only *Archer* and *Biter* of the British ships had seen service on this route, while HMS *Dasher*, which had also been intended for this task, was lost in March 1943 after an internal explosion. The British blamed the loss on the in-adequacy of the American aircraft fuel system.

The successes of the Escort Groups in April and May 1943 were the result of this new tactic. Seen overall, however, the use of the escort carriers in such small numbers was only of limited importance – judging by the number of CVEs which arrived subsequently. When they arrived in greater num-bers, the decisive turn in the North Atlantic took place, and from mid-1943 German submarine operations in mid-Atlantic necessarily declined.

Further efforts and discussions on the part of the Royal Navy concerning the construction of more escort carriers eventually led to increased use of British CVEs with the Escort Groups, and also in supporting amphibious landings. This book does not include a description of their development, as it only details the escort carriers built by the USA for Great Britain. It is interesting to note that in addition to British units, about a dozen American CVEs, constantly rotating, took part at various times in the wide-ranging convoy escort operations in the North Atlantic and later principally in the mid-Atlantic. The reader is referred to the relevant section of the tables in *Aircraft Carriers of the US Navy* for further details.

The successes of the American CVE groups operating mainly in the Mediterranean and the South Atlantic were apparent, but the most recent research has shown that an important reason for this success was fundamentally that the British managed to decode the German radio messages over long periods, so that the positions of the German submarines in the Atlantic were frequently known. In this way the CVEs and their escort vessels could be steered towards the supply points for the German submarines. After the Summer of 1943 the Allies' tasks were divided. The Americans were to operate in mid- and South Atlantic, while the British and Canadians maintained Escort Groups in the North Atlantic, in which CVEs were also employed to a limited extent. From Autumn 1943 British 'Merchant Aircraft Carriers' accompanied the convoys to provide protection. These vessels only shipped four aircraft, but could also carry a normal cargo. They were civilian-manned, except for the gun crews and the small aircraft sections, which were under naval control.

Let us return now to further consideration of the development of American CVE classes. The invasion of North Africa was over, but by the end of 1942 the Americans only had *Enterprise* and *Saratoga* of their large aircraft carriers in the Pacific; consequently the versatile CVEs of the *Sangamon* class were moved to the Pacific to provide reinforcement. The careers of these four ships show how intensive a rôle they had to play in the Pacific War.

In the meantime President Roosevelt decided to have more escort aircraft carriers built. In this he was especially influenced by the proposals for rationalization made by shipyard owner Henry J Kaiser, who had presented a detailed plan for the mass production of escort carriers in his yard at Vancouver, Washington. After contracts had been signed, the 50 CVEs of the *Casablanca* class were

built there, all of which were delivered within one year – from July 1943 to July 1944; a unique achievement, which had a decisive influence on the further operation of the US carrier force. At a trial displacement of about 9570 tons, these ships had a top speed of 19.3kts. The crew numbered 110 officers and 750 men, while the aircraft capacity was 12 torpedo bombers and 16 fighters, which were launched by means of a single hydraulic catapult.

In January 1943 contracts were signed for the first units of a further CVE class, in this case the design being carried out by the Navy itself, utilizing experience gained with the previous class. The lead ship, USS *Commencement Bay* (CVE-105), was commissioned at the end of 1944. With a trial displacement of 23,100 tons and a speed of 19kts, these ships were roughly comparable to the *Sangamon* class. Nine more units of this class were completed by the end of the War, although most of them saw no active service.

After the *Sangamon* class took part in the invasion of North Africa, eight CVEs did effective service in supporting the landings on the Gilbert and Marshall Islands, in which ships of the first three classes were present.

The variety of possible uses of these versatile ships also manifested itself in the reclassification which took place on two occasions. AVG and ACV were categories of auxiliary ships, but from July 1943 the ships were rated as CVEs, and therefore 'combatants'. At the end of 1944 a type command 'Escort Carrier Force, Pacific' was formed, whose first commander, Rear Admiral C T Durgin, had already pointed out the limitations of the use of CVEs after the invasion of North Africa. Their low speed, lack of armor, and weak armament made it dangerous to use them where a confrontation with a superior enemy was likely. The fate of TU-77.4.3 ('Taffy 3') at the hands of Japanese battleships and heavy cruisers in the battle off Samar on 25 October 1944, during the Leyte operations, made this only too obvious. However, within more powerful groups, or with adequate protection from their own air and naval forces, the CVEs were capable of carrying out all the tasks of their 'big brothers', within the limitations of the ships' capabilities. The purpose of establishing the new type command mentioned above was to create a more effective plan of operation with better defined objectives, which would fit in with the requirements of the fast carrier battle groups. Rear Admiral Durgin controlled all the CVEs in the Pacific with the exception of those which had been given training and transport rôles. Other high points of CVE operation included:

1) The landing on Mindoro in December 1944
2) The landing on Luzon in January 1945, where 17 escort carriers of TG-77.4 were subjected to constant heavy attack by Kamikaze aircraft
3) Further landings on the Philippine Islands, also in January 1945, in which six CVEs were used
4) Support for the landing on Iwo Jima in February 1945
5) Support for the landing on Okinawa from March 1945 onward, involving 18 CVEs of TG-52.1

One of the earlier sections in the book has already provided details of total losses and damage suffered by escort carriers. Five of the CVEs which were sunk were lost in the Pacific, and only one in the Atlantic. During the war years and shortly before, the US Navy commissioned 77 escort carriers with a further nine being completed after the end of the War. A total of 38 escort carriers built in the United States were loaned to the Royal Navy, of which four were lost in action. Of the tasks set, the escort carriers proved best suited to:

1) Transporting aircraft and their personnel
2) Hunting submarines inside and outside the convoys
3) Providing aerial support for amphibious landings

A small number of them were converted for special purposes after the War, and served until the end of the 1960s.

At this time the era of the small carrier seemed to have finally come to an end in favor of very large Super Carriers. Yet not 10 years after the cancellation of the last of these 'jeep carriers', as they were jokingly – but respectfully – called, there is a renewed need for smaller, economical carriers, which are now intended to support vertical take-off aircraft and increase the number of aircraft platforms available for naval use. At the time this book was concluded, there were no *definite* projects within the US Navy, although various preliminary studies are in hand – especially by other nations, such as Great Britain, Italy and Spain. The last-named three countries are already building VTOL and helicopter carriers.

Escort Carrier Classes

Explanatory Notes

1) In the title to the individual ships, the identification number is given with the name which the ship had when *contracted for*. All other alterations to classification are detailed in the summary in the tabular section

2) The title includes each name which the ship was allocated at any time in her naval service, printed in chronological order

3) Names carried previously as merchant ships are given in italics in the text

4) The information on the squadrons carried by the ships has been collected from various publications. It is by no means complete. The month and year given do not always correspond with the date that the squadron was embarked on the ship, but the earliest month of which there is evidence that the squadron was present. In particular the information under July 1943 and March 1944 often only represents the date when command of the squadrons was to be assumed, which usually occurred several months before the ship was ready for service. In many cases the squadron was not in fact embarked if the proposed use for the ship had changed in the meantime. This applies in particular to the later units of the *Casablanca* class, which were eventually allotted mainly transport duties

5) In many cases the dates given for camouflage schemes are taken from photographic evidence; where assumptions have been made, or uncertainty exists, this is always indicated

Long Island Class and USS Charger (CVE-30)

Early in 1941 the US Navy obtained six modern merchant ships in order to convert them to escort carriers, following the pattern of the first British escort carrier HMS *Audacity*, which had been the captured German merchant ship *Hannover* before being converted. The average time for conversion was just 75 working days in dock. The lead ship of the class was given the identification AVG-1, and the mercantile name *Mormacmail* was changed to USS *Long Island*. *Long Island* had been of the standard C3 cargo (M) ship type, while the remaining five ships were of the C3 P & C (M) type. They were all sister ships of the *Mormacmail*, and had been launched between 1939 and 1941. They were intended for loan to the Royal Navy under a lend/lease arrangement, and were given the identification BAVG-1 to -5. The conversion of these ships showed certain differences compared with USS *Long Island*, as will be seen later. According to the Treaty conditions, the US Navy also undertook the training of the British escort carrier pilots. HMS *Charger* (BAVG-4) was selected as the training ship, and was retained in the USA, where she was reclassified in 1942 as AVG-30, but kept her name when taken over by the US Navy. During the rest of the War USS *Charger* served chiefly as a training ship for British aircraft crews.

A flight deck consisting of wooden planks was installed over the major part of the hull of the USS *Long Island*, at the front edge of which, under the level of the deck, a narrow bridge was fitted. A hangar and aircraft repair shops were provided in the after half of the ship, between the flight deck and the hull. The hangar was open at the forward end. The remaining British conversions received a slightly larger hangar and flight deck extending further forward, on which a catapult was fitted.

Compared with USS *Long Island*, the British conversions had a longer flight deck and a small island on the starboard side of the flight deck. Later, in the Autumn of 1942, *Long Island* was also modified, the flight deck being extended forward. The bridge was removed, leaving only a navigation position on either side. The ship was also fitted with a catapult and radar, and the 20mm AA armament was strengthened by five guns. As *Charger*'s

USS *Long Island* (CVE-1) after the extension of the flight deck forward, which was carried out in Autumn 1942. At the same time the ship was fitted with a short radar mast and an SC antenna, which was replaced by SC-2 before the end of the War.

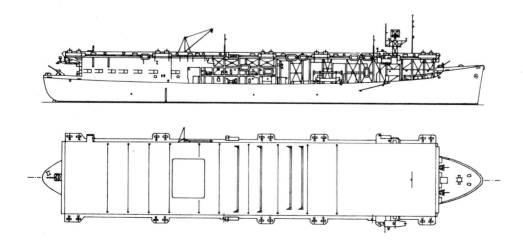

rôle was limited to that of training ship, she was not modernized during the rest of the War. In *Long Island*'s case, the conversion meant that 21 aircraft could be carried.

It should be noted at this point that only the first six British conversions were coded BAVG (al-though BAVG-6 belonged to the succeeding *Bogue* class!), while all later ships were loaned to the Royal Navy as AVG or ACV. This becomes more plausible when one realizes that AVG-2 to -5 existed in addition to BAVG-2 to -6 – in theory, at least – as will be shown later.

USS Long Island (AVG-1)

Conversion from merchant ship *Mormacmail* at Newport News SB & DD

SERVICE HISTORY
Mid-1941   East Coast; series of tests to evaluate possibility of using aircraft on converted freighters
May 1942   West Coast; brief Pacific operations
August 1942   Aircraft transport in the South Pacific for the Marine Corps; Guadalcanal
1942-43   Pilot training, West Coast
1944-45   Transport of aircraft and personnel to the Pacific
September 1945   Participation in 'Magic Carpet' operation
26 March 1946   Withdrawn from service; stricken

AIRCRAFT, SQUADRONS
Summer 1942   VGS-1 with SOC-3s and F2As
December 1941   VS-201 with 7 F2As and 13 SOCs = 20

August 1942   Ferry duties: 19 F4Fs and 12 SBDs = 31 Marine Corps aircraft

CAMOUFLAGE
1942   Possibly Measure 12 with color patches
December 1942   Possibly Measure 14
1944   Measure 32/9a

RADAR
December 1942   SC
1944   SC-2

USS *Long Island*, the US Navy's first escort carrier, here as AVG-1, photographed on 7 August 1941, four months before the USA entered the War. Note the bridge, visible here below the two aircraft, and the boats located forward of it on the deck. The code letters LI are painted on both ends of the flight deck, which has not yet been extended, and they are legible from forward or aft; this feature and the arresting wires stretched across the whole length of the deck indicates that even escort carriers were expected to cope with landings over the bow at that time.
USN (BfZ collection)

Quarter view of *Long Island*, around mid-1942. Note the simple signal masts and the bridge wings projecting beyond the sides. The ship carries a camouflage scheme similar to the one featured at that time by USS *Wasp* (CV-7) and USS *Hornet* (CV-8), and hence might be the early Measure 12.
USN (BfZ collection)

This photograph of *Long Island* was taken on 19 December 1942, after a period in Mare Island Navy Yard. The bridge was sacrificed in favor of an extended flight deck, so that from now on the ship was conned from bridge wings on either side. The paint scheme is evidently the Ocean Gray of Measure 14. Note the newly installed radar mast with SC antenna.
USN (BfZ collection)

HMS Charger (BAVG-4) – USS Charger (AVG-30)

Formerly merchant ship *Rio de la Plata*. Conversion at Newport News SB & DD. To Royal Navy as HMS *Charger* (BAVG-4). Returned to US Navy on 4 October 1941. Reclassified as AVG-30 on 24 January 1942, placed in service with the US Navy on 3 March, retaining the name

SERVICE HISTORY
Training of pilots and carrier crews for the whole of the war in Chesapeake Bay; except:
October 1942 Training cruise to Bermuda

September 1945 Training cruise to Guantanamo, Cuba
15 March 1946 Withdrawn from service; stricken

CAMOUFLAGE
1942 Measure 22

RADAR
1942 Presumably SC, SG
1944 SC-2

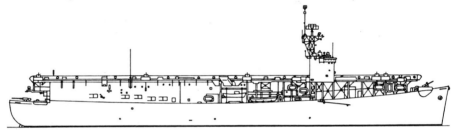

This drawing of USS *Charger* (CVE-30) clearly shows the differences from her sister ship *Long Island*: a somewhat longer flight deck, gun tubs for the 3in mounts, and the presence of a small island, here with SC-2 radar, installed in 1944.

Here the regulations relating to Measure 22 have been followed correctly. USS *Charger* (ACV-30), the odd man out in hull number terms, photographed in 1942. The close kinship with *Long Island* is unmistakeable, although the differences are equally obvious: longer hangar, extending from the fantail to amidships, and a small island instead of the navigating bridge wings.
USN (BfZ collection)

AVG-2 to AVG-5

These hull numbers were officially allocated, but they were never given to a ship. In mid-1941 that is, before the USA entered World War II, it had already been planned to convert four medium-sized passenger ships to auxiliary aircraft carriers – as in the German Navy. These conversions were authorized, and initial material orders were placed. However, by December 1941 these conversion ideas had been abandoned, and the first three ships were converted into troop transports, which better suited their design.

Washington became USS *Mount Vernon* (AP-22) in 1942; *Manhattan* became USS *Wakefield* (AP-21) in 1942; *America* became USS *West Point* (AP-23) in 1942.

The conversion of the passenger liner *Kungsholm* was also suspended in December 1941.

As replacements, 21 hulls of standard C3 type freighters were selected to be completed as escort carriers (*Bogue* class). To these were added the four conversions from T3 tankers (*Sangamon* class). Later a further 24 units of the *Prince William* class (Standard C3-S-A1 type) were completed as CVEs, although only *Prince William* herself remained with the US Navy, the others being loaned to the Royal Navy.

At that time there was talk of using the large passenger ships *Normandie, President Coolidge, Lurline, Mariposa* and *Monterey* as auxiliary aircraft carriers, but these plans failed to materialize.

USS *Charger*, taken on 28 January 1944, with camouflage and Measure 22 still in evidence. The dark blue identification number on the flight deck is scarcely visible, but the white deck markings are very clear, in contrast. 20mm AA guns can be picked out in their gun tubs. *USN official*

Bogue/Prince William Class

The C3-S-A1 type merchant ships which were planned for completion as AVGs had not all been launched when modifications for their new rôle began. Hence the conversion measures could be carried out more rapidly than had been possible with the preceding class. A characteristic of this class was the enclosed aircraft hangar, which extended under the wooden flight deck. Two aircraft elevators connected the hangar to the flight deck. Galleries and several sponsons were fitted to the side of the ships at the level of the main deck, one function being to accommodate AA machine guns. *Bogue, Card* and *Core* had two catapults at the forward end of the aircraft deck, while most of the other ships of the class had to make do with one. In contrast with the *Long Island* class, which were diesel-powered, steam turbines were chosen for these ships. Exhaust gases were vented via small smoke ducts on both sides of the flight deck, slightly aft of amidships. If normal flight operations were envisaged, the ships could carry 28 aircraft, but there was space for up to 90 aircraft in the hangar and on the flight deck for transport purposes. The original AA armament of two quadruple 40mm mounts was later reinforced with four twin mounts, two of them at the forward end of the flight deck, with the other two aft on the main deck. An average of ten additional 20mm AA guns were also installed. A radar system was part of the basic equipment of the ships.

Many sources make a distinction between the *Bogue* and the *Prince William* classes. In reality USS *Prince William* (CVE-31) was virtually identical to USS *Bogue*, the main difference being the arrangement of the 40mm AA armament. This ship was also the sole member of its class which stayed with the US Navy; all the succeeding units up to CVE-54 were loaned to the Royal Navy.

The construction times for the ships of this class (and for the succeeding *Casablanca* class) give a clear indication of the extent to which the Americans had increased their shipbuilding capacity to meet war demands. The whole class, of 45 units, was completed in slightly less than a year, and at such a pace that most of the ships were delivered in the decisive year of 1943. The initial building times of almost 15 months were reduced to barely 8½ months for the last units.

Four ships of this class were reactivated in 1958, manned by civilian crews of the MSTS and used thereafter as aircraft ferries – including participation in the Vietnam War.

In 1942, when more and more shipbuilding capacity was needed, a redistribution of building contracts became necessary, which resulted in many ships being finished in a different yard from that in which they were started. The building contracts for CVE-31 to -44 and CVE-46 to -54 were transferred to Todd, Pacific on 1 May 1942. CVE-45 was to have been built by Commercial Iron Works, but was transferred to Todd, Pacific after being laid down. CVE-31 was started at Todd, but was then transferred for completion at Puget Sound Navy Yard on 1 June 1942. CVE-32 was also begun at Todd, but then sent to Willamette Iron for completion. CVE-33 was not even begun at Todd, but transferred to Puget Sound Navy Yard on 1 June 1942. In the same way CVE-40 went directly to Willamette on 24 July 1942. CVE-37 was launched at Todd, but the ship went to Commercial Iron Works for completion on 22 December 1942. CVE-45 was 'redirected' twice before finally being allocated to Willamette for construction on 24 July 1942. CVE-47 was launched at Todd, Pacific, but the completion contract went to Commercial Iron Works on 17 June 1943.

HMS Archer (BAVG-1)

Conversion from merchant ship *Mormacland* at Newport News SB & DD. Transferred to Royal Navy on 17 November 1941. Returned to US Navy on 9 January 1946. Stricken 26 February 1946

HMS *Archer* (BAVG-1). The similarity to the class ship USS *Long Island* is unmistakable, but the island is very small, with an additional small mast behind it. Camouflage is to a British design, and the ship flies the White Ensign, but the aircraft on board are American.
USN (Barilli collection)

HMS Avenger (BAVG-2)

Conversion from merchant ship *Rio Hudson* at Bethlehem, Staten Island. Transferred to Royal Navy on 2 March 1942. Torpedoed 15 November 1942 and sunk at Gibraltar. Stricken 16 May 1944

HMS Biter (BAVG-3) – Dixmude

Conversion from merchant ship *Rio Parana* at Atlantic Basin Iron Works. Transferred to Royal Navy on 5 May 1942. Returned 9 April 1945, loaned to France on same day, as *Dixmude*. Served as aircraft ferry. Later aircraft transport between USA and Indo-China. 1959 depot ship at St Mandrier. Returned to USA 10 June 1966. Sunk in 1966 as test target

This fine quarter view of *Dixmude* shows the after gun mounting with the British 4in gun, and the separate electronics mast. The radar antenna on the island mast is the American SA.
H Emery (BfZ collection)

HMS Charger (BAVG-4) – USS Charger (AVG-30)

Conversion from merchant ship *Rio de la Plata* at Newport News SB & DD. Transferred to Royal Navy September 1941. Commissioned as HMS *Charger*. Returned to US Navy 4 October 1941. Classified as AVG-30 24 January 1942, commissioned in US Navy 3 March 1942 (See also AVG-30)

HMS Dasher (BAVG-5)

Conversion of merchant ship *Rio de Janeiro* at Tietjen and Lang DD Co, transferred to Royal Navy 2 July 1942. Destroyed 27 March 1943 by internal explosion. Stricken 2 June 1945

HMS Tracker (BAVG-6)

Of *Bogue* type. Completed by Willamette Iron. Transferred to Royal Navy 31 January 1943.

Returned to US Navy on 29 November 1946. Stricken 21 January 1946

The first of four ships built at Ingalls, and subsequently transferred to the Royal Navy, was HMS *Battler* (BAVG-6), of the *Bogue* type. At this early stage only 20mm AA guns are on board.
Ingalls

USS Altamaha (AVG-6) – HMS Battler

Acquired by US Navy 31 October 1942, transferred to Royal Navy the same day. Returned 12 February 1946

USS Barnes (AVG-7) – HMS Attacker

Laid down as merchant ship *Steel Artisan*, then renamed USS *Barnes*. Transferred to Royal Navy as HMS *Attacker* 30 September 1942. Returned to US Navy 5 January 1946

USS Block Island (AVG-8) – HMS Trailer – HMS Hunter

Laid down as merchant ship *Mormacpenn*. Renamed USS *Block Island* when taken over by US Navy. Transferred to Royal Navy as HMS *Trailer* on 9 January 1943. Renamed HMS *Hunter* in 1943. Returned to US Navy 29 December 1945

USS Bogue (AVG-9)

Laid down as merchant ship *Steel Advocate*

SERVICE HISTORY

February 1943 Atlantic; hunter-killer operations with several convoy escort cruises. Seven German submarines sunk by ship's aircraft.
February 1944 Transportation of USAAF aircraft to Scotland
March 1944 Resumption of anti-submarine operations in North Atlantic
September 1944 Training cruises, East Coast
February 1945 Transportation of USAAF aircraft to Scotland
April 1945 Resumption of anti-submarine operations

tions
July 1945 Pacific; one cruise to Alaska
From September 1945 'Magic Carpet' operations
30 November 1946 Withdrawn from service; reserve fleet

AIRCRAFT, SQUADRONS
March-July 1943 VC-9 with 12 F4Fs and 12 TBFs = 24
September-December 1943 VC-19 with 9 FMs and 13 TBFs = 22
March 1944 VC-95 with 9 FMs and 12 TBFs = 21

Left: USS *Bogue*, here as ACV-9, photographed on 3 November 1942 in Puget Sound, about 6 weeks after commissioning. The dark paintwork evidently corresponds to Measure 14. SG, SC and YE antennas are visible. *USN (BfZ collection)*

USS *Bogue*, taken somewhere in the Atlantic on 20 June 1943, carrying Measure 22 camouflage. The photo provides a good view of the after gun mounts. The port 5in gun is trained outboard, and the director mounts are located behind the 40mm AA guns. *USN official*

April 1944 VC-19 with 9 FMs and 13 TBFs = 22

May-July 1944 VC-69 with 9 FMs and 12 TBMs = 21

August-September 1944 VC-42 with 9 FMs and 14 TBMs = 23

April-May 1945 VC-19 with 3 FMs and 16 TBMs = 19

CAMOUFLAGE
September 1942 Probably Measure 14
June 1943 Measure 22
January 1944 Measure 32/4a
1945 Presumably Measure 21

RADAR
November 1942 SC, SG, YE

USS Breton (AVG-10) – HMS Chaser

Laid down as merchant ship *Mormacgulf*. Transferred to Royal Navy as HMS *Chaser* 9 April 1943. Returned 12 May 1946

USS Card (AVG-11)

SERVICE HISTORY

May-June 1943 Atlantic; troop and aircraft transport from New York to Casablanca

July-October 1943 TG-21.14; anti-submarine warfare operations. Four German submarines sunk during first operational cruise

October-November 1943 Second anti-submarine operation. Four more submarines sunk

November 1943 to February 1944 Third anti-submarine operation

March-May 1944 Transport operations, East Coast to Casablanca

June 1944 TG-22.10; anti-submarine operations

September 1944 TG-22.2; two further operations

February 1945 Aircraft transport to Liverpool

March-May 1945 Training ship for pilot qualifications

June 1945 Pacific; supply transport to Pearl Harbor and Guam

August-December 1945 Three 'Magic Carpet' operations in Pacific

13 May 1946 Withdrawn from service; reserve fleet

1 July 1958 Reactivated as T-CVU-11 for MSTS Pacific

2 May 1964 Sunk on even keel at Saigon pier by mine. Raised, and repaired

11 December 1964 Further transport duties

1966 New starboard stack between island and stern, removal of the four side stacks

10 March 1970 Withdrawn from service; stricken

AIRCRAFT, SQUADRONS

July-September 1943 VC-1 with 6 F4Fs and 11 TBFs = 17

September-November 1943 VC-9 with 6 F4Fs and 12 TBFs = 18

November 1943-January 1944 VC-55 with 9 FMs and 12 TBFs = 21

July 1944 VC-12 with 9 FMs and 12 TBMs = 21

CAMOUFLAGE

March 1943 Measure 22

1944 Possibly Measure 32/4a

RADAR

March 1943 SC, SG, YE

1944 SK, SG, YE

All three drawings show USS *Card* (CVE-11) in 1944, after SK has replaced SC radar. The mast forward of the first 40mm twin, and the second, slightly raised 40mm AA mount were absent from *Breton*, *Nassau*, *Barnes*, and possibly some other ships of this class employed in the Pacific. The pole topmast behind the SK unit was slightly longer on the CVEs operating in the Pacific.

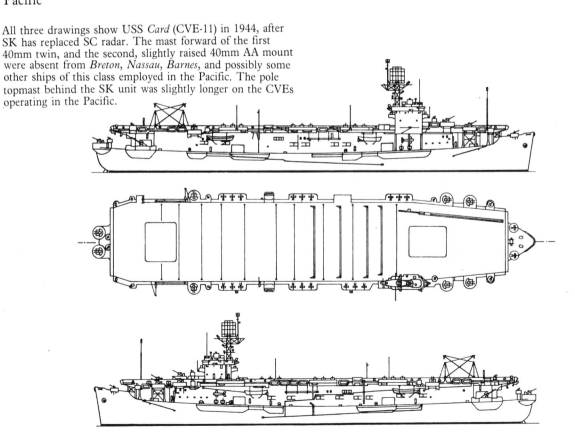

USS *Card* (ACV-11) with Measure 22 camouflage and SK
radar, which was fitted in early 1943 during a refit: 13
aircraft can be counted on the flight deck.
USN official

USS *Card* (CVE-11), camouflaged to Measure 32/4a.
USN (Barilli collection)

USS Copahee (AVG-12)

Laid down as merchant ship *Steel Architect*.
Converted at Puget Sound Navy Yard

SERVICE HISTORY
September 1942 Pacific; aircraft transport to Guadalcanal
1943-1945 Various transport cruises between West Coast and the Pacific combat areas
September-December 1945 'Magic Carpet' missions between Saipan, Guam, Eniwetok, Philippines and the West Coast
5 July 1946 Withdrawn from service; reserve fleet

AIRCRAFT, SQUADRONS
At some time CVEG-50 is said to have been on board
November 1942 VGS-12 with F4Fs and TBFs

CAMOUFLAGE
September 1942 and July 1943 Presumably Measure 14
After July 1943 Measure ?

RADAR
August 1942-May 1943 SC, SG, YE
July 1943 SK, SG, YE

Above: USNS *Card* is the legend on the port side, evidence that the ship is manned by a civilian MSTS crew. This photograph may have been taken after 1966, when *Card* was used for transport duties to Vietnam. Note the new, longer stack forward of the starboard crane, the reinforcing ribs on the side of the island, and the navigation radar antenna typical of many MSTS ships.
USN official

Top right: USS *Copahee* (ACV-12) leaves San Francisco Bay on 9 May 1943, with a deck load of various aircraft types, heading for the Pacific. SC radar can be seen on the mast. The strong sunshine makes the Ocean Gray paintwork appear lighter than it really is.
Centre and bottom right: Just two months later: after a refit in Mare Island Navy Yard, *Copahee* shows off her SK antenna. The single color paint scheme has been retained. Three captive barrage balloons are visible above the ship. The 'zipper' along the hull side is formed by recently added external aircraft fuel lines. The bow and stern views of *Copahee* were also taken on 14 July 1943. The SK antenna with BT-5 IFF supplement is clearly visible.
USN (BfZ collection)

USS Core (AVG-13)

SERVICE HISTORY
February 1943   Pacific; pilot qualifications
April 1943   Atlantic; pilot training cruises
June 1943   TG-21.12; anti-submarine operations. Two German submarines sunk on first operational cruise
August-September 1943   Second and third operational cruises. Three submarines sunk, then continued anti-submarine operations
December 1943   Aircraft transport, East Coast to Liverpool
April 1944   TG-21.16; transport cruise to Glasgow
August 1944   Anti-submarine operations and training cruises
June 1945   Pacific; aircraft transport to Pearl Harbor and Samar
October 1945-January 1946   'Magic Carpet' to Yokohama, total of two cruises
4 October 1946   Withdrawn from service; reserve fleet
1 July 1958   Reactivated; MSTS civilian crew
25 November 1969   Withdrawn from service; stricken

AIRCRAFT, SQUADRONS
June-November 1943   VC-13 with 6 F4Fs and 12 TBFs = 18
April-May 1945   VC-12 with 3 FMs and 16 TBMs = 19

CAMOUFLAGE
January 1943 and November 1943   Measure 22
1944   Measure 32/4a

RADAR
January 1943   SC, SG, YE

Aerial photo of USS *Core* (CVE-13), taken on 19 November 1943 with the high contrast surfaces of camouflage Measure 22. An SK radar antenna is already fitted.
USN official

A few CVEs served in the 1950s and 1960s as aircraft transports, and carried a civilian crew of Military Sea Transport Command — abbreviated to MSTS. Some of them were slightly modified, and this drawing shows how USNS *Core* (T-AKV-41) looked in 1968. Note the rib-like reinforcements on the island side, the enlarged stack and the large crane on the former flight deck.

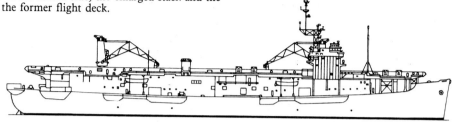

USS *Core* approaches her anchorage in Saigon harbor on 17 June 1966, now under the MSTS command. At that time the ship carried more than 70 aircraft needed for the war in Vietnam. Note the windbreak on the forward end of the flight deck, the extended stack and the radar antenna, fitted higher than on *Card*.
USN official

USS Croatan (AVG-14) – HMS Fencer

Transferred to Royal Navy as HMS *Fencer* 1 March 1943. Returned 21 December 1946

USS Hamlin (AVG-15) – HMS Stalker

Transferred to Royal Navy as HMS *Stalker* 21 December 1942. Returned 29 December 1945

USS Nassau (AVG-16)

Conversion completed at Puget Sound Navy Yard

SERVICE HISTORY

October 1942 Pacific; two aircraft transport missions to the New Hebrides

April 1943 Pilot training cruises West Coast; VC-21 on board, cruise to Alaska with TG-51.1

May 1943 Attu

June 1943 Aircraft transport to Australia

July 1943 Return to West Coast

October 1943 Aircraft transport to Samoa

December 1943-February 1944 TG-51.2; Marshall Islands

From March 1944 VC-66 disembarked; transport of aircraft and personnel to the Marshall Islands, New Guinea, Admiralty Islands and New Hebrides

September 1944 TG-30.8; transport of replacement aircraft and crew for Fleet Carriers, also air cover for supply groups

October 1944 Carolines with TG-38.1 and 38.3; transport of replacement aircraft for the Fleet Carriers. Until the end of the War, several transport cruises to Guam, Marcus, Samar and Saipan

28 October 1946 Withdrawn from service; reserve

AIRCRAFT, SQUADRONS

November 1942 As ferry 38 F4Fs, SBDs and TBDs of the Marine Corps

April 1943 VC-21 with FMs and TBMs

July 1943 (intended) VC-18 with 2 F4Fs and 9 TBFs = 11

November-December 1943 As ferry: 22 F6Fs of VF-1

January-March 1944 VC-66 with 14 FMs and 9 TBMs = 23

CAMOUFLAGE

September and December 1942 Presumably Measure 14

April 1944 Measure 32/2a

November 1945 Presumably Measure 21

RADAR

April 1942 SC, SG, YE

November 1945 SK, SG, YE

This photo of USS *Nassau* (CVE-16) was taken in April 1944. The freshly applied colors of Measure 32 are well defined, as is the port arrangement of design 2a. *USN official*

USS *Nassau* returns to San Francisco on 21 November 1945 with a deck load of various types of aircraft. The Measure 21 paintwork is badly weathered.
J A Casoly

USS St George (AVG-17) – HMS Pursuer

Laid down as merchant ship *Mormacland*. Transferred to Royal Navy as HMS *Pursuer* 14 June 1943. Returned 12 February 1946

USS Altamaha (AVG-18)

Completed at Puget Sound Navy Yard

SERVICE HISTORY
September 1943 Pacific; aircraft transport between West Coast and the Pacific islands
March 1944 VC-66 embarked at Pearl Habor
April 1944 Anti-submarine operations near the Marshall Islands
May 1944 West Coast shipyard
November 1944-February 1945 Supply to the Third Fleet, including damage by hurricane on 18 December 1944
Until August 1945 Transport cruises between California and Pearl Harbor
1945-1946 'Magic Carpet' operations after the end of the War, between Okinawa and the West Coast

27 September 1946 Withdrawn from service; reserve fleet

AIRCRAFT, SQUADRONS
March-April 1944 VC-66 with 12 FMs and 9 TBMs = 21

CAMOUFLAGE
September 1942 and July 1943 Presumably Measure 14
1945 Presumably Measure 21

RADAR
July 1943 SC, SG, YE
1945 SK, SG, YE

USS Prince William (AVG-19) – HMS Striker

Transferred to Royal Navy as HMS *Striker* 28 April 1943. Returned 12 February 1946

USS Barnes (AVG-20)

SERVICE HISTORY
1943 Pacific; transport cruises, West Coast to Western Pacific
November-December 1943 Tarawa, Gilbert Islands
September-October 1944 Carolines, Luzon
August-November 1945 Occupation of Japan
March 1946 Return to West Coast
29 August 1946 Withdrawn from service; reserve

AIRCRAFT, SQUADRONS
July 1943 VC-34 with 1 FM and 6 TBFs = 7
November-December 1943 As ferry: 22 F6Fs of VF-1
March 1944 As ferry: VF-34 with 30 F6Fs
February 1945-July 1945 VF-82

CAMOUFLAGE
March 1943 Dazzle pattern Measure ?
1944-1945 Presumably Measure 21

RADAR
March 1943 SC, SG, YE

Left: USS *Altamaha* (CVE-18) with a deck load of P-51 fighter aircraft, destined for the USAAF in the Pacific. This photograph was taken on 16 July 1943 off San Francisco, and it shows that SC radar was fitted at this time. The paintwork is already badly weathered. Numerous 20mm Oerlikons can be seen, in addition to the 40mm twin AA guns.
USN (BfZ collection)

Above: USS *Barnes* (CVE-20), evidently painted Ocean Gray to Measure 14. If this is so, the photograph would date from around February 1943, ie as commissioned. Further evidence for this is the presence of the SC antenna. However, if credence is given to the dating of another photo, the ship must have been repainted in March 1943 to an unknown 'dazzle pattern'. If this photo really shows the Navy Blue paintwork of Measure 21, the date would then be early to mid-1945, although this would imply that SC radar was never replaced by SK, which seems improbable.
USN official

USS Block Island (AVG-21)

SERVICE HISTORY
May 1943 Atlantic; until the Summer two aircraft transport missions to Ireland, thereafter anti-submarine operations. Two German submarines sunk
29 May 1944 Sunk by submarine torpedo north-west of Canary Islands

AIRCRAFT, SQUADRONS
July 1943 VC-25 with 6 FMs and 12 TBFs = 18
December 1943-February 1944 VC-58 with 9 FMs and 12 TBFs = 21
February-March 1944 VC-6 with 9 FMs and 12 TBFs = 21

April-May 1944 VC-58 with 9 FMs and 12 TBFs = 21
May 1944 VC-55 with 9 FMs and 12 TBFs = 21

CAMOUFLAGE
October 1943 Measure 22

RADAR
October 1943 SK, SG, YE

The date of this picture of USS *Block Island* (CVE-21) is also unknown. Presumably it was taken in late 1943, judging by the SK antenna, and Measure 22. At least 13 20mm AA guns can be made out.
USN official

HMS Searcher (AVG-22)

Completed at Commercial Iron Works. No American name. Transferred to Royal Navy as HMS *Searcher* 7 April 1943. Returned to US Navy on 29 November 1945

USS Breton (AVG-23)

SERVICE HISTORY
1943-1944 For the whole of the War transport operations within 'Carrier Transport Squadron Pacific'

June-August 1944 Saipan, Tinian, Philippines, Bonin Islands

April 1945 Okinawa, thereafter occupation of Japan

September-November 1945 'Magic Carpet' operations

30 August 1946 Withdrawn from service; reserve fleet

1 July 1958 Reactivated for the MSTS

26 October 1970 Withdrawn from service; stricken

AIRCRAFT, SQUADRONS
July 1943 VC-16 with 36 F6Fs and 18 F4Fs, apparently (probably transport)

March 1944 VF-33 with 24 F6Fs

March-April 1945 As ferry: transportation of F4Us and F6Fs

CAMOUFLAGE
December 1943 Presumably Measure 14

November 1945 Presumably Measure 21

RADAR
November 1945 SK, SG, YE

December 1949 As previously

USS *Breton*, taken on 17 November 1945 on her return to San Francisco Bay from a 'Magic Carpet' operation. The dark blue paintwork corresponds to Measure 21. *J A Casoly*

USNS *Breton* (T-CVE-23). Note the different appearance after reactivation in 1958 — the ship's cranes fitted subsequently, the slightly lengthened stacks and the lack of heavier radar antennas and any kind of armament. The aircraft, probably destined for use in Vietnam, comprise a B-26 bomber, and several A-1 Skyraiders. *MSTS official*

HMS Ravager (AVG-24)

Completed at Willamette Steel. Transferred to Royal Navy 25 April 1943. Apparently was to have been named HMS *Charger*. Returned to US Navy 27 February 1946

USS Croatan (AVG-25)

SERVICE HISTORY

July 1943 Atlantic
August 1943 Anti-submarine escort of convoys
October 1943 Two aircraft transport missions to North Africa
From January 1944 Anti-submarine warfare, several operations
September-November 1945 Pilot qualifications, East Coast
November 1945 'Magic Carpet' between East Coast and France
20 May 1946 Withdrawn from service; reserve fleet
16 June 1958 Reactivated for MSTS as T-CVHE-25
1 July 1958 Reclassified T-CVU-25
27 October 1964 Transferred to NASA with civilian crew. Served for a time as a sea-going launch platform for experiments in the South Pacific. Rocket launchers were fixed at the stern and around the after elevator and tracking antennas were installed. This was all removed by May 1965

From 20 May 1965 Renewed normal aircraft ferry service for the MSTS. Starboard stack as USS *Card* (CVE-11).
1970 Withdrawn from service; stricken

AIRCRAFT, SQUADRONS

July 1943 VC-19 with 6 FMs and 12 TBFs = 18
April-May 1944 VC-42 with 9 FMs and 11 TBMs = 20
June 1944 VC-95 with 9 FMs and 10 TBFs = 19
March-April 1945 VC-55 with 3 FMs and 16 TBMs = 19

CAMOUFLAGE

May 1943 Measure 22

RADAR

May 1943 SC, SG, YE
1944 SK, SG, YE

USS *Croatan*, here still classified as ACV-25, photographed on 20 May 1943 off Restoration Point, Wisconsin. The picture shows the ship just four weeks after commissioning, at which time it is clear that Measure 22 was carried. The SC radar antenna is still on the mast, but it was replaced by SK later.
USN (BfZ collection)

Left and above: These two photos show the appearance of USNS *Croatan* as T-AKV-43 in the period 1964-65, when the ship was in the service of the National Space Administration (NASA), acting as a test platform for various experiments. The stacks were extended, and show some similarity to those of the *Independence* class. Note the two heavy cranes and the numerous calibration devices and antennas distributed over the deck.
MSC

USS Prince William (AVG-31)

Laid down as AVG-31. Completed at Puget Sound Navy Yard

SERVICE HISTORY
July 1943 Pacific; aircraft transport missions between West Coast, New Caledonia, Samoa, Espiritu Santo
April 1944 Short stay on West Coast, transport mission to Australia
May 1944 Transfer to Atlantic
July-August 1944 Pilot qualifications in Chesapeake Bay, one aircraft transport mission to Casablanca
October 1944-January 1945 Training carrier
June 1945 Return to Pacific; aircraft transport missions to Hawaii until end of War

Right: USS *Prince William* (ACV-31), the only American representative of the second series of the *Bogue* class, pictured off Puget Sound Navy Yard on 15 April 1943, one week before commissioning, painted in Measure 14. *USN (BfZ collection)*

Below: This aerial picture of *Prince William* dates from 7 August 1943, and shows 17 aircraft on deck, which are being transported to an operational base in the Pacific. The wings of the transport aircraft were removed prior to loading. At a later time CVE-31 was given a 'dazzle pattern' camouflage scheme. *USN official*

September 1945 Seven months of 'Magic Carpet' operations
April 1946 Transfer to Atlantic
29 August 1946 Withdrawn from service; reserve fleet

AIRCRAFT, SQUADRONS
July 1943 VC-64 with 11 FMs and 4 TBFs = 15

CAMOUFLAGE
April 1943 Presumably Measure 14
1944 Measure ?

RADAR
April 1943 SC or SC-2, SG, YE
1944 SK, SG, YE

USS Chatham (AVG-32) – HMS Slinger

Laid down as USS *Chatham* (AVG-32). Completed at Willamette Iron. Transferred to Royal Navy as HMS *Slinger* 11 August 1943. Returned to US Navy on 27 February 1946.

USS Glacier (AVG-33) – HMS Atheling

Laid down as AVG-33 and commissioned on 3 July 1943. Withdrawn from service 31 July 1943 and transferred to Royal Navy as HMS *Atheling* (CVE-33). Returned 13 December 1946

HMS *Atheling* (AVG-33) belonged to the second group of the *Bogue* class, all of which, with the exception of USS *Prince William* (AVG-31), flew the British flag. This photo was taken in 1947 in Valletta harbor, Malta.
Pavia (BfZ collection)

USS Pybus (AVG-34) – HMS Emperor

Laid down as AVG-34. Commissioned 31 May 1943. Withdrawn from service 6 August 1943 and transferred to Royal Navy as HMS *Emperor*. Returned 12 February 1946

USS Baffins (AVG-35) – HMS Ameer

Laid down as AVG-35. Commissioned 28 June 1943. Withdrawn from service 19 July 1943 and transferred to the Royal Navy as HMS *Ameer*. Returned 17 January 1946

USS Bolinas (AVG-36) – HMS Begum

Laid down as AVG-36. Commissioned 22 July 1943. Withdrawn from service 2 August 1943 and transferred to Royal Navy as HMS *Begum*. Returned 4 January 1946

USS Bastian (AVG-37) – HMS Trumpeter

Laid down as USS *Bastian* (ACV-37). Completed as Commercial Iron Works. Transferred to Royal Navy as HMS *Trumpeter* 4 August 1943. Was to have been called HMS *Lucifer*. Returned 6 April 1946

USS Carnegie (AVG-38) – HMS Empress

Commissioned as CVE-38 on 9 August 1943. Withdrawn from service 12 August 1943 and transferred to Royal Navy as HMS *Empress* on same day. Returned 4 February 1946

USS Cordova (AVG-39) – HMS Khedive

Laid down as ACV-39. Transferred to Royal Navy 25 August 1943 as HMS *Khedive*. Returned 26 January 1946

USS Delgada (AVG-40) – HMS Speaker

Laid down as ACV-40. Transferred to Royal Navy as HMS *Speaker* on 20 November 1943. Returned 27 July 1946

USS Edisto (AVG-41) – HMCS Nabob

Laid down as ACV-41. Transferred to Royal Canadian Navy as HMCS *Nabob* (CVE-41) on 7 September 1943, but remained under operational control of the Royal Navy. Torpedoed 22 August 1944, was not repaired; sold 1947

USS Estero (AVG-42) – HMS Premier

Laid down as ACV-42. Completed at Commercial Iron Works. Transferred to Royal Navy as HMS *Premier* on 3 November 1943. Returned 12 April 1946

USS Jamaica (AVG-43) – HMS Shah

Laid down as ACV-43. Transferred to Royal Navy as HMS *Shah* on 27 September 1943. Returned 6 December 1945

USS Keweenaw (AVG-44) – HMS Patroller

Laid down as ACV-44. Transferred to Royal Navy as HMS *Patroller* on 22 October 1943. Returned 13 December 1946

USS McClure (AVG-45) – USS Prince – HMS Rajah

Laid down as USS *McClure* (ACV-45). Renamed USS *Prince* on 13 December 1943. Transferred to Royal Navy as HMS *Rajah* on 17 January 1944. Returned on 13 December 1946

USS Niantic (AVG-46) – HMS Ranee

Laid down as ACV-46. Transferred to Royal Navy as HMS *Ranee* on 8 November 1943. Returned 21 November 1946

USS Perdido (AVG-47) – HMS Trouncer

Laid down as ACV-47. Transferred to Royal Navy as HMS *Trouncer* on 31 January 1944. Returned 3 March 1946

USS Sunset (AVG-48) – HMS Thane

Laid down as ACV-48. Transferred to Royal Navy as HMS *Thane* on 19 November 1943. Severely damaged by submarine torpedo 15 January 1945. Officially returned 5 December 1945

USS St Andrews (AVG-49) – HMS Queen

Laid down as ACV-49. Transferred to Royal Navy as HMS *Queen* 7 December 1943. Returned 31 October 1946

USS St Joseph (AVG-50) – HMS Ruler

Laid down as ACV-50. Transferred to Royal Navy as HMS *Ruler* 22 December 1943. Returned 29 January 1946

This picture of HMS *Ranee* (AVG-46) with pendant number
03 dates from 1945. Note the American radar antenna SK
with IFF supplement plus the aircraft homing beacon YE.
The ship's paintwork shows the effects of the long period of
operation.
BfZ collection

HMS *Ruler* (AVG-30) with freshly painted British
camouflage scheme and the typically large pendant number,
applied to the hull forward, in contrast to the American
practice of painting it on the island.
USN (Barilli collection)

HMS *Smiter* (AVG-52) flying the Royal Navy's White
Ensign and recognition signal flags. The camouflage scheme
is British as are the markings of the aircraft on board. 20mm
AA guns can be made out in the side galleries.
USN (Barilli collection)

USS St Simon (AVG-51) – HMS Arbiter

Laid down as ACV-51. Transferred to Royal Navy
as HMS *Arbiter* 31 December 1943. Returned 3
March 1946

USS Vermillion (AVG-52) – HMS Smiter

Laid down as ACV-52. Transferred to Royal Navy
as HMS *Smiter* 20 January 1944. Returned 6 April
1946

USS Willapa (AVG-53) – HMS Puncher

Laid down as ACV-53. Transferred to Royal Navy
as HMS *Puncher* 5 February 1944. Returned to US
Navy on 17 January 1946

USS Winjah (AVG-54) – HMS Reaper

Laid down as ACV-54. Transferred to Royal Navy
as HMS *Reaper* 18 February 1944. Returned to US
Navy on 20 May 1946

Sangamon Class

This class evolved in parallel with the *Bogue* class. With further C3 commercial ship hulls unavailable, the US Navy decided in 1942 to convert four completed oilers of the T3-S2-A1 type. These ships were begun as tankers for the merchant navy, then taken over and commissioned by the Navy in 1940-41 after completion, then to be converted into ACVs in 1942.

The engines-aft arrangement made it convenient to locate the exhaust uptakes right at the stern, where they were fitted horizontally at the edge of the flight deck. These ships were larger than the first two classes and of higher performance. The hangar was enclosed, and could accommodate 30 aircraft. Two catapults were fitted forward, although the second catapult was not installed until late Autumn 1944. The hull side was flat, with no sponsons, unlike the *Bogue* class. Several openings in the sides, which was a feature of this class, provided better ventilation of the hangar. In the course of the War some of the ships were fitted with two extra quadruple 40mm and six twin mounts, plus about ten 20mm AA guns. Up to 34 aircraft could be carried during normal flying operations.

As will be seen later, these four CVEs were used in combat far more often than the other ships of the type, which were very often restricted to transport duties for long periods. These ships often operated together in a group, in the Atlantic and, later, in the Pacific, where they worked as part of CARDIV 22.

USS Sangamon (AO-28/AVG-26)

Completed as mercantile tanker *Esso Trenton*. Taken over by the US Navy 27 October 1940. Classified as AO-28 on 12 April 1941, and renamed USS *Sangamon*. Commissioned 23 October 1941 as AO-28. Reclassified as AVG-26 on 14 February 1942; AVG conversion carried out at Newport News SB & DD.

SERVICE HISTORY
25 August 1942   Commissioned as AVG-26
October 1942   Atlantic; TF-34 in 'Operation Torch'
November 1942   Return to East Coast. Transfer to Pacific
January 1943   Pacific. CARDIV 22; New Hebrides, eight months in the Solomons
August 1943   Espiritu Santo
September 1943   West Coast shipyard
November 1943   Espiritu Santo, TF-53, Tarawa
January 1944   West Coast, Pearl Harbor, Kwajalein
February 1944   Eniwetok, Pearl Harbor shipyard
March-April 1944   TG-50.15; Admiralty Islands, supplying Fleet Carriers at the Palau Islands

June 1944   TF-53; Kwajalein, Marianas; TF-52 at Saipan
July 1944   Saipan
August 1944   Guam, Marcus
September 1944   Morotai
October 1944   TG-77.4 at Leyte ('Taffy 1'); participation in battle off Samar; damaged 19 October 1944 by aircraft bombs, 25 October 1944 by Kamikaze
November 1944   West Coast shipyard, second catapult installed
February 1945   Training of VC-33 at Hawaii
March 1945   TU-52.1.1 off the Japanese home islands
April 1945   TU-52.1.3; Okinawa, damaged by Kamikaze on 4 May 1945 (11 dead, 25 missing, 21 seriously wounded)
June 1945   Pearl Harbor via Ulithi; transfer to East Coast for docking
August 1945   Repairs stopped at news of Japan's surrender
24 October 1945   Withdrawn from service; scrapped

AIRCRAFT, SQUADRONS
November 1942 VGF-26 with 12 F4Fs and VGS-26 with 9 SBDs and 9 TBFs = 30
July 1943 CVEG-26 with VF-26 (17 F4Fs) and VC-26 (9 SBDs and 8 TBFs) = 34
November-December 1943 VC-26 with 12 F6Fs, 9 SBDs and 9 TBFs = 30
January-February 1944 CVEG-37 with VF-37 (12 F6Fs) and VC-37 (9 SBDs and 10 TBFs/TBMs) = 31
July-August 1944 CVEG-37 with VF-37 (22 F6Fs) and VT-37 (9 TBFs/TBMs) = 31

October 1944 CVEG-37 with VF-37 (17 F6Fs) and VT-37 (9 TBMs) = 26
March-April 1945 VC-33 with 24 F6Fs and 6 TBMs = 30

CAMOUFLAGE
1942-43 Presumably Measure 14

RADAR
1942 SC, SG, YE
October 1943 SC-2, SG, YE

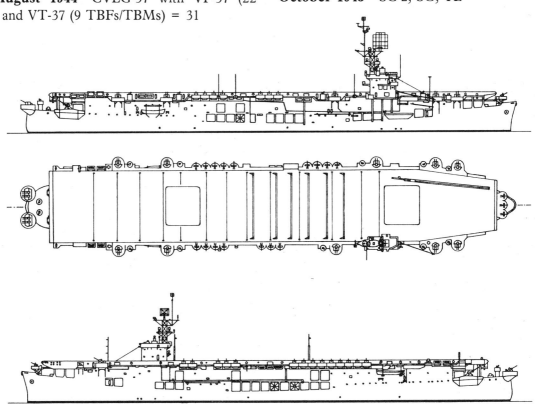

The port side profile shows the appearance of all four units of the *Sangamon* class at the time of the first Atlantic operations. Initially there were only 8 40mm AA guns in twin mounts, and SC radar. Starboard side profile and deck plan show USS *Santee* (CVE-29) in 1945, with strengthened 40mm AA armament and SK radar.

This aerial picture of USS *Sangamon* shows that the arrangement of the openings along the starboard side of the hangar differs slightly from that on the port side.
USN official

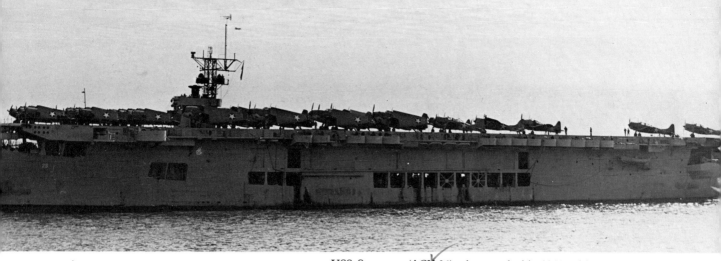

USS *Sangamon* (ACV-26), photographed in 1942, with Measure 14 camouflage. The SC radar antenna visible here was replaced by SC-2 in 1943. The director unit on the bridge was presumably removed later. The long row of ten similar openings along the hangar is a distinctive feature of this class.
USN (BfZ collection)

USS Suwannee (AO-33/AVG-27)

Completed as mercantile tanker *Markay*. Taken over by US Navy as AO-33 on 12 April 1941, renamed USS *Suwannee*. Commissioned as AO-33 on 9 July 1941. Reclasssified as AVG-27 on 30 January 1942 and subsequently converted to AVG at Newport News SB & DD

SERVICE HISTORY
24 September 1942 Commissioned as AVG-27
November 1942 Atlantic; invasion of North Africa, return to East Coast
December 1942 Pacific; South Pacific, Guadalcanal, Solomons
January 1943 New Caledonia, remained there for 7 months
October 1943 West Coast
November 1943 Gilbert Islands, Tarawa, Makin
December 1943 West Coast
January 1944 Hawaii, Marshall Islands, Roi, Namur
February 1944 Kwajalein, Eniwetok
March 1944 Pearl Harbor, Palau Islands
April 1944 Solomons, Hollandia
June 1944 Saipan, Marianas, Guam; aerial and submarine escort
September 1944 Morotai
October 1944 Leyte; TG-77.4 ('Taffy 1') during the battle off Samar; seriously damaged by dive bombers on 25 and 26 October 1944
November 1944 West Coast shipyard
February 1945 Tulagi via Pearl Harbor, then to Okinawa via Ulithi
April 1945 Okinawa, Japanese home islands
24 May 1945 At Okinawa, damaged by internal explosion

June 1945 Leyte, Borneo
August 1945 Okinawa
September 1945 Return to East Coast
October 1946 Stand-by reserve
28 October 1946 Withdrawn from service; reserve fleet

AIRCRAFT, SQUADRONS
November 1942 VGF-27 (11 F4Fs), VGF-28 (12 F4Fs), VGS-27 (9 TBFs), VGS-30 (6 F4Fs) = 38
December 1942 VGF-27 with 18 F4Fs and VGS-27 with 15 TBFs = 33
July 1943 CVEG-27 with VF-27 (18 F4Fs) and VT-27 (15 TBFs) = 33
November-December 1943 CVEG-60 with VF-60 (12 F6Fs) and VC-60 (9 SBDs and 9 TBFs) = 30
January-February 1944 As previously
April-May 1944 VC-3
July-August 1944 CVEG-60 with VF-60 (22 F6Fs) and VT-60 (9 TBMs) = 31
October 1944 As previously
March-April 1945 CVEG-40 with VF-40 (17 F6Fs) and VT-40 (10 TBMs) = 27
November 1945 VGF-27 with 18 F4Fs and VGS-27 with 15 TBFs = 33

CAMOUFLAGE
October 1943 Presumably Measure 14
March 1945 Possibly Measure 22

RADAR
1944 SC-2, SG, YE
March 1945 SK, SG, YE

This photograph of USS *Suwannee* (CVE-27) dates from 12 October 1943, when the ship was already in the Pacific. The wartime censor has touched out the radar equipment. *USN official*

USS Chenango (AO-31/AVG-28)

Completed in 1939 as mercantile tanker *Esso New Orleans*. Classified as AO-31 on 12 April 1941, renamed USS *Chenango*, taken over by US Navy 31 May 1941. Commissioned as AO-31 on 20 June 1941. Withdrawn from service 16 March 1942, reclassified as AVG-28 on same day, on commencement of conversion at Bethlehem, Staten Island

SERVICE HISTORY
October 1942   Atlantic; invasion of North Africa
December 1942   Pacific; convoy escort at Guadalcanal
August 1943   West Coast shipyard
October 1943   Gilbert Islands
From January 1944   Roi, Kwajalein, Eniwetok, Hollandia
July 1944   Marianas
October 1944   Leyte; participation in the battle off Samar ('Taffy 1')
November 1944   Aircraft transport for Fleet Carriers at Leyte
March 1945   Okinawa; 9 April 1945 damaged by own aircraft crashing onto ship
July 1945   Supplying the Third Fleet
November 1945   'Magic Carpet' mission from Okinawa and Pearl Harbor to West Coast
14 August 1946   Withdrawn from service; reserve fleet

AIRCRAFT, SQUADRONS
November 1942   Transport of 76 P-40s for the USAAF
January 1943   VGF-28 with 11 F4Fs and VGS-28 with 8 SBDs and 9 TBFs = 28
July 1943   CVEG-28 with VF-28 (18 F4Fs) and VC-28 (9 SBDs and 8 TBFs) = 35
November 1943-February 1944   CVEG-35 with VF-35 (12 F6Fs) and VC-35 (9 SBDs and 9 TBFs/TBMs) = 30
July-August 1944   CVEG-35 with VF-35 (22 F6Fs) and VT-35 (9 TBMs) = 31
October 1944   As previously
March-July 1945   CVEG-25 with VF-25 (18 F6Fs) and VT-25 (12 TBMs) = 30
August 1945   CVEG-33 with F6Fs and TBMs

CAMOUFLAGE
September 1943   Presumably Measure 14
July 1945   Presumably Measure 21

RADAR
1942-43   SC, SG, YE

Above: USS *Chenango* (CVE-28), around 1943. The former oiler had her engines aft, hence the position of the two short stacks visible here. The 5in/51 guns seen here are the older model, as used in older battleships on casemate mountings. Note the exposed mounts for the 40mm and 20mm AA guns.
USN official

Right: This photograph of USS *Chenango* may have been taken in mid-1945.
USN official

USS Santee (AO-29/AVG-29)

Completed as mercantile tanker *Esso Seakey* in 1939. Taken over by US Navy 30 October 1940, commissioned as USS *Santee* (AO-29). Reclassified as AVG-29 on 9 January 1942 on commencement of conversion at Norfolk Navy Yard

SERVICE HISTORY
24 August 1942 Commissioned as AVG-29
September 1942 Atlantic; TF-22
30 October 1942 TG-34.2; damaged by own aircraft bomb dropped by mistake. Continued to West Africa
November 1942 Return to East Coast
January 1943 To Brazil; TU-23.1.6; patrols in South Atlantic
March 1943 Return to East Coast
June-July 1943 To Casablanca
July-November 1943 Anti-submarine operations south of the Azores; occasional air cover for USS *Iowa* (BB-61), with President F D Roosevelt on board

December 1943 TG-21.11
January 1944 Aircraft transport to Glasgow; return to East Coast
February 1944 Return to Pacific via Panama Canal
March 1944 Aircraft transport to Pearl Harbor; to Fifth Fleet west of the Palau Islands, with the three sister ships to form CARDIV 22; New Hebrides
April 1944 New Guinea, Hollandia
June 1944 Transportation of aircraft crews of Marine Air Group 21 to Guam
September 1944 TF-77; Morotai
October 1944 Philippines, Leyte; participation in the battle off Samar ('Taffy 1'); damaged by submarine and aircraft torpedo on 25 October 1944
November 1944 Docked, repairs in Pearl Harbor
December 1944 West Coast shipyard
February 1945 Pearl Harbor
March 1945 Leyte

April 1945 Okinawa and East China Sea, Japanese home islands

July 1945 Air cover during minesweeping operations around Okinawa, Guam; damaged by own aircraft whose arresting hook was broken

August 1945 Saipan, Leyte

September 1945 Evacuation of American, British and Dutch prisoners of war from Formosa to Manila; occupation of Japan

October 1945 'Magic Carpet' missions to Pearl Harbor and Guam

March 1946 Return to East Coast

21 October 1946 Withdrawn from service; reserve fleet

AIRCRAFT, SQUADRONS

November 1942 VGF-29 with 14 F4Fs and VGS-29 with 9 SBDs and 8 TBFs = 31

June-August 1943 VF-29 with 12 F4Fs and VC-29 with 9 SBDs and 13 TBFs = 34

April-October 1944 CVEG-26 with VF-26 (24 FMs) and VT-26 (9 TBFs/TBMs) = 33

March-July 1945 CVEG-24 with VF-24 (18 F6Fs) and VT-24 (12 TBMs) = 30

July-August 1945 CVEG-26 with VF-26 (F6Fs) and VT-26 (TBMs)

CAMOUFLAGE

September 1942 Measure 17

October 1943 Possibly Measure 14

RADAR

October 1943 SC, SG, YE

1945 SK, SG, YE

This identification photograph of USS *Santee* (ACV-29), taken in September 1942, shows clearly the camouflage design of Measure 17, which was the same to port and starboard.
USN (BfZ collection)

This photo of USS *Santee*, now classified as CVE-29, was
taken on 12 October 1943, and shows a rather curious
deviation from the regulations regarding Measure 22, giving
the impression that the waterline was painted too high. Later
we will make the same observation about another CVE, but
it is possible that this is a different camouflage measure
whose number is not known.
USN (BfZ collection)

Casablanca Class

All 50 ships of this class were completed from unfinished hulls of MARCOM S4-S2-BB3 type merchant ships. The Navy officially took over each ship on the day of commissioning.

This class is an example of the USA's ability to realize its full economic and manpower potential in times of war and emergency. It is a considerable feat to complete and equip 50 ships of this size in just under one year and the nickname 'jeep carriers' referred not only to their small dimensions but also to their rapid sequence of completion. The Kaiser yard in Vancouver rationalized construction as far as possible, and the building tables at the end of the book show that the schedule for laying down, launching and completion was enforced to the day. The longest building time was eight months, the shortest 3½! To complete the picture, it must be mentioned here that the US Navy had to fulfil numerous other building programs at the same time, including hundreds of destroyers and escort ships, submarines, cruisers and many other new ship types and conversions.

In contrast to the first two AVG classes, no ships of this class were loaned to the Royal Navy. All of them spent most of their time in the Pacific, carrying out a multitude of tasks.

Ships of this class had one catapult and two elevators. A characteristic feature was the flat transom, above which the single 5in/38 gun was fitted in a gun tub. In addition there were numerous AA mounts located under the flight deck edges, in contrast to the *Sangamon* class.

There was evidently a bottleneck in the supply of turbine propulsion systems, and therefore the choice of reciprocating engines was inevitable, driving two screws. The two exhaust uptakes emerged under the flight deck on each side, towards the stern.

A few ships of this class were reactivated at the start of the Korean War, in which they were used principally as aircraft ferries under a civilian MSTS crew.

HMS Ameer (AVG-55) – USS Alazon Bay – Casablanca

Laid down as HMS *Ameer*. Renamed USS *Alazon Bay* on 23 January 1943, then *Casablanca* on 3 April 1945

SERVICE HISTORY
August 1943 Pacific; training ship for escort carrier crews
August 1944 Aircraft transport to the Western Pacific
October 1944 Training ship again
From March 1945 Transport missions to Guam

September 1945 'Magic Carpet' missions between Pacific Islands, Japan and the West Coast
10 June 1946 Withdrawn from service; reserve fleet

CAMOUFLAGE
1943 Measure 14
1944 Measure 32/12a

RADAR
August 1944 SC-2, SG, YE

One of the first photos of USS *Casablanca* (CVE-55). At this time the ship carried SC-2, SG and YE antennas, all of which have been removed by the wartime censor. Note the large number of mounts for the 40mm and 20mm AA armament.
'Our Navy' photo

USS Liscome Bay (AVG-56)

Launched as ACV-56

SERVICE HISTORY
October 1943 Pacific; CARDIV 24, only one operation
November 1943 TF-52; air support at the Gilbert Islands
24 November 1943 Sunk by submarine torpedo in the Gilbert Islands area (Rear Admiral Mullinnix, Captain Wiltsie, 53 officers and 591 men lost, 272 men saved)

AIRCRAFT, SQUADRONS
July-November 1943 VC-39 with 11 FMs, 2 SBDs and 9 TBMs = 22
November 1943 VGF-56 with 16 FMs and VGS-56 with 12 TBMs = 28

CAMOUFLAGE
September 1943 Presumably Measure 14

RADAR
September 1943 SC-2, SG, YE

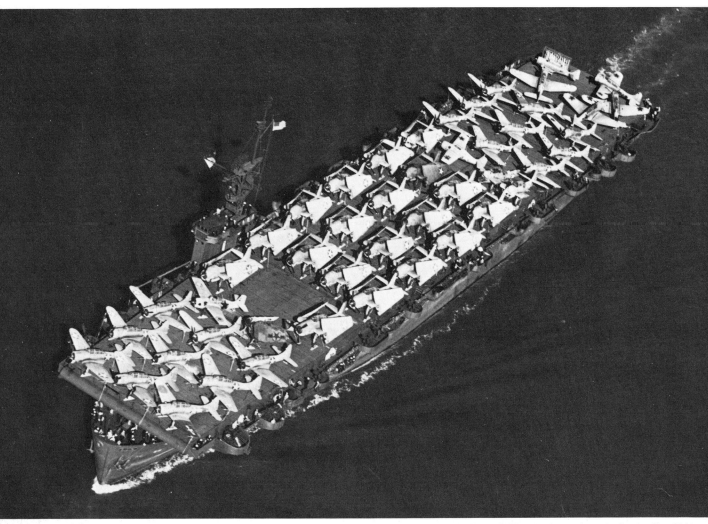

USS *Liscome Bay* (CVE-56), pictured on 20 September 1943, ie about six weeks after commissioning, with SBD and TBM aircraft of VC-39 on board. From this viewpoint the dark paintwork of Measure 14 matches the environment very well, while the aircraft stand out too strongly. The SC-2 radar antenna can just be made out.
USN official

USS Alikula Bay (AVG-57) – Coral Sea – Anzio

Laid down as USS *Alikula Bay* (ACV-57). Renamed *Coral Sea* 3 April 1943. Commissioned as USS *Coral Sea* (CVE-57), renamed *Anzio* on 15 September 1944

SERVICE HISTORY
November-December 1943   Pacific; Makin
January-February 1944   Kwajalein
March 1944   Emirau
April-May 1944   Aitape, New Guinea
June-July 1944   Saipan
August-September 1944   West Coast shipyard, return to Pacific as USS *Anzio*

December 1944   Anti-submarine escort at Leyte and Luzon
February-March 1945   Anti-submarine escort at Iwo Jima
March-June 1945   Anti-submarine escort and air support at Okinawa
July-August 1945   Anti-submarine escort around the Japanese home islands. Four Japanese submarines sunk since November 1944
September 1945   Two 'Magic Carpet' missions from Okinawa, until December 1945
December 1945   West Coast
5 August 1946   Withdrawn from service; reserve fleet

AIRCRAFT, SQUADRONS
July 1943 VC-33 with 6 FMs, 1 SBD and 12 TBFs = 19
November-December 1943 VC-33 with 16 FMs and 12 TBFs = 28
January-February 1944 VC-33 with 5 FMs, 9 F4Fs and 12 TBFs/TBMs = 26
July-August 1944 VC-3 with 14 FMs and 12 TBFs/TBMs = 26
October 1944-March 1945 VC-82 with FMs and TBMs
March-August 1945 VC-13 with 12 FMs and 12 TBMs = 24
August-September 1945 VC-66 with FMs and TBMs

CAMOUFLAGE
1943 Measure 22
October 1944 Measure 32/12a

RADAR
October 1944 SC-2, SG, YE

The date of this picture of CVE 57 is not known, but it was certainly while she still carried the name *Coral Sea*. Note the two elevator shafts, with the elevator platforms in the lowered position. The catapult track can be seen on the forward part of the flight deck.
USN (BfZ collection)

Above: Details of the stern of *Anzio*, shown on 6 October 1944, shortly after being renamed, and after the application of camouflage to Measure 32/12a. SG and YE antennas are clearly visible on the mast.
USN (BfZ collection)

Left: USS *Anzio* goes the way of all old iron ships, seen here under tow in 1960, bearing a non-standard hull number on her bow.
BfZ collection

USS Anguilla Bay (AVG-58) – Corregidor

Laid down as USS *Anguilla Bay* (ACV-58). Was to have been transferred to the Royal Navy as HMS *Atheling*, but remained with the US Navy, CVE-33 being transferred instead. Renamed USS *Corregidor* on 3 April 1943; launched under this name

SERVICE HISTORY

October 1943 Pacific; CARDIV 24 in Pearl Harbor

November-December 1943 Gilbert Islands, then an aircraft transport mission from the West Coast

January-March 1944 Marshall Islands

March-April 1944 Emirau

April 1944 Hollandia

June 1944 Saipan

July 1944 Guam, then to West Coast shipyard

October-November 1944 Pilot qualifications

January 1945 Anti-submarine operations between Pearl Harbor and Eniwetok

March-April 1945 Anti-submarine operations in Marshall Islands

May-September 1945 Pilot qualifications from Pearl Harbor

October 1945 'Magic Carpet' operation from Pearl Harbor to West Coast

30 July 1946 Withdrawn from service; reserve
19 May 1951 Reactivated as T-CVE-58 for the MSTS; transport missions to Korea
1958 Lebanon crisis in Mediterranean
4 September 1958 Withdrawn from service

AIRCRAFT, SQUADRONS

July 1943 VC-41 with 11 F4Fs and 6 TBFs = 17
November-December 1943 VC-44 with 16 FMs and 12 TBFs = 28
January-February 1944 VC-44 with 6 FMs, 3 F4Fs and 11 TBFs/TBMs = 20
March 1944 VC-41 with 12 FMs, 3 F4Fs and 10 TBFs/TBMs = 25
July-August 1944 VC-41 with 14 FMs and 12 TBMs = 26
November-December 1944 VC-83 with FMs and TBMs
January-May 1945 VC-42 with FMs and TBMs

CAMOUFLAGE
1944 Measure ?

RADAR
? SK

USS *Corregidor* (CVE-58) with enclosed bridge and some of the 40mm AA guns mothballed.
'Our Navy' photo

Although steaming under the command of the then MSTS,
T-CVE-58 *Corregidor* still features the large hull number on
the island. This picture dates from March 1957, and was
taken off Capetown. Note the extended stacks.
Davis collection

USS Atheling (AVG-59) – Mission Bay

Laid down as USS *Atheling* (ACV-59). Renamed
USS *Mission Bay* 3 April 1943

SERVICE HISTORY
December 1943 Atlantic; escort duty and anti-
submarine operations, then return to East Coast
February 1944 Transport of aircraft and crews
via South Africa to India
March 1944 Arrival in India
May-June 1944 One Atlantic operation
September 1944 Anti-submarine operations in
South Atlantic
February 1945 Escort for the cruiser USS
Quincy (CA-71) returning President Roosevelt
from the Yalta Conference
March 1945 Return to East Coast
April-May 1945 Anti-submarine operations in
North Atlantic
July-December 1945 East Coast training opera-
tions

1946 Still in service, but in stand-by reserve
21 February 1947 Withdrawn from service;
reserve fleet

AIRCRAFT, SQUADRONS
July-August 1943 (intended) VC-58 with 6 FMs
and 10 TBFs = 16
December 1943 VC-8 with FMs and TBFs
September-October 1944 VC-36 with 9 FMs
and 12 TBMs = 21
March-April 1945 VC-95 with 9 FMs and 10
TBFs = 19

CAMOUFLAGE
1943 Measure 22
August 1944 Measure ?

RADAR
August 1944 SK, SG, YE

Above: USS *Mission Bay* (CVE-59), photographed in August 1944. This camouflage is probably Measure 32, design 4a.
USN official

Right: USS *Mission Bay*, taken in Mirao harbor in Japan on 28 February 1960, awaiting scrapping. The mothballed 40mm AA guns are still on board.
N Itoki (BfZ collection)

USS Astrolabe Bay (AVG-60) – Guadalcanal

Laid down as USS *Astrolabe Bay* (ACV-60). Renamed USS *Guadalcanal* on 3 April 1943

SERVICE HISTORY
November 1943   Atlantic; flagship of the anti-submarine TG-21.12
From January 1944   Anti-submarine operations in the Atlantic, off the West African coast, during which the German submarine *U-505* captured in May 1944
From December 1944   Pilot qualifications, East Coast and Caribbean
15 July 1946   Withdrawn from service; reserve fleet

AIRCRAFT, SQUADRONS
July-August 1943   (intended) VC-36 with 6 FMs and 11 TBFs = 17
March-April 1944   VC-58 with 9 FMs and 12 TBFs/TBMs = 21
May-June 1944   VC-8 with 9 FMs and 12 TBMs = 21

CAMOUFLAGE
September 1944 and April 1945   Measure ?

RADAR
1944   SK, SG, YE

USS *Guadalcanal* (CVE-60) in September 1944, taken from a height of just 200 feet somewhere in the Atlantic, showing the same camouflage scheme as *Mission Bay*, if slightly less weather-beaten. The dark deck number is hard to see against the dark blue flight deck.
USN official

USS Bucareli Bay (AVG-61) – Manila Bay

Laid down as USS *Bucareli Bay* (ACV-61). Renamed USS *Manila Bay* on 3 April 1943

SERVICE HISTORY

November-December 1943   Pacific; one transport mission with damaged aircraft from Pearl Harbor to the West Coast
January-February 1944   Flagship of CARDIV 24, TF-52; Marshall Islands, Kwajalein, Eniwetok, Majuro
March 1944   Espiritu Santo; TF-37, Kavieng, Solomons, Rabaul
April 1944   New Guinea, Hollandia
May 1944   Pearl Harbor, shipyard
June 1944   Aircraft transport to the Marianas; return with wounded to Pearl Harbor
July 1944   West Coast
October 1944   Leyte; TG-77.4 ('Taffy 2'), battle off Samar, Cebu
December 1944   Mindoro
January 1945   Philippines
5 January 1945   Damaged by Kamikaze (14 dead, 52 wounded); Lingayen

February 1945   West Coast shipyard
May 1945   Hawaii, Western Pacific
June 1945   Okinawa, Guam, Eniwetok
August 1945   TF-44; Aleutians
September 1945   Occupation of North Japan
October 1945   'Magic Carpet', working from Eniwetok, total of three missions
February 1946   East Coast
31 July 1946   Withdrawn from service; reserve fleet

AIRCRAFT, SQUADRONS

July 1943   (intended) VC-31 with 6 FMs and 12 TBFs = 18
January-July 1944   VC-7 with 16 FMs and 12 TBFs = 28
October 1944   VC-80 with 16 FMs and 12 TBMs = 28
January 1945   VC-80 with 20 FMs and 12 TBMs = 32
June-September 1945   VC-71 with FMs and TBMs

USS *Manila Bay* (CVE-61), taken in 1944.
'Our Navy' photo

HMS Begum (AVG-62) – USS Natoma Bay

Laid down as HMS *Begum*. Renamed USS *Natoma Bay* on 3 April 1943, and transferred to the US Navy. CVE-36 was transferred to the Royal Navy in her place

SERVICE HISTORY
November 1943 Pacific; transport of aircraft and crews to Hawaii
January 1944 Flagship of CARDIV 24, TG-51.2; Marshall Islands
March 1944 TF-37; Kavieng, Solomons
April 1944 TF-78; New Guinea
May 1944 Pearl Harbor
June 1944 Aircraft transport to the Marianas
July 1944 West Coast
September 1944 Pilot qualifications for squadron VC-81
October 1944 Third Fleet, TG-77.4; Philippines; flagship of TU-77.4.2. ('Taffy 2') at Leyte, battle off Samar
December 1944 Mindoro
January 1945 CARDIV 25; Luzon landings
February 1945 TU-52.2.1; Iwo Jima
June 1945 Okinawa
7 June 1945 Damaged by Kamikaze, then to Guam

August 1945 West Coast
November-December 1945 'Magic Carpet' mission from the Philippines
February 1946 Transfer to East Coast
20 May 1946 Withdrawn from service; reserve fleet

AIRCRAFT, SQUADRONS
July 1943 (intended) VC-55 with 6 FMs and 12 TBFs = 18
January-February 1944 VC-63 with 12 FMs and 12 TBMs = 24
April-May 1944 VC-63 with 28 FMs and 18 TBMs = 46 (evidently as transport)
October 1944 VC-81 with 16 FMs and 12 TBMs = 28
January 1945 VC-81 with 20 FMs and 12 TBMs = 32
March-July 1945 VC-9 with FMs and TBMs

CAMOUFLAGE
March 1945 Measure ?

RADAR
March 1945 SK, SG, YE

The camouflage scheme is scarcely visible in this picture of USS *Natoma Bay* (CVE-62), taken in the Pacific on 1 March 1945.
USN official

USS Chapin Bay (AVG-63) – Midway – St Lo

Laid down as USS Chapin Bay (ACV-63), renamed USS *Midway* on 3 April 1943. Later launched under this name and commissioned. Renamed USS *St Lo* on 15 September 1944

SERVICE HISTORY
1943-1944   Pacific; two transport missions to Pearl Harbor, one to Australia
June 1944   'Carrier Support Group 1'; Saipan
July 1944   Eniwetok, Tinian
August 1944   Manus
September 1944   TF-77; Morotai, Palau Islands (renamed *St Lo*)
October 1944   Leyte; TU-77.4.3 ('Taffy 3')
25 October 1944   Sunk by Kamikaze hit during battle off Samar

AIRCRAFT, SQUADRONS
July 1943   (intended) VC-42 with 6 FMs and 12 TBFs/TBMs = 18
March 1944   VC-65 with 12 FMs and 9 TBMs = 21
June-August 1944   VC-65 with 12 FMs and 9 TBMs = 21
October 1944   VC-65 with 17 FMs and 12 TBMs = 29

CAMOUFLAGE
April 1944   Measure 32/15a

RADAR
?   SK

USS *Midway* (CVE-63), pictured on 7 April 1944, which was renamed *St Lo* only a few months later, shortly before being sunk in the battle off Samar. The freshly painted camouflage design 15a of Measure 32 is a great help in identification. The radar antennas have been touched out by the wartime censor.
USN official

USS Didrickson Bay (AVG-64) – Tripoli

Laid down as USS *Didrickson Bay* (ACV-64), and commissioned under that name. Renamed USS *Tripoli* on 6 November 1943

SERVICE HISTORY

January 1944 Builders' trials, followed by period in dock, during which: explosion (1 fatally wounded); commissioning delayed

February 1944 Transfer to East Coast

March 1944 VC-13 on board; TG-21.15; anti-submarine operations in the area of the Cape Verde Islands

April 1944 Supply stop in Recife, Brazil, thereafter further anti-submarine operations; return to East Coast

May 1944 VC-6 on board; anti-submarine operations around the Cape Verde Islands, convoy escort at Nova Scotia

June 1944 Return to East Coast

Until July 1944 Training cruises East Coast

August 1944 Operations from Recife, Brazil (one German submarine sunk); Fourth Fleet, TG-37.7

September 1944 Return to Recife; anti-submarine operations together with USS *Mission Bay* (CVE-59)

October 1944 A further operation from Recife

November 1944 Return to East Coast

January 1945 Transfer to West Coast via Panama Canal

February 1945 Pacific; VC-8 transported to Hawaii, aircraft transport to Roi

August 1945 Training operations from Pearl Harbor until end of War; one 'Magic Carpet' mission to West Coast

September 1945 Night qualification cruises from Pearl Harbor, until November

November 1945 One more 'Magic Carpet' mission

January 1946 Transfer to East Coast

22 May 1946 Withdrawn from service; reserve fleet

5 January 1952 Reactivated for MSTS, serving as aircraft ferry. Total of 44 transport missions to Europe, Mediterranean and Japan in the following six years

25 November 1958 Withdrawn from service; stricken

AIRCRAFT, SQUADRONS

July 1943 (intended) VC-66 with 10 FMs and 3 TBFs = 13

March 1944 VC-13 with 9 FMs and 12 TBFs = 21

August-October 1944 VC-6 with 13 FMs and 17 TBMs = 30

RADAR

1944 SK, SG, YE

March 1952 As previously

Two months after reactivation: USS *Tripoli* (CVE-64), photographed off New York in March 1952. Despite the MSTS command and civilian crew, the ship still carries full radar equipment and armament. The upper bridge is now protected by metal plating.
Ted Stone (BfZ collection)

USS Dolomi Bay (AVG-65) – Wake Island

Laid down as ACV-65. Renamed USS *Wake Island* on 3 April 1943, and commissioned later under this name

SERVICE HISTORY
December 1943 Pacific; West Coast initially
January 1944 East Coast via Panama Canal
February 1944 TG-27.2; freight and personnel transport to India via Brazil and South Africa
March 1944 Arrival in India; departure across Indian Ocean after unloading
April 1944 Arrival East Coast
June 1944 TG-22.6; anti-submarine operations in Atlantic (one German submarine sunk)
July 1944 Casablanca, anti-submarine operations around the Azores and north-west Africa
August 1944 Return to East Coast
March-October 1944 Pilot qualifications, East Coast
November 1944 West Coast via Panama Canal
December 1944 Pacific; transport of aircraft to the Admiralty Islands via Pearl Harbor
January 1945 TG-77.4; liberation of Philippines; rescue of survivors from USS *Ommaney Bay* (CVE-79); Ulithi
February 1945 Iwo Jima, air support
March 1945 Ulithi, air support at Okinawa with TG-52.1
April 1945 Okinawa
3 April 1945 Damaged by two Kamikazes, then to Guam for repair of damage

May 1945 Return to Okinawa
June 1945 One aircraft and munitions transport mission from Guam to Okinawa
July 1945 West Coast
August 1945-January 1946 Pilot qualification cruises
5 April 1946 Withdrawn from service; stricken

AIRCRAFT, SQUADRONS
July 1943 (intended) VC-63 with 3 F4Fs, 6 FMs, 6 SBDs and 5 TBFs – 20
June-August 1944 VC-58 with 9 FMs and 12 TBMs = 21
January 1945 VOC-1 with 23 FMs and 12 TBMs = 35
March-April 1945 VOC-1 with 26 FMs and 6 TBMs = 32

CAMOUFLAGE
November 1944 and January 1945 Measure 33/10a

RADAR
January 1945 SC, SG, YE

USS *Wake Island* (CVE-65), pictured on 9 November 1944 after a refit at Norfolk Navy Yard. The camouflage scheme, to Measure 33/10a, has been freshly applied. Numerous life rafts line the edge of the flight deck. *USN offical*

USS Elbour Bay (AVG-66) – White Plains

Laid down as USS *Elbour Bay* (ACV-66). Renamed USS *White Plains* on 3 april 1943 and later commissioned under this name

SERVICE HISTORY

January-February 1944 Pacific; aircraft transport to the Marshall Islands
March 1944 West Coast
April 1944 Pilot qualification cruises on West Coast; embarked own aircraft squadron VC-4
May 1944 Training cruises from Pearl Harbor
June 1944 Saipan, Rota, Tinian, New Hebrides
August-September 1944 Fifth Fleet; Marianas; Third Fleet; Palau Islands, Ulithi
October 1944 Seventh Fleet; Leyte TU-77.4.3 ('Taffy 3')
25 October 1944 Damaged by Kamikaze and gunfire during battle off Samar
November 1944 Pearl Harbor, repairs to damage
From January 1945 Until end of war transport missions to Okinawa, Roi, Guam, Saipan, Ulithi, Samar, Leyte and Manus

August 1945 West Coast shipyard
September-October 1945 First 'Magic Carpet' mission to Okinawa: 800 men carried without installation of additional accommodation. Thereafter extra equipment to enable further transport cruises
10 July 1946 Transfer to East Coast, withdrawn from service; reserve fleet

AIRCRAFT, SQUADRONS

July 1943 (intended) VC-68 with 1 F4F, 2 FMs, 3 SBDs and 2 TBMs = 8
March 1944 (intended) VC-68 with 12 FMs and 9 TBMs = 21
April-August 1944 VC-4 with 16 FMs and 9 TBFs/TBMs = 25
October 1944 VC-4 with 16 FMs and 12 TBMs = 28
March-June 1945 As ferry: F4Us and F6Fs

CAMOUFLAGE
November 1943 Presumably Measure 14
1944 Measure 33/10a

RADAR
?

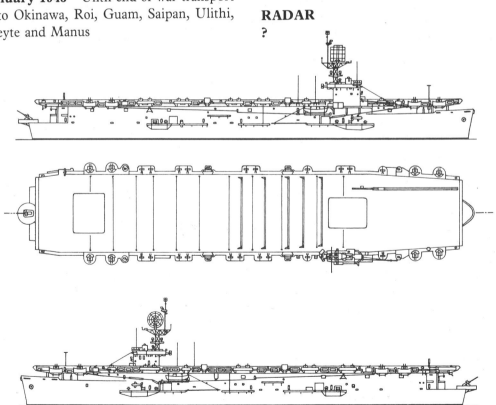

The only significant differences among the *Casablanca* class CVEs were in the radar antennas. The starboard side profile and the deck plan show USS *White Plains* (CVE-66); most of the ships between CVE-55 and -97 looked like this, with the exception of CVE-65, which still featured SC at the end of the war, and CVE-96 which still had SC-2 in 1945. The first four units of this class were also fitted with SC-2. The port side elevation shows the typical appearance of later ships, from USS *Kwajalein* (CVE-98) to USS *Munda* (CVE-104).

Right: USS *White Plains* (CVE-66). The mast visible over the after part of the ship belongs to a different vessel. *Davis collection*

Below: USS *Solomons* (CVE-67) leaves San Diego for Pearl Harbor on 30 December 1943, camouflaged to Measure 22. *USN official*

HMS Emperor (AVG-67) – USS Nassuk Bay – Solomons

Laid down as USS *Nassuk Bay* (ACV-67), but was to be transferred to the Royal Navy as HMS *Emperor*. CVE-34 was transferred instead. Renamed USS *Solomons* on 6 November 1943, and later commissioned under this name

SERVICE HISTORY
January 1944 Pacific; one transport mission with aircraft and crew from Pearl Harbor to West Coast
February 1944 To East Coast via Panama Canal
March 1944 Fourth Fleet in Atlantic; aircraft transport to Brazil and anti-submarine operations
June 1944 Return to East Coast
October 1944 Aircraft transport to Casablanca
November 1944 Return to East Coast; pilot training on the East Coast for the rest of the War

15 May 1946 Withdrawn from service; stricken

AIRCRAFT, SQUADRONS
July 1943 (intended) VC-65 with 2 F4Fs, 6 FMs, 5 SBDs and 5 TBMs = 18
March 1944 (intended) VC-9 with 13 FMs and 18 TBFs/TBMs = 31
June 1944 VC-9 with 9 FMs and 12 TBFs/TBMs = 21

CAMOUFLAGE
January 1944 Measure 22
1944 Measure 32/4a

RADAR
January 1944 SK, SG, YE

USS Kalinin Bay (AVG-68)

Laid down as ACV-68

SERVICE HISTORY
January 1944 Pacific; supply of the Fleet Carriers; with VC-3 anti-submarine escort at Marshall Islands, for several months
June 1944 Aircraft transport mission to Eniwetok
October 1944 Air support at Leyte, TU-77.4.3 ('Taffy 3')

25 October 1944 Severely damaged by Kamikaze and gunfire (only 5 dead and 55 wounded) during battle off Samar
November 1944 West Coast shipyard, repairs to damage
From January 1945 Aircraft transport to Pearl Harbor and Guam
From September 1945 Three 'Magic Carpet' missions to Samar and Pearl Harbor
December 1945 Flight deck damaged by typhoon
February 1946 Transfer to East Coast
15 May 1946 Withdrawn from service; stricken

AIRCRAFT SQUADRONS
April-August 1944 VC-3 with 14 FMs and 9 TBMs = 23
October 1944 VC-3 with 16 FMs and 12 TBFs/TBMs = 28

RADAR
January 1944 SK, SG, YE

An aerial photograph of USS *Kalinin Bay* (CVE-68), taken on 17 January 1944. The deck load is protected by windbreaks.
USN official

USS Kasaan Bay (AVG-69)

Laid down as ACV-69

SERVICE HISTORY
January 1944 Pacific; transport of aircraft and personnel to Pearl Harbor
February 1944 Transfer to East Coast
May 1944 Atlantic; aircraft transport to Casablanca
July 1944 Air and anti-submarine escort in Mediterranean
August 1944 Invasion of Southern France
October 1944 Aircraft transport from the East Coast to Casablanca
January 1945 Transfer to the Pacific; aircraft transport for the Fleet Carriers
February 1945 Pilot training duties
June 1945 Escort missions, Marshall Islands and Marianas
September 1945 'Magic Carpet' missions to

Saipan, Philippines and Hawaii
January 1946 Transfer to East Coast
6 July 1946 Withrawn from service; reserve fleet

AIRCRAFT, SQUADRONS
July 1943 (intended) VC-69 with 6 FMs and 2 TBFs = 8
March 1944 (intended) VC-12 with 9 FMs and 12 TBMs = 21
June-August 1944 VF-74 with 24 F6Fs
June-September 1945 VC-72 with FMs and TBMs

CAMOUFLAGE
January 1944 Measure 32/4a

RADAR
January 1944 SK, SG, YE

USS *Kasaan Bay* (CVE-69) with camouflage to Measure
32/4a.
Barilli collection

Kasaan Bay was scrapped in Germany. This photo was
taken in Hamburg in March 1960. Here again the 40mm AA
guns are under the hemisperical preservation hoods.
Bödecker and Drauz (BfZ collection)

USS Fanshaw Bay (AVG-70)

Laid down as ACV-70

SERVICE HISTORY

April 1944   Pacific; flagship of CARDIV 25; anti-submarine escort at Majuro

June 1944   Saipan

17 June 1944   Damaged by aircraft bombs at the Marianas

October 1944   Leyte; TU-77.4.3 ('Taffy 3')

25 October 1944   Damaged by gunfire during battle off Samar

November 1944   Pearl Harbor, repairs to damage

March 1945   Flagship of CARDIV 26; Japanese home islands

August 1945   Occupation of North Japan

October-November 1945   Return to West Coast with troops on board

14 August 1946   Withdrawn from service; reserve fleet

AIRCRAFT, SQUADRONS

March 1944   VC-4 with 12 FMs and 8 TBMs = 20

June-September 1944   VC-68 with 16 FMs and 12 TBMs = 28

September-November 1944   VC-66 with FMs and TBMs

February-March 1945   VC-8 with FMs and TBMs

March-August 1945   VOC-2 with 24 FMs and 6 TBMs = 30

August-September 1945   VC-10 with FMs and TBMs

CAMOUFLAGE

January 1944   Measure 22

RADAR

January 1944   SK, SG, YE

USS *Fanshaw Bay* (CVE-70), the 'lucky' ship of 'Taffy 3' in the battle off Samar, sustaining only relatively minor damage. This photograph was taken on 17 January 1944, during her first transport operation in the Pacific area. Measure 22 camouflage.
USN official

USS Kitkun Bay (AVG-71)

Laid down as ACV-71

SERVICE HISTORY

January-March 1944 Pacific; one transport mission to the New Hebrides

May 1944 Flagship of CARDIV 26; training cruises with VC-5, based at Pearl Harbor

June 1944 Tinian, Saipan

August 1944 Guam

September 1944 Palau Islands

October 1944 Leyte; TU-77.4.3 ('Taffy 3')

25 October 1944 Battle off Samar, during which damaged by Kamikaze; initial repairs to damage at Marcus

January 1945 Aircraft transport for the invasion of Luzon

8 January 1945 Damaged by Kamikaze near the Philippines (16 dead, 37 wounded)

February 1945 Via Leyte to West Coast ship-yard, repairs to damage

From June 1945 Third Fleet; support for Fleet Carriers off the Japanese home islands

August 1945 TF-44; Adak, Alaska

October 1945 'Magic Carpet'; return of American prisoners of war from Honshu. Further cruises from Pearl Harbor and Okinawa

19 April 1946 Withdrawn from service; stricken

AIRCRAFT, SQUADRONS

May-August 1944 VC-5 with 12 FMs and 8 TBMs = 20

August-November 1944 VC-5 with 14 FMs and 12 TBMs = 26

November 1944-February 1945 VC-91 with 17 FMs and 11 TBMs = 28

May-September 1945 VC-63 with FMs and TBMs

CAMOUFLAGE

February 1944 Presumably Measure 14

RADAR

February 1944 SK, SG, YE

On 10 February 1944 USS *Kitkun Bay* (CVE-71) was employed on a transport mission in the Pacific when this picture was taken. The Measure 14 camouflage looks very light-colored in parts where it reflects the sunshine. *USN official*

USS Fortezela Bay (AVG-72) – Tulagi

Laid down as USS *Fortezela Bay* (ACV-72). Renamed USS *Tulagi* on 6 November 1943, and later commissioned under this name

SERVICE HISTORY
January 1944   Pacific; aircraft and personnel transport to Hawaii
March 1944   Transfer to East Coast via Panama Canal
June 1944   Aircraft transport to Casablanca, return to East Coast
July 1944   Flagship TG-27.7; mission to Oran and Malta
August 1944   Preparation and participation in the invasion of Southern France
September 1944   Return to East Coast
October 1944   Transfer to West Coast; aircraft transport to Hawaii
November 1944   Anti-submarine training cruises from Pearl Harbor
December 1944   Anti-submarine operations at the Palau Islands and South Marianas
January 1945   Philippines
February 1945   Ulithi
March 1945   Air support at Iwo Jima; Ulithi
March-June 1945   Okinawa
June 1945   Return to West Coast
September 1945   Aircraft transport from Samar

January 1946   Return to West Coast
30 April 1946   Withdrawn from service; stricken

AIRCRAFT, SQUADRONS
March 1944   (intended) VC-15 with 9 FMs and 12 TBMs = 21
July 1944   VGF-1 with 24 F6Fs
December 1944-March 1945   VC-92 with 11 FMs and 12 TBMs = 23
April-July 1945   VC-92 with 19 FMs and 12 TBMs = 31

CAMOUFLAGE
May 1944   Measure ?

RADAR
May 1944   SK, SG, YE

USS *Tulagi* (CVE-72), seen here on 31 May 1944 from USS *Mission Bay* (CVE-59), during an aircraft transport mission to Casablanca. The camouflage measure, probably 32, design 4a, is the same as that of *Mission Bay* and *Guadalcanal*, and it seems to have been specially designed for Atlantic conditions. There is a windbreak to protect the deck load. *USN official*

USS Gambier Bay (AVG-73)

Laid down as ACV-73

SERVICE HISTORY
February 1944 Pacific; aircraft transport to Pearl Harbor, and for USS *Enterprise* (CV-6)
May 1944 TG-52.11; Marianas
June 1944 Air support at Saipan
July 1944 Tinian
September 1944 Palau Islands
October 1944 Leyte; TU 77.4.3 ('Taffy 3')
25 October 1944 Sunk by gunfire during battle off Samar

AIRCRAFT, SQUADRONS
March-August 1944 VC-10 with 16 FMs and 12 TBMs = 28
October 1944 VC-10 with 18 FMs and 12 TBMs = 30

CAMOUFLAGE
February 1944 Presumably Measure 14
1944 Measure 32/15a

RADAR
February 1944 SK, SG, YE

Two months after commissioning, USS *Gambier Bay* (CVE-73) is pictured on 19 February 1944, still with Ocean Gray paintwork. During the battle off Samar, in which the ship was sunk, *Gambier Bay* carried Measure 32/15a camouflage.
USN official

USS Nehenta Bay (AVG-74)

Laid down as CVE-74. Was to have been transferred to Royal Navy as HMS *Khedive*, but CVE-39 was transferred instead

SERVICE HISTORY

February 1944   Pacific; aircraft and personnel transport to Pearl Harbor

March-April 1944   Aircraft and personnel transport to Hawaii

June 1944   TF-51; Marianas

July 1944   Guam, Saipan

August 1944-January 1945   Third Fleet; Carolines, Philippines, Chinese coast, Palau Islands

18 December 1944 and 17 January 1945   Damaged by typhoons on two occasions

February 1945   West Coast shipyard

May 1945   Okinawa

June-August 1945   Third Fleet; Japanese home islands

September 1945   Pearl Harbor; 'Magic Carpet' missions to the Marshall Islands and to the Philippines

January 1946   Transfer to East Coast

15 May 1946   Withdrawn from service; reserve fleet

AIRCRAFT, SQUADRONS

June 1944-February 1945   VC-11 with 12 FMs and 9 TBMs = 21

April-September 1945   VC-8 with FMs and TBMs

CAMOUFLAGE

March 1944   Measure 22

RADAR

March 1944   SK, SG, YE

On 15 March 1944, at the end of a refit, USS *Nehenta Bay* (CVE-74) undertakes a transport mission at the end of which the ship took part in the Okinawa operation. A few flying boats and transport aircraft are visible on deck, plus one B-26 bomber. Design 22 camouflage.
USN official

USS Hoggatt Bay (AVG-75)

Laid down as CVE-75

SERVICE HISTORY
March 1944 Pacific; aircraft and personnel transport to Pearl Harbor
May-June 1944 Anti-submarine operations in south-west Pacific, based at Pearl Harbor
July-August 1944 Marianas
November 1944 Air support in the Philippines
December 1944-January 1945 Lingayen
15 January 1945 Damaged by explosion
February 1945 West Coast shipyard
May-June 1945 Okinawa
June 1945 Leyte
September 1945 Occupation of Japan
October 1945 'Magic Carpet' operation
20 July 1946 Withdrawn from service; reserve fleet

AIRCRAFT, SQUADRONS
May-December 1944 VC-14 with 12 FMs and 9 TBMs = 21
December 1944-February 1945 VC-88 with 16 FMs and 12 TBMs = 28
April-September 1945 VC-99 with FMs and TBMs

CAMOUFLAGE
January 1944 Presumably Measure 14

RADAR
January 1944 SK, SG, YE

USS *Hoggatt Bay* (CVE-75), taken in January 1944, around the time she was commissioned. The dark paintwork is presumably that of Measure 14.
USN official

USS Kadashan Bay (AVG-76)

Laid down as CVE-76

SERVICE HISTORY
March-April 1944 Pacific; two transport missions with a total of 154 aircraft to Espiritu Santo
May 1944 West Coast shipyard
July 1944 To CARDIV 27 at Pearl Harbor
September 1944 Palau Islands
October 1944 Leyte; TG-77.4, battle off Samar ('Taffy 2')
January 1945 Philippines
8 January 1945 Damaged by Kamikaze hit
February 1945 West Coast shipyard
April-July 1945 Aircraft transport for Third Fleet
From September 1945 'Magic Carpet' missions to Guam, Okinawa and China
January 1946 Transfer to East Coast
14 June 1946 Withdrawn from service; reserve

AIRCRAFT, SQUADRONS
August-December 1944 VC-20 with 15 FMs and 11 TBMs = 26
January-February 1945 VC-20 with 24 FMs and 11 TBMs = 35

CAMOUFLAGE
June 1944 Measure 33/10a
December 1946 Presumably Measure 21

RADAR
June 1944 SK, SG, YE
December 1946 As previously

USS *Kadashan Bay* (CVE-76), photographed on 4 December 1946 while bringing aircraft back from the Pacific area. The strong sunlight causes heavy shadows.
USN official

USS Kanalku Bay (AVG-77) – Marcus Island

Laid down as USS *Kanalku Bay* (CVE-77). Renamed USS *Marcus Island* on 6 November 1943, and launched later under this name

SERVICE HISTORY

May-July 1944 Pacific; transport missions in South Pacific
August-September 1944 Tulagi; flagship of CARDIV 27, Palau Islands, Peleliu, Angnar
October 1944 Admiralty Islands; TU-77.4.2 ('Taffy 2') at Leyte, battle off Samar; Mindoro
December 1944 Lingayen, Luzon
18 December 1944 Damaged by typhoon near the Philippines
February 1945 Ulithi; flagship of CARDIV 24
March 1945 Japanese home islands
May 1945 Transport of damaged aircraft from Guam to West Coast
July 1945 One further transport mission to Pearl Harbor and Guam
September-December 1945 Several 'Magic Carpet' missions
February 1946 Transfer to East Coast
12 December 1946 Withdrawn from service; reserve

AIRCRAFT, SQUADRONS

August 1944 VC-21 with 12 FMs and 11 TBMs = 23
January-February 1945 VC-21 with 24 FMs and 9 TBMs = 33
February-April 1945 VC-87 with 20 FMs and 12 TBMs = 32
April-July 1945 VOC-1 with FMs and TBMs

CAMOUFLAGE

May 1944 Measure 32/15a

RADAR

May 1944 SK, SG, YE

USS *Marcus Island* (CVE-77). This photo dates from 8 May 1944, and was taken off the coast of California. The camouflage is that of Measure 32/15a.
USN (BfZ collection)

USS Kaita Bay (AVG-78) – Savo Island

Laid down as USS *Kaita Bay* (CVE-78). Renamed USS *Savo Island* on 6 November 1943, and later launched under this name

SERVICE HISTORY
March-July 1944   Pacific; two aircraft transport missions to the south-west Pacific
July 1944   Aircraft squadron on board
August 1944   Third fleet, Pearl Harbor
September 1944   Peleliu
October 1944   Seventh Fleet; TG-77.4 battle off Samar ('Taffy 2')
November 1944   Escort missions
December 1944   Landings on Mindanao
January 1945   Lingayen, Philippines
5 January 1945   Damaged by Kamikaze hit
March-April 1945   Okinawa
May 1945   West Coast shipyard
July 1945   Transport missions to Pearl Harbor
August 1945   Transport mission to the Aleutians, occupation of North Japan
September 1945   Three 'Magic Carpet' operations to Guam, Pearl Harbor and Okinawa
January 1946   Transfer to East Coast
12 December 1946   Withdrawn from service; reserve fleet

AIRCRAFT, SQUADRONS
August-December 1944   VC-27 with 16 FMs and 12 TBMs = 28
January-February 1945   VC-27 with 19 FMs and 12 TBMs = 31
February-May 1945   VC-91 with 20 FMs and 15 TBMs = 35
August-September 1945   VC-3 with FMs and TBMs

CAMOUFLAGE
February 1944   Presumably Measure 14
September 1945   Probably Measure 22

RADAR
February 1944   SK, SG, YE
September 1945   As previously

This view of USS *Savo Island* (CVE-78) was taken off the coast of Washington State on 27 February 1944, three weeks after she was commissioned. The deck markings are still missing, and the 40mm AA guns are under canvas covers. *USN (BfZ collection)*

USS Ommaney Bay (AVG-79)

Laid down as CVE-79

near Philippines, and sunk on same day by own forces

SERVICE HISTORY
March 1944 Pacific; aircraft transport to Australia
April 1944 West Coast, pilot training cruises
June-August 1944 Training cruises from Pearl Harbor
September 1944 Palau Islands
October 1944 Leyte; TU-77 4 2, battle off Samar ('Taffy 2')
December 1944 Mindanao
4 January 1945 Total loss from Kamikaze hit

AIRCRAFT, SQUADRONS
August-December 1944 VC-75 with 16 FMs and 11 TBMs = 27
January 1945 VC-75 with 19 FMs and 12 TBMs = 31

CAMOUFLAGE
July 1944 Measure 32/15a

RADAR
July 1944 SK, SG, YE

Above: Aerial photograph of USS *Ommaney Bay* (CVE-79), taken in Hawaiian waters on 6 July 1944. Camouflage to Measure 32/15a.
USN official

Right: This photo, taken on 4 January 1945, shows the destructive effect of the Kamikaze strike on USS *Ommaney Bay*, as a result of which the ship had to be abandoned and sunk by US forces. The port side camouflage design 15a is still visible on the bow.
D McPherson

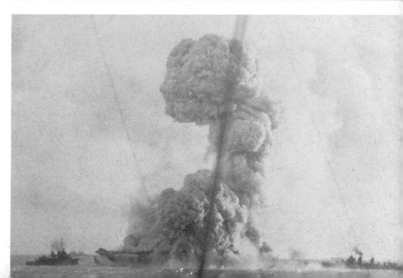

USS Petrof Bay (AVG-80)

Laid down as CVE-80

SERVICE HISTORY
March 1944 Pacific; aircraft and personnel transport to Espiritu Santo
April 1944 Transfer of aircraft to Fleet Carriers; Truk
May 1944 Majuro; West Coast
August 1944 Pearl Harbor, TG-32.4; Guadalcanal, Tulagi
September 1944 TU-32.7.3; Peleliu
October 1944 Leyte; TU-77.4.1 ('Taffy 1'), battle off Samar
November 1944 Leyte; TU-77.4.5
January 1945 TG-77.4; Philippines
February 1945 TG-52.19, Iwo Jima
March 1945 Guam, Ulithi; TU-52.1.2 Okinawa
May 1945 Guam
June 1945 West Coast shipyard
August 1945 Pearl Harbor, Tokyo Bay; 'Magic Carpet', also from Guam
January 1946 West Coast

February 1946 Transfer to East Coast
31 July 1946 Withdrawn from service; reserve

AIRCRAFT, SQUADRONS
August-December 1944 VC-76 with 16 FMs and 10 TBMs = 26
January-March 1945 VC-76 with 20 FMs and 12 TBMs = 32
March-April 1945 VC-93 with 16 FMs and 12 TBMs − 28
May-July 1945 VC-90 with FMs and TBMs

CAMOUFLAGE
March 1944 Presumably Measure 14
1944 Measure 33/10a

RADAR
March 1944 SK, SG, YE

USS *Petrof Bay* (CVE-80), pictured exactly one month after commissioning, on 18 March 1944, without aircraft embarked. Note the rails around the elevator shafts.
USN (BfZ collection)

USS Rudyerd Bay (AVG-81)

Laid down as CVE-81

SERVICE HISTORY

April-May 1944 Pacific; aircraft transport to Espiritu Santo

July 1944 Training cruises, West Coast; aircraft transport to Majuro

August 1944 Eniwetok; TG-30.8

September 1944 Air cover for supply groups at the Palau Islands

January 1945 Philippines, South China Sea, Ulithi

February 1945 Saipan; TG-51,17, Iwo Jima

March-April 1945 TG-52.2; Iwo Jima, Ulithi; TU-52.1.2, Okinawa; TG-50

May 1945 TG-50.8; Japanese home islands, Okinawa; Guam; VC-85 squadron transported to West Coast; then shipyard

August 1945 Aircraft transport to the Marshall Islands, VC-33 transported to Okinawa, and another squadron taken to West Coast

October 1945 'Magic Carpet' operations

February 1946 Transfer to East Coast

11 June 1946 Withdrawn from service; reserve fleet

AIRCRAFT, SQUADRONS

March-August 1944 VC-77 with 12 FMs and 9 TBFs/TBMs = 21

March-July 1945 VC-96 with 20 FMs and 11 TBMs = 31

CAMOUFLAGE

1944 Measure 32/15a

RADAR

1944 SK, SG, YE

USS *Rudyerd Bay* (CVE-81), date of photograph unknown. Camouflage Measure 32/15a. Note the light-colored side markings on the flight deck. The radio aerials are folded down horizontally in preparation for an aircraft landing. *USN official*

USS Saginaw Bay (AVG-82)

Laid down as CVE-82

SERVICE HISTORY
April 1944 Pacific; aircraft and personnel transport to Pearl Harbor
May-July 1944 Pilot training cruises on West Coast; second transport mission to Pearl Harbor; aircraft transport to Eniwetok and Majuro
August 1944 Palau Islands
October 1944 Leyte
January 1945 Lingayen, Ulithi
March 1945 Okinawa
May 1945 West Coast shipyard
August 1945 Aircraft transport to Guam; West Coast
September 1945 'Magic Carpet' missions to Samar, Philippines, Okinawa
February 1946 Transfer to East Coast
19 June 1946 Withdrawn from service; reserve fleet

AIRCRAFT, SQUADRONS
March-October 1944 VC-78 with 15 FMs and 12 TBMs = 27
January-March 1945 VC-78 with 20 FMs and 12 TBMs = 32
March-May 1945 VC-88 with 20 FMs and 12 TBMs = 32

CAMOUFLAGE
April 1944 Measure ?

RADAR
April 1944 SK, SG, YE

USS *Saginaw Bay* (CVE-82) with a camouflage measure of unknown designation. There are also light-colored, dotted lines on the sides of the flight deck.
Davis collection

USS Sargent Bay (AVG-83)

Laid down as CVE-83

SERVICE HISTORY

August 1944 Pacific; one transport mission to the central Pacific; then Third Fleet; Pearl Harbor, Eniwetok, Manus

November 1944-January 1945 Air cover for supply groups in the Philippines

3 January 1945 Damaged in collision with USS *Robert F Kellar* (DE-419)

February 1945 Iwo Jima

March-June 1945 Okinawa; two weeks at Guam

June 1945 Leyte

August 1945 West Coast shipyard

October 1945 Two 'Magic Carpet' missions to Hawaii

November-December 1945 Two 'Magic Carpet' missions to Eniwetok and Okinawa

March 1946 Transfer to East Coast

23 July 1946 Withdrawn from service; reserve fleet

AIRCRAFT, SQUADRONS

March 1944-February 1945 VC-79 with 10 FMs, 4 F4Fs and 9 TBFs/TBMs = 23

March-July 1945 VC-83 with 16 FMs and 12 TBMs = 28

July-August 1945 VC-33 with FMs and TBMs

CAMOUFLAGE

May 1944 Measure 32/15a

September 1945 Presumably Measure 21

RADAR

May 1944 SK, SG, YE

September 1945 As previously

The bow and stern of USS *Sargent Bay* (CVE-83), taken on 30 May 1944 off the California coast. The camouflage Measure 32/15a is easy to identify, especially on the stern. Part of the 40mm AA armament is still under canvas covers, as is the after 5in/38 gun.
USN (BfZ collection)

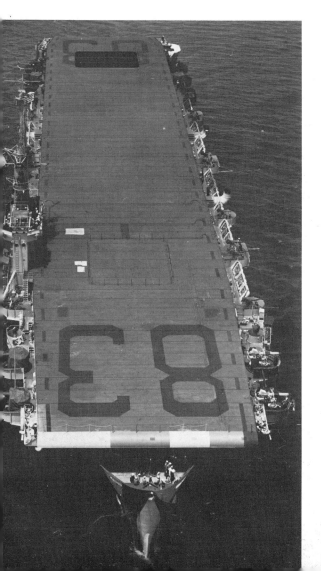

Above: This picture of USS *Sargent Bay* might have been taken around the end of the War, when the Navy Blue of the ship's hull (Measure 21) was combined with a light-colored island on a few escort carriers.
USN official

Left: Another stern view of *Sargent Bay* with Measure 21 paintwork, which is clearly a shade darker than the matt Sea Blue of the deck. The picture was taken on 29 September 1945 off the California coast.
USN (BfZ collection)

USS Shamrock Bay (AVG-84)

Laid down as CVE-84

SERVICE HISTORY

September-October 1944 Training cruises on West Coast, then transfer to East Coast; Atlantic; two aircraft transport missions to Casablanca

November 1944 Transfer to West Coast with VC-44

December 1944 Pacific; transport of VC-93 to Hawaii; VC-42 disembarked, VC-94 embarked

January 1945 Philippines, then TG-77.17 at Ulithi

February 1945 To Iwo Jima with TU-50.8.25

March 1945 To Okinawa with TU-52.1.1

May 1945 Guam

June 1945 TU-32.1.1; Japanese home islands, return of aircraft engines to West Coast, VC-96 disembarked

August 1945 Aircraft transport operations to Guam

October 1945 Three 'Magic Carpet' missions to Pearl Harbor, Okinawa, Honshu

March 1946 Transfer to East Coast

6 July 1946 Withdrawn from service; reserve

AIRCRAFT, SQUADRONS

March 1944 VC-80 with 12 FMs and 9 TBMs = 21

November 1944 VC-42

January 1945 VC-94 with 20 FMs and 12 TBMs = 32

March-May 1945 VC-94 with 18 FMs and 12 TBMs = 30

May 1945 VC-96 with 20 FMs and 11 TBMs = 31

CAMOUFLAGE

April 1944 and February 1945 Measure 33/10a

RADAR

October 1944 SK, SG, YE

USS *Shamrock Bay* (CVE-84), photographed off the American East Coast on 23 October 1944 from a height of 400 feet. Camouflage Measure 33/10a. The dotted flight deck edge markings are supplemented by a center line.

USN (BfZ collection)

USS Shipley Bay (AVG-85)

Laid down as CVE-85

SERVICE HISTORY
May-October 1944 Aircraft transport operations to Pearl Harbor and in the South Pacific; Majuro, Guadalcanal, Tulagi
October 1944 Supply to fast carrier groups of TF-38 at the Philippines
February-April 1945 Training cruises from Pearl Harbor
April 1945 To Okinawa via Guam
16 May 1945 Damaged in collision near Okinawa
June 1945 Japanese home islands
July 1945 West Coast shipyard
September 1945 'Magic Carpet' missions to Pearl Harbor, Okinawa, Kwajalein
February 1946 Transfer to East Coast
28 June 1946 Withdrawn from service; reserve fleet

AIRCRAFT, SQUADRONS
March 1944 (intended) VC-81 with 12 FMs and 9 TBFs/TBMs = 21
May-July 1945 VC-97 with 14 FMs and 12 TBMs = 26

CAMOUFLAGE
May 1944 Measure 32/15a

RADAR
May 1944 SK, SG, YE

USS *Shipley Bay* (CVE-85), at anchor off Majuro Atoll. The photo was taken on 18 May 1944, when *Shipley Bay* had come from the West Coast of the USA with a deck load of aircraft, destined for the Marshall Islands. The camouflage, to Measure 32/15a, is still in good condition.
USN official

USS Sitkoh Bay (AVG-86)

Laid down as ACV-86

SERVICE HISTORY

1944   Pacific; supply operations for the Third and Seventh Fleet
From January 1945   Supply for the Third Fleet in the Philippines, Iwo Jima and Okinawa
August 1945   TG-30.8; occupation of Japan
September 1945   'Magic Carpet' missions to Guam, Samar, Philippines, Okinawa and Pearl Harbor
30 November 1946   Withdrawn from service; reserve
29 July 1950   Reactivated as T-CVE-86 for the MSTS at start of Korean War; cruises between West Coast and Japan. Support of UN troops (evidently retained armament, despite having civilian crew)
March 1951   Aircraft transport to Saigon
27 July 1954   Withdrawn from service; reserve fleet

AIRCRAFT, SQUADRONS

March 1944   (intended) VC-82 with 7 FMs, 5 F4Fs and 6 TBMs = 18
March-June 1945   Transport of Marine Corps F4Us and F6Fs

CAMOUFLAGE

1943   Measure 14
August 1945   Presumably Measure 21

RADAR

August 1945   SK, SG, YE
September 1945   As previously

During the Korean war, USS *Sitkoh Bay*'s duties were similar to those carried out during the Second World War. This photo, taken around 1951, shows the ship after reactivation as T-CVE-86. The deck is loaded with various types of aircraft, many of them so large that their wings project out over the edges of the flight deck. The after 40mm twin AA guns remained preserved after reactivation. The forward guns and the SK radar antenna are in full working order.
USN official

This photo of *Sitkoh Bay* dates from 6 November 1953. The after 40mm twins, which had previously been mothballed, have been removed by this time, and their gun tubs are empty. The gun tub for the 5in gun, the catapult and the SK antenna are still present. Although the ship nominally had a civilian crew, it can be assumed that there were also Navy personnel on board to operate the guns and radars. *Davis collection*

USS Steamer Bay (AVG-87)

Laid down as CVE-87

SERVICE HISTORY
May 1944   Pacific; transport of aircraft and personnel of MAG-61 to New Hebrides; Espiritu Santo
June-July 1944   West Coast, aircraft transport to the Marshall Islands, Majuro
August 1944   Aircraft transport to Manus; transport of replacement aircraft and pilots for TF-38 to the Palau Islands and the Philippines
November 1944   Pearl Harbor shipyard
January 1945   TG-77.4, Lingayen
February 1945   Ulithi, Iwo Jima
March 1945   Leyte, Okinawa
April-May 1945   Okinawa
25 April 1945   Damaged in collision with USS *Hale* (DD-642) off Okinawa
16 June 1945   Damaged by aircraft accident, also at Okinawa
June 1945   Guam, repairs to damage; Third Fleet; Japanese home islands, Ulithi
August 1945   Ulithi, Guam, Pearl Harbor, West Coast shipyard
October 1945   'Magic Carpet' missions
January 1947   Withdrawn from service; reserve fleet

AIRCRAFT, SQUADRONS
March 1944   (intended) VC-83 with 4 FMs, 8 F4Fs and 8 TBFs/TBMs = 20
December 1944-February 1945   VC-90 with 16 FMs and 12 TBMs = 28
March-May 1945   VC-90 with 19 FMs and 12 TBMs = 31

CAMOUFLAGE
1943-April 1944   Presumably Measure 14
July 1944   Measure 32/12a

RADAR
July 1944   SK, SG, YE

Above: This photo of USS *Steamer Bay* (CVE-87) was taken on 22 April 1944. The dark paintwork is presumably that of Measure 14; three months later a 'dazzle pattern' was applied.
USN official

Right: This stern view of *Steamer Bay* was taken immediately after a refit on 17 July 1944, during which camouflage Measure 32/12a was applied. Here the centerline marking is light-colored, but the deck-edge markings are dark.
USN (BfZ collection)

USS Tananek Bay (AVG-88) – Cape Esperance

Laid down as CVE-88. Renamed USS *Cape Esperance* before keel was laid

SERVICE HISTORY
May 1944   Pacific; transport missions to the South Pacific bases
From November 1944   TG-30.8; Leyte, Luzon, during which replacement aircraft transferred to Fleet Carriers; several transport missions between the West Coast and the Western Pacific area
18 December 1944   Damaged by typhoon near Philippines
From September 1945   Return of aircraft and troops to West Coast
22 August 1946   Withdrawn from service; reserve fleet

5 August 1950   Reactivated for the MSTS, but evidently still with armament; numerous transport missions to Korea, Thailand, Hongkong, Europe and Pakistan
15 January 1959   Withdrawn from service

AIRCRAFT, SQUADRONS
March 1944   (intended) VC-84 with 7 FMs, 5 F4Fs and 9 TBFs/TBMs = 21

USS *Cape Esperance* (CVE-88) was another of the escort carriers which were reactivated for transport duties in the Korean War after just four years in reserve, and which retained (in part) the weapons and electronics fitted previously. This photograph dates from around 1952 when the after 40mm twins were still mothballed.
USNI collection

This photograph of *Cape Esperance* dates from much later, as the ship remained in service until the end of 1958. As can be determined, the state of the ship corresponds to the CVEs/AKVs reactivated later: the gun tubs are empty and the SK radar antenna has been removed. A R-4D Skytrain and several jet fighters are on the flight deck, at the forward end of which is a windbreak.
Real Photographs

USS Takanis Bay (AVG-89)

Laid down as CVE-89

SERVICE HISTORY
May-August 1945 Pilot qualification cruises, West Coast
September 1945 'Carrier Transport Squadron': installation of berths for 800 passengers; participation in 'Magic Carpet', total of five cruises to Hawaii and Japan, until January 1946
1 May 1946 Withdrawn from service; reserve fleet

AIRCRAFT, SQUADRONS
May 1944 (intended) VC-85 with 5 FMs, 6 F4Fs and 9 TBFs/TBMs = 20

CAMOUFLAGE
May 1944 Presumably Measure 14

USS *Takanis Bay* (CVE-89), photographed from a height of about 350 feet on 8 May 1944. Note the four short, angled stacks at the flight deck edges.
USN official

USS *Takanis Bay* on 23 May 1946 in Puget Sound Navy Yard during inclination experiments. She had evidently been painted peacetime-gray to Measure 13 by that time. The mast on the right of the picture belongs to a battleship of the *Colorado* class and since *West Virginia* did not have a basket mast after her conversion, the ship must be either *Colorado* or *Maryland*, both of which remained in service until 1947.
USN (BfZ collection)

USS Thetis Bay (AVG-90)

Laid down as CVE-90

SERVICE HISTORY

June 1944 Pacific; transport of aircraft and personnel to Makin, Majuro and Kwajalein, returning with troops going on leave and aircraft needing repair

August-September 1944 Three further transport missions to Hawaii and the Marshall Islands

December 1944 January 1945 Two transport missions to New Guinea

June-August 1945 TG-30.8 at Guam; transfer of replacement aircraft to Fleet Carriers

September 1945 Return to West Coast, then participation in 'Magic Carpet' operations within TG-16.12, until January 1946

7 August 1946 Withdrawn from service; reserve

June 1955 Conversion to helicopter carrier at San Francisco Naval Shipyard

20 July 1956 Commissioned as USS *Thetis Bay* (CVHA-1)

28 May 1959 Reclassification as LPH-6

From August 1956 Under command of the Amphibious Force, Pacific, not the Naval Air Force, Pacific

December 1961 Atlantic

October 1962 Stand-by reserve during the Cuba crisis

1963 Security ship in Hamburg during the visit of President John F Kennedy to West Germany and West Berlin

1 March 1964 Withdrawn from service; stricken (the last ship of the former *Casablanca* class)

August 1965 As the ship had not yet been scrapped, transfer to the Spanish Navy was considered, but this idea was abandoned

1966 Broken up

AIRCRAFT, SQUADRONS

March 1944 (intended) VC-86 with 11 FMs and 9 TBFs/TBMs = 20

CAMOUFLAGE

December 1945 Presumably Measure 21

RADAR

December 1945 SK, SG, YE

1956-1963 SPS-12, SPS-10

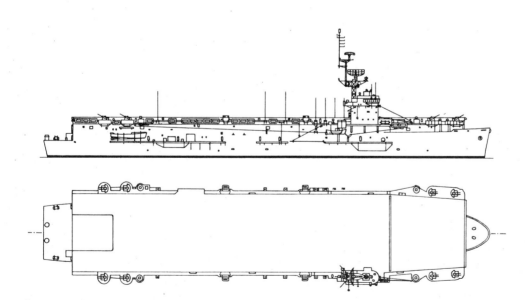

USS *Thetis Bay* (CVE-90), as in 1956 and later, after being converted to the US Navy's first helicopter carrier, with the temporary hull number CVHA-1, later changed to LPH-6. The shortening of the flight deck forward and aft is evident, as is the after elevator (now open on one side), the slightly modified bridge, the lattice mast and the loss of the gun tubs for 20mm guns. *Thetis Bay* was the only former CVE which ever carried the SPS-12 radar antenna.

Above: USS *Thetis Bay* (CVE-90), seen here on her return from the Pacific theatre on a 'Magic Carpet' operation, photographed on 12 December 1945 in San Francisco Bay. The AA guns are under covers, numerous members of the armed forces are standing on the flight deck, and are looking forward to their homecoming. The paint scheme is almost certainly that of Measure 21.
J A Casoly

Below: The conversion of *Thetis Bay* to helicopter carrier was one of only two CVE conversions, but one which gave the ship a very different appearance. This is not so obvious in broadside as in these bow and stern views of the vessel, taken on 15 August 1956 off San Francisco Navy Yard. In particular the extended bridge and the broadside view of SPS-10 (top) and SPS-12 (lower) radar antennas, are clearly visible here. Suspended from the port side of the mast is a flood-lighting installation for illuminating the flight deck. The stern view shows that the gun tub and mount for the 5in gun has been removed. The platform of the after helicopter elevator is in the lowered position.
USN (BfZ collection)

These two quarter views show more details of the 'open' elevator, with the platform in the lowered position. These two photographs were also taken in San Francisco Bay on 15 August 1956.
USN (BfZ collection)

These two pictures of *Thetis Bay* provide another impression of the extent of the alterations brought about by the conversion. The top photograph was taken on 17 September 1956. The forward elevator and the catapult were removed, and the flight deck shortened at the stern, to 'open' the after side of the second elevator – seen here with centreline markings. Note the deck code CVHA, and the hull number 1 painted on the island. The bottom photograph, also taken in 1956, shows two dark-painted helicopters of the Marine Corps, and two light-colored Navy machines. On the port side the hull number 1 is painted almost on the edge of the island, where it is scarcely possible to make it out.
Real Photographs (Davis collection)

Four years later: *Thetis Bay* is now classified as LPH, and carries the new hull number 6, visible in three places. The following features are clearly visible: the forward 40mm AA mounts, now in an extended gallery, the radio aerials folded down on either side of the flight deck, and the additional small ordnance elevator on the port edge of the flight deck, well aft. This photograph dates from 5 June 1960. The ship was taking part in the 'Rose Festival' of Portland, Oregon, and the crew was formed up in greeting to the town.
USN (BfZ collection)

In Summer 1963 *Thetis Bay* acted as guardship during President John F Kennedy's visit to West Germany and West Berlin. This photograph was taken during the ship's employment in Hamburg.
BfZ collection

USS Ulitka Bay (AVG-91) – Makassar Strait

Laid down as CVE-91. Renamed USS *Makassar Strait* before keel was laid

SERVICE HISTORY
June 1944   Pacific; transport missions to Pearl Harbor and to the Marshall Islands
July 1944   West Coast
September -October 1944   Aircraft transport to Hawaii and to the Admiralty Islands
October 1944-January 1945   Pilot qualification cruises from Pearl Harbor

February-April 1945   Eniwetok; TG-50.8; Okinawa, Japanese home islands
May 1945   Pilot training cruises
August-October 1945   West Coast; pilot training cruises
November 1945   'Magic Carpet' operations to Kwajalein, twice to Guam
9 August 1946   Withdrawn from service; reserve fleet

AIRCRAFT, SQUADRONS
March 1944   (intended) VC-87 with 12 FMs and 9 TBFs/TBMs = 21
February-May 1945   VC-97 with 14 FMs and 12 TBMs = 26

CAMOUFLAGE
1944   Measure 32/16a

RADAR
1944   SK, SG, YE

USS *Makassar Strait* (CVE-91), taken around 1944, with weathered paintwork to Measure 32/16a. *Davis collection*

USS Windham Bay (AVG-92)

Laid down as CVE-92

SERVICE HISTORY
June-July 1944   Pacific; after training cruises, to 'Carrier Transport Squadron' at Pearl Harbor; aircraft transport to Majuro. Transport of VMF(N)-532 to Saipan; return with captured Japanese weapons and aircraft
August 1944   West Coast shipyard
September 1944   Transport missions to the Admiralty Islands, to the New Hebrides, and to New Guinea
October 1944   Return to West Coast
November 1944   Transport cruise to the Admiralty Islands
December 1944   West Coast shipyard; further transport mission to Midway
January 1945   Aircrew training cruise to Hawaii
February 1945   Aircraft transport for Fleet Carriers of TF-58 at Iwo Jima

March-June 1945   The same at Okinawa
5 June 1945   Damaged by typhoon
July-August 1945   West Coast shipyard, repairs to damage; aircraft transport of VMF-312 to Guam, return of aircraft and personnel from Samar
October 1945   'Magic Carpet' missions from Pearl Harbor
Around January 1947   Withdrawn from service; reserve fleet
31 October 1951   Reactivated for the MSTS
1959   Stricken

AIRCRAFT, SQUADRONS
March 1944   (intended) VC-88 with 2 FMs, 10 F4Fs and 9 TBFs/TBMs = 21

RADAR
1944   SK, SG, YE
1952   As previously

This photograph of USS *Windham Bay* (CVE-92) dates from 1952, when the ship was acting as an aircraft transport under the MSTS. As with many other escort carriers which operated under the MSTS at this time, there is the large hull number on the island, SK, SG and YE antennas, and only half the 40mm AA guns are in operational condition. *USNI collection*

USS Woodcliff Bay (AVG-93) – Makin Island

Laid down as CVE-93. Renamed USS *Makin Island* before the keel was laid

SERVICE HISTORY
June 1944 Pacific; aircraft transport to Pearl Harbor, Majuro, Kwajalein
November 1944 Ulithi; escort protection at the invasion of Leyte; Luzon
December 1944 Flagship TG-77.4
January 1945 Lingayen
February 1945 Iwo Jima
March 1945 Okinawa
June 1945 Guam
July 1945 East China Sea, Japanese home islands
August 1945 Okinawa
September 1945 Occupation of Honshu
November-December 1945 One 'Magic Carpet' mission to Shanghai
19 April 1946 Withdrawn from service; reserve fleet

AIRCRAFT, SQUADRONS
March 1944 (intended) VC-90 with 14 FMs and 9 TBFs/TBMs = 23
November 1944-January 1945 VC-84 with 16 FMs and 12 TBMs = 28
March-April 1945 VC-84 and VC-91 with 16 FMs and 11 TBMs = 27

CAMOUFLAGE
February 1945 Measure ?
November 1945 Presumably Measure 21

RADAR
February 1945 SK, SG, YE

On 28 February 1945, when this photo was taken USS *Makin Island* (CVE-93) was still camouflaged, although the designation is not known.
US official

Amateur photographer J A Casoly from San Francisco, who died a few years ago, was skipper of a harbor tug, and we owe a debt of gratitude to him for systematically photographing all the ships returning to this port at the end of the War. For example, he proved that most of these ships were painted to Measure 21, that is Navy Blue, at that time, including USS *Makin Island* (CVE-93), shown here on 17 November 1945.
J A Casoly

USS Alazon Bay (AVG-94) – Lunga Point

Laid down as CVE-94. Renamed USS *Lunga Point* before keel was laid

SERVICE HISTORY

Mid-1944 Pacific; aircraft transport to New Guinea
October 1944 CARDIV 29; Leyte
November 1944 Manus
December 1944-January 1945 Lingayen, Ulithi
February 1945 Iwo Jima
21 February 1945 Damaged by Kamikaze hit at Iwo Jima
March 1945 Okinawa, Japanese home islands
July-August 1945 Chinese coast, Okinawa; evacuation of allied prisoners from Japan
October 1945 Departure from Tokyo Bay for Pearl Harbor
November 1945 'Magic Carpet' operations
24 October 1946 Withdrawn from service; reserve fleet

AIRCRAFT, SQUADRONS

March 1944 (intended) VC-91 with 4 FMs, 8 F4Fs and 9 TBFs/TBMs = 21
November 1944-February 1945 VC-85 with 14 FMs and 12 TBMs = 26
March-April 1945 VC-85 with 18 FMs and 12 TBMs = 30
June-September 1945 VC-98 with FMs and TBMs

CAMOUFLAGE
1944 Measure 33/18a

USS *Lunga Point* (CVE-94) featuring Measure 33/18a camouflage, although the darkest area of the camouflage looks more like the Dull Black of Measure 32. *USN (BfZ collection)*

USS Alikula Bay (AVG-95) – Bismarck Sea

Laid down as CVE-95 and launched as USS *Alikula Bay*. Renamed USS *Bismarck Sea* on 16 May 1944, a few days before commissioning

SERVICE HISTORY

July-August 1944 Escort operation between the West Coast and the Marshall Islands
From November 1944 Seventh Fleet; Leyte
February 1945 Iwo Jima
21 February 1945 Sunk at Iwo Jima after Kamikaze hit (318 dead)

AIRCRAFT, SQUADRONS

March 1944 (intended) VC-92 with 11 FMs, 1 F4F and 9 TBFs/TBMs = 21
January-February 1945 VC-86 with 16 FMs and 12 TBMs = 28
February 1945 VC-81

CAMOUFLAGE
June 1944 Presumably Measure 14

RADAR
June 1944 SK, SG, YE

USS *Bismarck Sea* (CVE-95), seen somewhere in the Pacific area. Two aircraft are being transferred from a cargo lighter, using the ship's loading gear.
USN official

This photo of USS *Bismarck Sea* shows just how lively a platform a CVE could be in heavy seas. It was taken on 24 June 1944 from a height of 500 feet, and it is easy to see that aircraft operations on a CVE demanded not only a sufficiently strong headwind, but also depended on a minimum degree of stability on the ship's part.
USN official

USS Anguilla Bay (AVG-96) – Salamaua

Laid down as CVE-96. Renamed USS *Salamaua* before keel was laid

SERVICE HISTORY
August 1944 Pacific; aircraft transport to Pearl Harbor and New Guinea
November 1944 Ulithi, Palau, Philippines, Leyte
January 1945 Lingayen
13 January 1945 Damaged by Kamikaze at the Philippines (15 dead, 80 wounded); temporarily repaired
February 1945 West Coast shipyard
May 1945 Guam, Okinawa
5 June 1945 Damaged by typhoon; repairs at Guam
July 1945 Anti-submarine operations around the Marianas and Okinawa
August 1945 Okinawa, Leyte
September 1945 Tokyo Bay; three 'Magic Carpet' missions
9 May 1946 Withdrawn from service; stricken

AIRCRAFT, SQUADRONS
March 1944 (intended) VC-93 with 4 FMs 6 F4Fs and 10 TBFs/TBMs = 20
November 1944-February 1945 VC-87 with 14 FMs and 10 TBMs = 24
May-September 1945 VC-70 with FMs and TBMs

CAMOUFLAGE
1944 Measure 33/18a
November 1945 Presumably Measure 21

RADAR
November 1945 SC-2, SG, SPS-4, YE

This picture of USS *Salamaua* (CVE-96) dates from around the end of 1945. Evidence for this is the presence of SPS-4 radar on the forward mast platform, which might also have been known as SG-6 at that time. *Salamaua* is also one of the few *Casablanca* class CVEs to be equipped with SC-2 radar. The AA guns are covered, and there are all sorts of personnel bustling about on deck. Assuming that the picture was taken near the photographer's home of San Francisco, it can be inferred that the ship was returning from a 'Magic Carpet' operation.
D McPherson

USS Astrolabe Bay (AVG-97) – Hollandia

Laid down as CVE-97, and launched as USS *Astrolabe Bay*. Renamed USS *Hollandia* on 30 May 1944, two days before commissioning

SERVICE HISTORY
July 1944 Pacific; training cruise (and aircraft transport) to Espiritu Santo
Until April 1945 Several supply operations to Manus, Ulithi, Guam
April 1945 Okinawa
June-August 1945 Transport of replacement aircraft for the Fleet Carriers
September 1945 Four 'Magic Carpet' operations
February 1946 Final return to West Coast
17 January 1947 Withdrawn from service; reserve fleet

AIRCRAFT, SQUADRONS
March 1944 (intended) VC-94 with 3 FMs, 9 F4Fs and 10 TBFs/TBMs = 22
March-April 1945 Transport of F4Us and F6Fs for the Marine Corps

CAMOUFLAGE
September 1944 Measure ?
November 1945 Presumably Measure 21

RADAR
September 1944 SK, SG, YE

This photo of USS *Hollandia* (CVE-97) was taken on 18 September 1944 off the California coast, and shows the ship's 'dazzle pattern', of unknown designation. The SK radar antenna shows up well in the sunshine. Crew members are working on catapult maintenance. *USN (BfZ collection)*

USS Bucareli Bay (AVG-98) – Kwajalein

Laid down as USS *Bucareli Bay* (CVE-98). Renamed USS *Kwajalein* on 26 April 1944

SERVICE HISTORY

July 1944   Pacific; transport of aircraft, personnel and fuel to Espiritu Santo

August 1944   Aircraft transport to Guam; on return to West Coast, captured Japanese equipment brought back to USA

October 1944   Transport of replacement aircraft for Fleet Carriers of TF-38

18 December 1944   Damaged by typhoon near the Philippines

February 1945   West Coast shipyard

March-August 1945   Transport mission to Pearl Harbor, to Western Pacific and to the Fleet Carriers off the Japanese home islands

September 1945   Four 'Magic Carpet' operations

February 1946   Final return to West Coast

16 August 1946   Withdrawn from service; reserve fleet

AIRCRAFT, SQUADRONS

March 1944   (intended) VC-96 with 11 FMs and 9 TBMs = 20

CAMOUFLAGE

July 1944   Presumably Measure 21

RADAR

July 1944   SK-2, SG, YE

Top left: USS Hollandia, photographed on 29 November 1945. The larger hull number has not yet been applied to the island, although the war had been over for three months. *Davis collection*

Top right: USS *Kwajalein* (CVE-98) at high speed. *USN official*

Below: Bow view of *Kwajalein* during a transport mission, shown on 19 July 1944 from a height of about 300 feet. Paintwork to Measure 21. This shows clearly how the windbreak supports are anchored in the flight deck. *Kwajalein* was the first CVE of the *Casablanca* class to be fitted with SK-2 radar antenna. *USN (BfZ collection)*

USS Chapin Bay (AVG-99) – Admiralty Islands

Laid down as USS *Chapin Bay* (CVE-99). Renamed USS *Admiralty Islands* on 26 April 1944

SERVICE HISTORY

1944 Pacific; 'Carrier Transport Squadron, Pacific'; transport missions between West Coast and the Western Pacific

February 1945 Supply of TF-58 and TF-38

February-March 1945 Iwo Jima

March-June 1945 Okinawa, Japanese home islands, then West Coast shipyard

From September 1945 'Magic Carpet' operation

26 April 1946 Withdrawn from service; stricken

AIRCRAFT, SQUADRONS

March 1944 (intended) VC-97 with 4 FMs, 8 F4Fs and 9 TBFs/TBMs = 21

CAMOUFLAGE

November 1945 Presumably Measure 21

RADAR

August 1945 SK-2, SG, YE

Two views of USS *Admiralty Islands* (CVE-99). Both photographs were taken off the California coast on 30 August 1945. The war is over, and the gun mounts are covered. The deck number is absent here, but details of the deck markings are visible.
USN (BfZ collection)

CVE-99 returns to San Francisco from a 'Magic Carpet' mission on 25 November 1945. A large number of passengers are gathered on the flight deck. The ship's paintwork has suffered from the long voyage.
J A Casoly

USS Didrickson Bay (AVG-100) – Bougainville

Laid down as USS *Didrickson Bay* (CVE-100). Renamed USS *Bougainville* on 26 April 1944

SERVICE HISTORY
August 1944   Pacific; 'Carrier Transport Squadron, Pacific'; transport missions to Pacific islands
February 1945   To 'Service Squadron 6'; supply of TF-58 and TF-38
February-June 1945   Iwo Jima, Okinawa
5 June 1945   Damaged by typhoon at Okinawa
October 1945   Remained in Western Pacific
3 November 1946   Withdrawn from service; reserve fleet

AIRCRAFT, SQUADRONS
March 1944   (intended) VC-98 with 2 FMs, 10 F4Fs and 3 TBMs = 15

CAMOUFLAGE
January 1945   Measure 21

RADAR
January 1945   SK-2, SG, YE

The 100th CVE: USS *Bougainville* (CVE-100), pictured on 30 December 1944. One of the few official USN photos on which Measure 21 camouflage is expressly mentioned.
USN (BfZ collection)

USS Dolomi Bay (AVG-101) – Matanikau

Laid down as USS *Dolomi Bay* (CVE-101). Renamed USS *Matanikau* on 26 April 1944

SERVICE HISTORY

August 1944 Pacific; aircraft transport to the South Pacific and to the Admiralty Islands

September 1944 Return to West Coast with damaged aircraft

October 1944 Pilot qualification cruises until July 1945

July 1945 Aircraft transport to the Marshall Islands within 'Carrier Transport Squadron, Pacific'

August 1945 Roi, Kwajalein

September 1945 TF-4; Honshu

October 1945 Return to West Coast

November 1945 'Magic Carpet' mission to Saipan

December 1945 'Magic Carpet' mission to Guam

January 1946 'Magic Carpet' mission to China

February 1946 West Coast; inactive for eight months

11 October 1946 Withdrawn from service; reserve fleet

AIRCRAFT, SQUADRONS

March 1944 (intended) VC-99 with 3 F4Fs and ?

October 1944 VC-93

CAMOUFLAGE

1944 Measure 32/16a

July 1944 Presumably Measure 21

RADAR

July 1944 SK-2, SG, YE

USS Elbour Bay (AVG-102) – Attu

Laid down as CVE-102. Renamed USS *Attu* on 6 November 1943, before keel was laid

SERVICE HISTORY
August 1944 Transport missions to Pacific islands
February-June 1945 Transport missions to Iwo Jima and Okinawa
5 June 1945 Damaged by typhoon at Okinawa. 4000 men brought back after end of War in 'Magic Carpet' operations
8 June 1946 Withdrawn from service; stricken

Left:USS *Matanikau* (CVE-101) in the Pacific, photographed in July 1944. The modernised radar equipment, including SK-2, is clearly visible here. *USN official*

Right: An aerial view of USS *Attu* (CVE-102), off the California coast, dated 28 September 1944. Note the strong contrast between the colors of the camouflage design, the designation of which remains unknown. *USN (BfZ collection)*

Below: USS *Attu*, shown on 2 September 1945 during a personnel exchange with USS *Fox* (AG-85). *USN official*

CAMOUFLAGE
September 1944 Measure ?

RADAR
September 1944 SK-2, SG, YE

USS Alava Bay (AVG-103) – Roi

Laid down as USS *Alava Bay* (CVE-103)

SERVICE HISTORY
August-December 1944 Pacific; 'Carrier Transport Squadron, Pacific'; aircraft transport to Espiritu Santo, Manus, Eniwetok, Guam, to the Marshall Islands and to the Marianas; several months supply to the Fleet Carriers of TF-38 within TG-30.8
July 1945 Supply operations; Guam
August 1945 Occupation of Japan; 'Magic Carpet' missions
9 May 1946 Withdrawn from service; stricken

CAMOUFLAGE
1945-46 Presumably Measure 21

RADAR
1945-46 SK-2, SG, YE

USS *Roi* (CVE-103), photographed in 1945.
'Our Navy' photo

USS Tonowek Bay (AVG-104) – Munda

Laid down as CVE-104, renamed USS *Munda* before keel was laid

SERVICE HISTORY
August 1944 Pacific; 'Carrier Transport Squadron, Pacific'; aircraft transport to Espiritu Santo
December 1944 Second and third transport missions, later three more operations
July-August 1945 TG-30.8; transport of replacement aircraft and personnel for the Fleet Carriers of TF-38; Japanese home islands, then to Guam until Japan's capitulation
September 1945 Tokyo Bay
October 1945 'Magic Carpet' missions until January 1946
13 September 1946 Withdrawn from service; reserve fleet

CAMOUFLAGE
1945-46 Presumably Measure 21

RADAR
1945 SK-2, SG, YE

USS *Munda* (CVE-104), at anchor in San Francisco Bay in 1945. The large hull number is already painted on the island.
D McPherson

Commencement Bay Class

This was the last class of US Navy escort carriers, and also the only class which was purpose-designed from the outset. The design was closer in size to the *Sangamon* class, and bore much evidence of the experience gained with the previous classes. The greater length resulted in increased aircraft capacity, and two catapults were located on the forward flight deck. Steam turbine propulsion was adopted once more, although twin screw propulsion was retained. The construction of all the ships was again entrusted to a single yard, namely Todd Pacific of Tacoma, in Washington State. The extra refinement of the design necessarily incurred a longer building time, the average being 1¼ years.

The AA armament was subsequently increased, in this case by fitting a quadruple 40mm mount on the forecastle, two quadruples of the same caliber on the fantail and two twin mounts on the side galleries in a superfiring arrangement. A feature of this class was the two 40mm AA mounts on the flight deck forward of the small island.

The late completion of these ships – one unit in 1944, and nearly all the others in 1945 – made it possible to fit more modern radar and electronics. Only a few of these ships saw action in the Pacific, and since they were relatively little used, a small number of these ships remained in use in the active Fleet until well into the 1950s. Some of them were reactivated at the start of the Korean War, and another was converted for other purposes (AGMR). Two units were used as aircraft ferries during the Vietnam War.

Of the 23 ships of this class approved for building by the budgets of 1943 and 1944, 19 were completed. CVE-128 to 139, which were approved in the 1945 budget but never stated, were to have been an improved version of the *Commencement Bay* class.

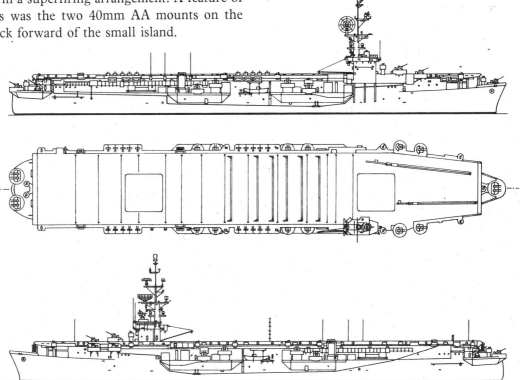

USS St Joseph Bay(ACV-105) – Commencement Bay

Laid down as USS *St Joseph Bay* (CVE-105), and launched with this name. Renamed USS *Commencement Bay* on 10 April 1944

SERVICE HISTORY
February-October 1945 Pacific; training ship for escort carrier crews, based at Puget Sound; also for pilots, operating for a short time from Pearl Harbor
30 November 1946 Withdrawn from service; reserve fleet

CAMOUFLAGE
October 1944 Measure 32/16a
December 1945 Measure 21

RADAR
October 1945 SK-2, SG, YE

This photo of USS *Commencement Bay* (CVE-105), the name ship of the class, was probably taken around the end of 1944. The port side pattern of the Measure 32/16a camouflage shows up very well.
USN official

Left: Starboard and deck elevations, showing the appearance of USS *Commencement Bay* (CVE-105) after completion in 1944. Note the converging catapults, the lifts located 6 feet to starboard of the centerline, and the large number of 20mm AA guns. The port profile shows the appearance of one of the late ships of the class, USS *Point Cruz* (CVE-119), which remained in active service until 1956. In her final period of service she carried SPS-6 and -10 radar, plus TACAN on the masthead. The 5in guns shown here were no longer mounted by then, in common with other active CVEs with Navy crews.

USS *Commencement Bay* (CVE-105) returns to San Francisco on 16 December 1945 with a small aircraft load. Note the effect of the dark paintwork to Measure 21, and the 40mm AA mounts fitted on the galleries. The white peacetime number on the island has already been applied.
J A Casoly

USS Sunset Bay (ACV-106) – Block Island

Laid down as USS *Sunset Bay* (CVE-106), and launched with this name. Renamed USS *Block Island* on 5 July 1944, in honor of the sunken CVE-21

SERVICE HISTORY
March 1945   Pacific
May 1945   Flight operations off Okinawa
May-June 1945   Leyte, Balikpapan
September 1945   After the end of the War, evacuation of prisoners of war from Formosa; remained in Far East until December 1945
December 1945   Return to West Coast
28 May 1946   Withdrawn from service; reserve
From 29 May 1946   Reserve as station ship of the Naval Academy at Annapolis, Maryland; used there as floating stationary class-rooms until 1950
1950   Transferred to reserve
28 April 1951   Reactivated, Atlantic
1951-1953   Local flight operations, East Coast
April-June 1953   Deployment to Europe
28 August 1954   Withdrawn from service; reserve fleet

22 December 1957   Classified as LPH-1
June 1958   Conversion to helicopter carrier suspended; instead USS *Thetis Bay* became CVHA-1, and later LPH-6

AIRCRAFT, SQUADRONS
May-August 1945   MCVG-1 with VMF-511 (F6Fs and F4Us) and VMTB-233 (TBMs)

CAMOUFLAGE
January 1945   Measure 33/18a

RADAR
January 1945   SK-2, SG, YE
January 1952   SPS-6, SPS-4, YE

Right: The second USS *Block Island* (CVE-106) was named in memory of her predecessor CVE-21, which was sunk by submarine torpedoes in the Atlantic in 1944. Both photographs were taken shortly after commissioning on 10 January 1945, and the freshly painted colors of Measure 33/13a are clearly discernible. The aerial picture provides a view of the convergent flight deck catapults.
USN (BfZ collection)

Above and left: These two photographs show *Block Island* seven years later, on 5 January 1952, off Philadelphia Navy Yard. The misty weather makes the peacetime gray paintwork appear darker than it really is. Note the SPS-6 and SPS-4 radar antennas, and the projecting galleries with their 40mm AA mounts. The two 5in guns are 'hidden' below the flight deck, and have restricted firing arcs. *USN (BfZ collection)*

Below: This aerial picture of *Block Island*, taken around 1952-54, makes very clear the alterations to the deck markings. The bow number is absent here. *USNI collection*

USS St Andrews Bay (ACV-107) – Gilbert Islands – Annapolis (AGMR-1)

Laid down as USS *St Andrews Bay* (CVE-107), renamed USS *Gilbert Islands* on 26 April 1944

SERVICE HISTORY
April 1945   Pacific; exercises at Hawaii
May-June 1945   Okinawa, ground support; Marine Corps squadrons on board
August 1945   Support for the Third Fleet off the Japanese home islands
October 1945   Occupation of Formosa
December 1945   Return to West Coast
21 May 1946   Withdrawn from service; reserve fleet
7 September 1951   Reactivated for the Korean War
August-September 1952   Transport of jet aircraft to Japan
October 1952   Return to East Coast
January 1954   Mediterranean deployment

15 January 1955   Withdrawn from service; reserve fleet
1 June 1961   Stricken
1 November 1961   Returned to official list, after being stricken; conversion planned to a Major Communications Relay ship (AGMR-1)
22 June 1963   Renamed USS *Annapolis*, after the Navy radio base there
7 March 1964   Commissioned as AGMR-1 after conversion
June 1965   Transfer to West Coast
September 1965   Action off Vietnam
20 December 1969   Withdrawn from service; reserve fleet

AIRCRAFT, SQUADRONS
May-August 1945   MCVG-2 with VMF-512 (FGs, F6Fs and F4Us) and VMTB-143 (TBMs)

CAMOUFLAGE
July 1945   Presumably Measure 21

RADAR
July 1945   SK-2, SPS-4, SG, YE
1963   SPS-10

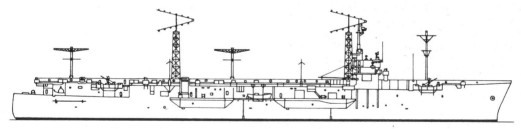

This is how ex-USS *Gilbert Islands* (CVE-107) looked after conversion into a relay ship, and after being renamed USS *Annapolis* (AGMR-1). The former flight deck was used as an antenna deck. *Annapolis* was the only former CVE to have 3in/50 guns on board.

Below: USS *Gilbert Islands* (CVE-107), photographed on 2 May 1945 and 18 July 1945; the Navy Blue paintwork of Measure 21 is clearly identifiable in the righthand picture. *USN (BfZ collection)*

Above: CVE-107 after completion of the conversion to Major Communication Ship (AGMR-1), renamed USS *Annapolis*. There are major changes evident in the ship's hull, bridge and deck. Although classed as an auxiliary ship after this conversion, *Annapolis* was fitted with four open double mounts with radar-controlled 3in/50 caliber guns — the only former CVE to be so equipped. Four antenna masts were fitted on the former flight deck, but a little space was left in the port midship area for a helicopter landing area. The photograph dates from 12 June 1964; the ship only served in the rôle for 4½ years.
USN official

Left: USS *Annapolis*, mothballed at San Diego, photographed in 1971. Note that the 3in guns were also preserved, while the electronic equipment was removed before preservation — as happened with all ships placed in reserve.
USN official (INRO collection)

USS Vermillion Bay (ACV-108) – Kula Gulf

Laid down as CVE-108. Renamed USS *Kula Gulf* on 6 November 1943, before keel was laid. Completed by Willamette Iron Works

SERVICE HISTORY
August 1945   Pacific; Seventh Fleet in Western Pacific
November 1945   Two 'Magic Carpet' missions from Guam
February 1946   Transfer to East Coast
3 July 1946   Withdrawn from service; reserve fleet
15 February 1951   Reactivated
August 1951   Aircraft transport to Casablanca
From September 1951   Pilot training for Korean operations
May 1952   Operations on the East Coast
January-July 1953   In shipyard
1953-1955   Participation in development work on anti-submarine warfare tactics; training cruises off East Coast

15 December 1955   Withdrawn from service; reserve fleet
30 June 1965   Reactivated as T-AKV-8, as aircraft ferry for the MSTS (crane installed to lift 150 tons; forward elevator enlarged); helicopter transport missions to Vietnam until 1970
1970   Withdrawn from service; stricken

AIRCRAFT, SQUADRONS
1945   (intended) CVEG(N)-63

CAMOUFLAGE
September 1945   Either Measure 22 or Measure 12

RADAR
September 1945   SK-2, SPS-4, SG, YE
October 1950   SPS-6, SPS-4, YE

Right: USS *Kula Gulf* (CVE-108), pictured on 5 September 1945, painted to Measure 22; in theory this could be a new form of Measure 12, but there is no further evidence for this. SG-6 or SPS-4 radar is barely visible in this side view. *USN official*

Below: Five years later: USS *Kula Gulf* possibly taken on 1 October 1950, that is, after her first reactivation, but before being commissioned for the second time. SPS-6 radar instead of SK-2. Navy aircraft on deck. *USN official*

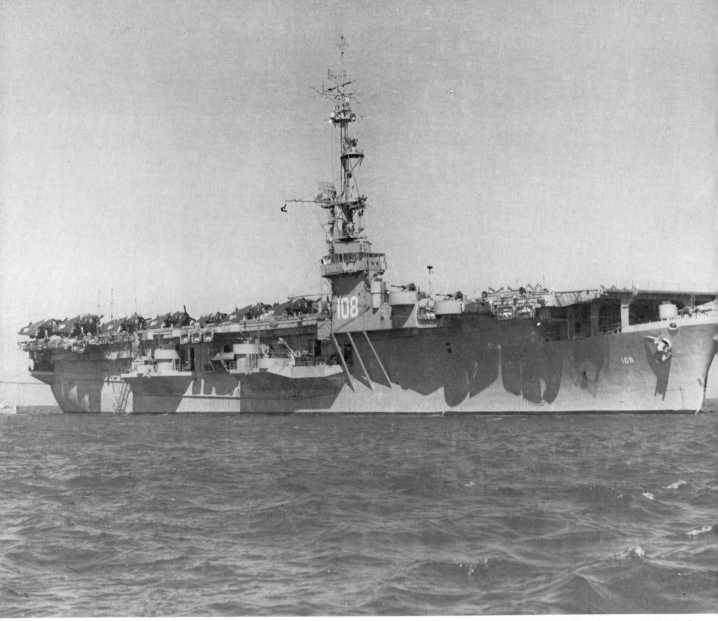

The appearance of USS *Kula Gulf* in the years 1951-54, that is, after the second reactivation. There are hardly any alterations worth noting compared with the previous photo. *USNI collection*

USS Willapa Bay (ACV-109) – Cape Gloucester

Laid down as USS *Willapa Bay* (CVE-109). Renamed USS *Cape Gloucester* on 26 April 1944 before being launched

SERVICE HISTORY
July 1945 Pacific; Third Fleet; Kamikaze defence, air cover for minesweeping operations along the Japanese coast
From September 1945 Four 'Magic Carpet' operations from Okinawa and Pearl Harbor to the West Coast
5 November 1946 Withdrawn from service; reserve fleet

1 July 1960 Returned to official list again one month after being stricken for first time on 1 June 1960. Not reactivated

AIRCRAFT, SQUADRONS
1945 MCVG-4 with VMF-351 (FGs and F6Fs) and VMTB-132 (TBMs)

CAMOUFLAGE
1945 Measure 22 or Measure 12

RADAR
March 1945 SK-2, SPS-4, SG, YE

USS *Cape Gloucester* (CVE-109), seen off the coast of
Washington State on 17 March 1945. The dividing line
between the two tones of the camouflage measure
(presumably Measure 22) is lower than usual here.
USN official

A fine picture of USS *Cape Gloucester* in 1971, laid up
shortly before being stricken from the official list. All the
40mm twin mounts are preserved, but the electronics have
been removed.
INRO collection

USS Winjah Bay (ACV-110) – Salerno Bay

Laid down as CVE-110. Renamed USS *Salerno Bay* on 6 November 1943, before keel was laid. Completed by Commercial Iron Works

SERVICE HISTORY
June 1945   Pacific; MCVEG-5 embarked
September 1945   Okinawa
December 1945   West Coast; transfer to East Coast, there pilot training cruises until 1947
4 October 1947   Withdrawn from service; reserve fleet
20 June 1951   Reactivated for US Navy
October 1951   CARDIV 18; routine operations
August 1952   TF-173; NATO manoeuvers off Norway
October 1952   Sixth Fleet in Mediterranean
December 1952   East Coast

16 February 1954   Withdrawn from service; reserve fleet

AIRCRAFT, SQUADRONS
June 1945   MCVEG-5 with VMF-514 and VMTB-144
Thereafter   MCVEG-3 with VMF-513 and VMTB-234

CAMOUFLAGE
May 1945 and May 1946   Measure 21

RADAR
June 1945   SK-2, SPS-4, SG, YE
1952   SPS-6, SPS-4, SG, YE

This photograph of USS *Salerno Bay* (CVE-110) was taken from an unusual angle off Portland, Oregon on 8 May 1945, eleven days before being commissioned. The hull numbers are still absent, and the Measure 21 paintwork appears lighter here because of the sunlight. The ship is fairly high in the water.
Commercial Iron Works (BfZ collection)

Above: A photo of USS *Salerno Bay* dating from 3 June 1945: converging catapult tracks, relatively clearly visible radar and electronics, radio aerials on the starboard side of the flight deck, and quadruple 40mm mounts at the bow and stern.
USN (BfZ collection)

Right: A further photo of USS *Salerno Bay*, taken on 2 June 1945, showing the concentration of ship's weapons on the stern, in the AA gun tubs on the side decks, and on the gallery along the flight deck. The directors for the after quadruple 40mm mounts are fitted inboard, and have a restricted field of view.
Commercial Iron Works (BfZ collection)

Below: Peacetime picture of *Salerno Bay* in 1951-53, as flagship of CARDIV 18, in service with the Atlantic Fleet. Radar systems SPS-6, SPS-4, SG and YE are on board. The command flag of a Rear Admiral is flying from the topmast.
USNI collection

USS Totem Bay (ACV-111) – Vella Gulf

Laid down as USS *Totem Bay* (CVE-111). Renamed USS *Vella Gulf* on 26 April 1944, before being launched

SERVICE HISTORY

May 1945 Pacific; one Marine Air Group embarked

June 1945 Training cruises from Pearl Harbor

July 1945 Guam, Rota, Pagan, Saipan

August 1945 Okinawa, occupation of Japanese home islands

September 1945 Tokyo Bay; return of 650 troops from Okinawa to West Coast via Pearl Harbor

October 1945-March 1946 West Coast; training ship for CVE crews

9 August 1946 Withdrawn from service; reserve fleet

1 November 1960 Returned to official list only a few months after being stricken for the first time

1964 Was to be converted to Major Communications Relay Ship after pattern of USS *Annapolis* (AGMR-1), approved in 1964 budget; plan abandoned in favour of ex-CVL-48 USS *Saipan*, already 60 per cent converted to CC-3, which was reclassified AGMR-2 and renamed USS *Arlington*

AIRCRAFT, SQUADRONS

July-September 1945 MCVEG-3 with VMF-513 (FGs, F6Fs and F4Us) and VMTB-134 (TBMs)

CAMOUFLAGE

August 1945 Measure 21

RADAR

August 1945 SK-2, SPS-4, SG, YE

USS *Vella Gulf* (CVE-111), taken on 25 August 1945 in Western Pacific waters. There is no camouflage pattern, despite the appearance to the contrary.
USN official

USS Frosty Bay (ACV-112) – Siboney

Laid down as USS *Frosty Bay* (CVE-112). Renamed USS *Siboney* on 26 April 1944, before being launched

SERVICE HISTORY
August-September 1945   Pacific; one transport mission to Pearl Harbor, then operations to Okinawa, via the Marshall Islands, Carolines and Philippines

SERVICE HISTORY
October 1945   In the area of the Japanese home islands; Tokyo Bay

January 1946   West Coast

February-April 1946   Operations in Western Pacific

June 1947   Transfer to Atlantic

November 1947   Withdrawn from service; reserve fleet

March 1948   Reactivated

May 1948   Aircraft transport to Turkey

October 1948   East Coast shipyard

January-December 1949   Withdrawn from service; reserve fleet

22 November 1950   Reactivated again for US Navy; Atlantic, East Coast

September-November 1951   Mediterranean deployment

January 1953   East Coast refit, followed by anti-submarine hunter-killer group on East Coast

September-December 1953   Mediterranean deployment

September 1954-January 1955   East Coast shipyard

1955-1956   East Coast operations

May-July 1956   Mediterranean deployment

31 July 1956   Withdrawn from service; reserve fleet

AIRCRAFT, SQUADRONS
September 1945   CVEG-36 with F6Fs and TBMs

RADAR
May 1951   SPS-6, SPS-4, SG, YE

USS *Siboney* (CVE-112) belongs to the small number of escort carriers which were reactivated twice in rapid succession after the end of the Second World War. This photo dates from the early post-war years 1945-48. For the first time we see the combination of radar antennas SK-2 and SP.
USNI collection

This aerial photograph of USS *Siboney* dates from 22 May 1951, that is, after the second reactivation. In place of SK-2 we now find SPS-6 radar, although SP is still on the forward mast platform. The bridge has been extended aft slightly. A few of the 40mm guns appear to be radar controlled.
USN official

This aerial picture of USS *Siboney* was taken a few years later, around the mid-1950s. Note the altered deck markings, the bridge extended to two levels, the new radar antenna arrangement, and the absence of the forward 40mm quadruple mounts. Here it is clear that the two aircraft elevators are located slightly to starboard of the centerline.
INRO collection

USS Hobart Bay (ACV-113) – Puget Sound

Laid down as USS *Hobart Bay* (CVE-113). Renamed USS *Puget Sound* on 5 June 1944, before being launched

SERVICE HISTORY
July 1945 Pacific; with embarked Marine Air Group
September 1945 Sailed via Hawaii for occupation of Japan
October-December 1945 Training cruises off the Philippines, Hong Kong and the Marianas
January 1946 Return of aircraft from Guam, then two 'Magic Carpet' missions to Pearl Harbor

and Okinawa, until February 1946
18 October 1946 Withdrawn from service; reserve fleet

AIRCRAFT, SQUADRONS
? VMTB-114

CAMOUFLAGE
June 1946 SK-2, SG, YE

RADAR
June 1946 SK-2, SG, YE

Two views of USS *Puget Sound* (CVE-113), an escort carrier which was in active service for only slightly more than one year. The photographs date from 29 June 1945, eleven days after commissioning. The SPS-4 radar antenna is absent here, as is the number on the hull side. The ship is steaming at a speed of 18 kts.
USN official

USS Mosser Bay (ACV-114) – Rendova

Laid down as CVE-114. Renamed USS *Rendova* on 6 November 1943 before keel was laid. Completed by Willamette Iron Works

SERVICE HISTORY
March 1946   Pacific; West Coast
April 1946   In service, but not in use; stationary flagship of CARDIV 15 until early in 1947
1947   Operations off West Coast and Hawaii
April 1948   Aircraft transport to Turkey via Panama Canal
July 1948   To West Coast, via Suez, Indian Ocean and Pacific
August 1948   Cruise to Tsingtau
January-April 1949   Western Pacific
October 1949   West Coast
27 January 1950   Withdrawn from service; reserve fleet
3 January 1951   Reactivated for US Navy

August 1951   Yokosuka, Okinawa, Kobe; embarked VMF-212 with F4U aircraft; Korea
December 1951   West Coast
January 1952   Training operations off West Coast
September 1952   Participation in atomic bomb test at Marshall Islands
1953   Restricted reserve status
1954   Fully active again; anti-submarine warfare operations in Western Pacific
June-October 1954   West Coast
30 June 1955   Withdrawn from service; reserve fleet

AIRCRAFT, SQUADRONS
August 1951   VMF-212 with F4Us
January 1954   TBM-3Ws and TBM-3Ss

RADAR
1951   SPS-6, SP, YE

This photo of *Rendova* (CVE-114) was probably taken in the early 1950s, after reactivation.
USN (BfZ collection)

USS Portage Bay (ACV-115) – Bairoko

Laid down as CVE-115. Renamed USS *Bairoko* on 5 June 1944, before keel was laid. Completed too late to take part in World War II

SERVICE HISTORY
1945-1949   Pacific; peace operations with two Far East cruises; participation in atomic bomb test
14 April 1950   Withdrawn from service; reserve fleet
12 September 1950   Reactivated for US Navy; Pacific
1950-1953   Three Western Pacific operations; air operations over Korea
9 May 1951   Explosion off Korea (5 dead and 14 injured)
August 1953   Return to West Coast
January 1954   Participation in hydrogen bomb experiments at Eniwetok island
18 February 1955   Withdrawn from service; reserve fleet

CAMOUFLAGE
1945   Measure 32/16a
October 1945   Measure 21, but with light colored island and mast

RADAR
July 1945   SK-2, SG, YE
October 1945   SK-2, SP, SG, YE

A picture of USS *Bairoko* (CVE-115) in the building yard, taken in mid-1945, evidently only a few days before commissioning. Freshly applied Measure 21 paintwork is visible, but the bow hull number is still absent, as is SP radar. The stacks appear to be longer here than on the other photographs.
USN (BfZ collection)

Just a few weeks later: USS *Bairoko* off the California coast
on 10 October 1945. After the end of the War the island was
painted light gray. Antennas for SP and YE are now clearly
visible; SK-2 is seen here in profile. Note the supports for
the island, where it projects over the edge of the deck.
USN (BfZ collection)

In September 1950, after only five months in reserve, USS
Bairoko was reactivated when this photo was taken. The
forward 40mm quadruple mount has been removed, and a
new radar has replaced SK-2, although its designation is still
not known. As far as we know, *Bairoko* was the only escort
carrier to feature this antenna. A few 40mm AA guns are
radar controlled, and a few 20mm Oerlikons are still on
board. Note the boats carried on deck.
USN (BfZ collection)

USS San Alberto Bay (ACV-116) – Badoeng Strait

Laid down as CVE-116. Renamed USS *Badoeng Strait* on 6 November 1944, before keel was laid. Completed by Commercial Iron Works

SERVICE HISTORY
March 1946 Pacific
20 April 1946 Withdrawn from service; reserve
6 January 1947 Reactivated; Pacific
June 1950 Test ship for anti-submarine warfare equipment; flagship of CARDIV 15 and 17 for a time
1950-1953 Three Korea operations with TF-95, TF-77; during which principal tasks were anti-submarine operations and ground support
April-September 1953 Shipyard, modernisation; introduction of new weapons and equipment for anti-submarine warfare

February-July 1956 Western Pacific
17 May 1957 Withdrawn from service; reserve

AIRCRAFT, SQUADRONS
1950-53 VMF-? with F4Us

CAMOUFLAGE
December 1945 Measure 21

RADAR
December 1945 SK-2, SP, SG, YE
January 1952 As previously
1956 SPS-6

USS Badoeng Strait (CVE-116), pictured in San Francisco Bay on 10 December 1945, just a month after commissioning. The Navy Blue paintwork of Measure 21 has suffered markedly.
J A Casoly

USS *Badoeng Strait*, nicknamed 'Bing Ding' by her crew, was one of the few escort carriers to remain on almost uninterrupted active service for more than eleven years. This aerial photo was taken on 13 January 1952, and shows the ship with a new identification number on the island, and some VMF-212 Marine Corps F4U Corsairs on board. SK-2 radar is still on the mast platform.
USN official

This photo of *Badoeng Strait* dates from 1956. The 5in guns are evidently no longer mounted, and SP radar has been removed and replaced by SPS-10 and SPS-6. YE has been relocated lower down.
Real Photographs

USS Saltery Bay (ACV-117) – Saidor

Laid down as CVE-117. Renamed USS *Saidor* on 5
June 1944, before keel was laid

SERVICE HISTORY
December 1945-March 1946 Pacific; operations from Pearl Harbor
April 1946 One week on the East Coast, then to Bikini
May-August 1946 Floating photographic laboratory for documentation of atomic bomb tests at Bikini

1947 West Coast
12 September 1947 Withdrawn from service, reserve fleet

RADAR
1945 SK-2, SP, SG, YE

USS *Saidor* (CVE-117), taken in the Pacific in 1945. *'Our Navy' photo*

USS Sandy Bay (ACV-118) – Sicily

Laid down as CVE-118. Renamed USS *Sicily* on 5
June 1944, before keel was laid. Completed by
Willamette Iron Works

SERVICE HISTORY
April 1946 West Coast
May 1946 Transfer to East Coast
September 1946 Cold weather training near
Newfoundland, until 1950
April 1950 Operations on East Coast; transfer to
West Coast

May 1950   Pacific

July 1950   First Korean operation

August 1950   Flagship of CARDIV 15; ground support in Korea

February 1951   West Coast

May-October 1951   Second Korean operation

May-December 1952   Third Korean operation

July 1953-February 1954   Western Pacific

5 July 1954   Withdrawn from service; reserve fleet

AIRCRAFT, SQUADRONS

August 1950   VMF-214 with F4Us

CAMOUFLAGE

June 1948   Possibly still Measure 21

RADAR

June 1948   SK-2, SP, SG, YE

March 1952-October 1953   SPS-6, SP, YE

Left: USS *Sicily* (CVE-118), taken in Hampton Roads off Norfolk, Virginia, on 6 June 1948.
W H Davis

Below: This aerial photo of USS *Sicily* shows the ship's appearance in the early 1950s, now with enclosed bridge, combination of SPS-6, SP and YE; the forward 40mm quadruple mount is now absent, and some of the 40mm twins are now radar controlled. There are some aircraft components lying on the flight deck: the wings of two aircraft and the radome (APS-20) of an early warning plane. Note the folding radio aerials on the starboard edge of the flight deck.
USNI collection

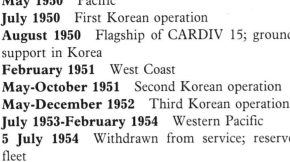

USS Trocadero Bay (ACV-119) – Point Cruz

Laid down as CVE-119. Renamed USS *Point Cruz* on 5 June 1944, before keel was laid

SERVICE HISTORY

October 1945-March 1946 Pacific; pilot training cruises on West Coast, thereafter aircraft transport to Western Pacific

30 June 1947 Withdrawn from service; reserve fleet

26 July 1951 Reactivated for US Navy and specialized for anti-submarine warfare operations

January 1953 Operations off Korea, based in Japan

December 1953 West Coast

August 1955 Western Pacific; Seventh Fleet, flagship of CARDIV 15

31 August 1956 Withdrawn from service; reserve fleet

23 August 1965 Reactivated as AKV-9 for the MSTS

September 1965 Reclassified as T-AKV-9; supply for the armed forces in south-east Asia, until 1970

1970 Withdrawn from service; stricken

RADAR

1953 SPS-6, SP, SG, YE

1955 As previously

Right: This photo of USS *Point Cruz* (CVE-119) dates from 1953. Radar combination is SPS-6/SP.
INRO collection

Below: In this photograph of USS *Point Cruz*, which must date from after 1953, the extended bridge, now one deck taller, is clearly visible.
USN official

This photo of USS *Point Cruz* may have been taken around 1954-55, after the 5in guns had been removed. At this time the ship was equipped with the radar combination SG/SPS-6/SP/TACAN.
Real Photographs

Above: USS *Point Cruz* on 23 June 1955, as an anti-submarine carrier, with S2A Trackers on board; these were still painted dark blue at the time they were introduced. Here the bow number is larger than the other number which had to be applied below the director mount, as there was insufficient room on the side of the island.
USN official

Left: This is how USS *Point Cruz* looked in the years 1965-70, while in the service of the MSTS. The double bridge remained, the radar equipment was simplified, the AA mounts removed. The ship is high in the water, and there is a deck load on the flight deck.
USNI collection

USS Mindoro (ACV-120)

Laid down as CVE-120

SERVICE HISTORY
February 1946 Atlantic; CARDIV 14; East Coast operations; pilot training cruises and anti-submarine exercises for the next 9 years
1950 and 1954 European and Mediterranean deployment

4 August 1955 Withdrawn from service; reserve fleet

RADAR
July 1949 SK-2, SP, SG, YE
1954 SPS-6, SP, SG, YE

Above: USS *Mindoro* (CVE-120), photographed in 1949. There is no identification number visible here.
USN official

Right: USS *Mindoro*, pictured on 28 April 1950. The forward 40mm quadruple mount had been removed by this time. A Blimp is tethered on the flight deck.
Breyer collection

USS *Mindoro*, seen from the air in the early 1950s, showing minor alterations to the bridge compared with the previous photograph. A few 40mm twins are now radar controlled. The ship has an anti-submarine hunter-killer air group embarked, with TBM-3W and TBM-3S aircraft.
USNI collection

USS *Mindoro*, pictured in 1954, now with colorful deck markings to indicate the flight deck centerline for new pilots, and SPS-6/SP/YE radar. The 5in guns have been removed.
Real Photographs

USS Rabaul (ACV-121)

Laid down as CVE-121. Completed by Commercial Iron Works. Completed and delivered, but never commissioned. Transferred to reserve after delivery to Navy

USS Palau (ACV-122)

Laid down as CVE-122

SERVICE HISTORY

May 1946 Atlantic, until 1947
May 1947 Immobilized, then a cruise to Africa
December 1947-March 1948 Immobilized again, but still in service
June 1948 Aircraft transport to Turkey, thereafter remained in Western Atlantic
April 1952 Sixth Fleet in Mediterranean, until June
June 1952 Second Fleet, East Coast; was to be withdrawn from service, but this was postponed
August-October 1953 Aircraft transport to Japan
15 June 1954 Withdrawn from service; reserve fleet

Right: USS *Palau* (CVE-122), pictured during the early post-war years.
BfZ collection

Below: USS *Palau* during the service period 1952-54. Radar combination SPS-6/SP/YE. Radio aerials at the deck edge.
USNI collection

RADAR
1946 SK-2, SP, SG, YE

USS Tinian (ACV-123)

Laid down as CVE-123. Completed, but never officially commissioned. Placed in reserve after delivery to Navy

The remaining four were laid down as CVE-124 to -127, but construction was suspended and the ships broken up

RADAR
February 1946   SK-2, SP, SG, YE

Left: USS *Tinian* (CVE-123), the second ship of the *Commencement Bay* class to be completed but not commissioned. The other ship was USS *Rabaul* (CVE-121). This photo was taken on 21 February 1946 during builders' trials. After delivery to the Navy, USS *Tinian* was immediately transferred to the reserve fleet.
D McPherson

And this is how *Tinian*, the last completed CVE, looked in preserved state as AKV-23. This photo dates from 26 November 1971, when *Tinian* had already been stricken from the official list.
L R Cote

USS Bastogne (ACV-124)
USS Eniwetok (ACV-125)
USS Lingayen (ACV-126)
USS Okinawa (ACV-127)

Aviation Support Ships

Introduction and Classification

From the very first years of American naval aviation there were aviation auxiliary ships, although they were of far more modest scope than during the Second World War and subsequent years. By 1920 there were the categories AV (for naval aircraft tender) and AZ for airship tender. There was only one airship tender (USS *Wright,* AZ-1), after which the abbreviation AZ soon disappeared from the classification list. The category AV was retained through the 1920s and 1930s, and included most of the ships of the Second World War. The class finally came to an end in the late 1960s, when the last 'seaplanes' were retired.

The AVs were, however, by no means the only ships to serve as support for aircraft and their crew. In particular, the American Army and Navy squadrons distributed all over the world often had to be supplied, maintained and repaired far from fixed, fully-equipped support bases; their crews had to be cared for and accommodated between individual operations, and the aircraft themselves had to be transported over great distances and brought to the advanced support bases. All this applied not only to shipboard naval aviation, but also to the Navy's land-based naval reconnaissance aircraft and aircraft of the US Army Air Force (USAAF). (It was only after the Second World War that there was an independent air force which operated as a self-contained arm of the armed forces.)

From the end of the 1930s, the need for the US Navy to create conditions for successful operation of all these aviation units led to a definite increase in the number of ships which later became known under the collective name of 'Aviation Auxiliaries'.

At present there are no categories of auxiliary ships which are *exclusively* concerned with aviation, but the following list shows every category of 'Aviation Auxiliary'. In alphabetical order:

AKV	Cargo Ships and Aircraft Ferries
APV	Transports and Aircraft Ferries
ARV	Aircraft Repair Ships
ARV(E)	Aircraft Repair Ships (Engine)
ARV(A)	Aircraft Repair Ships (Airframe)
ARVH	Aircraft Repair Ships (Helicopter)
AV	Seaplane Tenders
AVD	Seaplane Tenders (Destroyer)
AVP	Small Seaplane Tenders
AVB	Advanced Aviation Base Ships
AVS	Aviation Supply Ships
AVT	Auxiliary Aircraft Transports
AZ	Lighter-than-Air Aircraft Tender

The large number of ships within these categories can be divided into those specifically designed and built by the Navy for the purpose, and those that resulted from the conversion of other warships or commercial ships.

The following section presents the individual auxiliary ship categories and classes in general terms, while the complete construction data and technical information can be found at the end of the book. For this reason a summary of the individual ships' names in the index of ships' names is not needed.

Auxiliary Ship Categories and Classes

AKV – Cargo Ships and Aircraft Ferries

In this category there were four classes totalling 43 units, only a small number of which actually carried this code. The reader should bear in mind that from 1959 on nearly all the former escort carriers then in the reserve fleet were reclassified nominally as AKV, although most of them were never reactivated. In the Second World War only two ships carried this code.

Kitty Hawk Class
USS *Kitty Hawk* (AKV-1), ex-*Seatrain New York*
USS *Hammondsport* (AKV-2), ex-*Seatrain Havana*
The two ships of this class were still classed as aircraft transports (APV) up to 15 September 1943 (see also under APV). After the end of the War they were returned to their owners.

USS *Hammondsport* (AKV-2), here still classified as APV-2, with a load of carrier aircraft, whose wings are folded sideways, on the way to their operational base. *Davis collection*

Lt James E Robinson Class
USNS *James E Robinson* (T-AKV-3), ex-*Czechoslovakia Victory*
USNS *Pvt Joseph E Merrell* (T-AKV-4), ex-*Grange Victory*
USNS *Sgt Jack J Pendleton* (T-AKV-5), ex-*Mandan Victory*
Even before the Korean War the US Navy acquired three 'Victory' and two 'Liberty' freighters from the US Army, for use as aircraft ferries, under the code T-AKV. The three 'Victory' freighters belonged to the standard VC2-S-AP3 type, and they retained their Army names. These freighters were built at high speed during the Second World War, and the ruggedness of their construction is shown by the fact that all three ships survived to be reclassified as T-AKs in 1959. They then continued to serve the Military Sea Transportation Service (MSTS, later MSC) until 1974.

USS *Joseph F Merrell* (AKV-4), pictured on 21 January 1953.
Davis collection

The appearance of USS *Jack J Pendleton* (AKV-5) is typical of most of the 'Victory' freighters, built in very large numbers during the Second World War. The tubs for the guns fitted during the War are now empty. The navigation radar antenna was a feature of many MSTS ships for many years.
Davis collection

Albert M Boe Class
USNS *Albert M Boe* (T-AKV-6)
USNS *Cardinal O'Connell* (T-AKV-7)

These were two freighters which were taken over from the US Army by the Navy in May 1950. They belonged to the standard Type Z-EC2-S-C5 and retained their Army names. These ships also carried a civilian crew of the MSTS, and their length of time in Navy service was extremely short. Following the end of the Korean War they were stricken from the official list in March 1953.

USS *Cardinal O'Connell* (AKV-7), one of the standard 'Liberty' type vessels, which was also unarmed. Note the various types of king posts and derricks.
Davis collection

Kula Gulf Class

The only remaining class in the AKV category embraces 36 former escort carriers, all of which were reclassified as AKVs in May 1959. This was because it had become clear that, if reactivated, these ships could only have been used as aircraft ferries, since they lacked all the equipment needed to operate modern aircraft and helicopters. This class included a varied mixture of ships of the former CVE classes (*Commencement Bay, Casablanca* and *Bogue*), as can be seen from the list that follows:

USS *Kula Gulf* (AKV-8, ex-CVE-108)
USS *Cape Gloucester* (AKV-9, ex-CVE-109)
USS *Salerno Bay* (AKV-10, ex-CVE-110)
USS *Vella Gulf* (AKV-11, ex-CVE-111)
USS *Siboney* (AKV-12, ex-CVE-112)
USS *Puget Sound* (AKV-13, ex-CVE-113)
USS *Rendova* (AKV-14, ex-CVE-114)
USS *Bairoko* (AKV-15, ex-CVE-115)
USS *Badoeng Strait* (AKV-16, ex-CVE-116)
USS *Saidor* (AKV-17, ex-CVE-117)
USS *Sicily* (AKV-18, ex-CVE-118)
USS *Point Cruz* (AKV-19, ex-CVE-119)
USS *Mindoro* (AKV-20, ex-CVE-120)
USS *Rabaul* (AKV-21, ex-CVE-121)
USS *Palau* (AKV-22, ex-CVE-122)

USS *Tinian* (AKV-23, ex-CVE-123)
USS *Nehenta Bay* (AKV-24, ex-CVE-74)
USS *Hoggatt Bay* (AKV-25, ex-CVE-75)
USS *Kadashan Bay* (AKV-26, ex-CVE-76)
USS *Marcus Island* (AKV-27, ex-CVE-77)
USS *Savo Island* (AKV-28, ex-CVE-78)
USS *Rudyerd Bay* (AKV-29, ex-CVE-81)
USS *Sitkoh Bay* (AKV-30, ex-CVE-86)
USS *Takanis Bay* (AKV-31, ex-CVE-89)
USS *Lunga Point* (AKV-32, ex-CVE-94)
USS *Hollandia* (AKV-33, ex-CVE-97)
USS *Kwajalein* (AKV-34, ex-CVE-98)
USS *Bougainville* (AKV-35, ex-CVE-100)
USS *Matanikau* (AKV-36, ex-CVE-101)
USS *Commencement Bay* (AKV-37, ex-CVE-105)
USS *Block Island* (AKV-38, ex-CVE-106)
USS *Gilbert Islands* (AKV-39, ex-CVE-107)
USS *Card* (AKV-40, ex-CVE-11)
USS *Core* (AKV-41, ex-CVE-13)
USS *Breton* (AKV-42, ex-CVE-23)
USS *Croatan* (AKV-43, ex-CVE-25)

Only a few of these ships were employed in the 1960s as AKVs, as can be seen from the CVE service histories already detailed. The last units of this class were not stricken from the official list until the early 1970s.

APV – Transports and Aircraft Ferries

This category only encompassed one class with three ships during the Second World War. The code predated AKV, and was replaced by it. The reclassification as AKV was evidently no more than an example of bureaucracy, since the tasks of the APV and the AKV were the same. The code APV had been introduced in the late 1920s, but there were no ships in the category until in 1941.

The Kitty Hawk class
USS *Kitty Hawk* (APV-1), ex-*Seatrain New York*
USS *Hammondsport* (APV-2), ex-*Seatrain Havana*
USS *Lakehurst* (APV-3), ex-*Seatrain New Jersey*
These ships were railway ferries taken over by the Navy. APV-3 only carried this code for two months, before being once more reclassified as APM-1 on 3 December 1942. The first two ships, on the other hand, were reclassified from APV to AKV on 15 September 1943 (see AKV).

USS Lafayette (APV-4)
The only ship which was given the code APV – nominally, at least – was the French passenger liner *Normandie*, which was to be converted by the US Navy into a troop transport under the code AP-53. During conversion work in New York in Autumn 1942 the ship caught fire and capsized. About six months later she was raised, and it was planned to convert her into an APV, but the condition of the hull and propulsion system was so bad that the ship was never converted.

USS *Kitty Hawk* (APV-1) was the sister ship of *Hammondsport*. Note the two cranes and the clumsy, inelegant appearance of the ships of this class. *Davis collection*

Right: In contrast to the innocuous appearance of USS *Cardinal O'Connell* (AKV-7), this 'Liberty' freighter is heavily armed, because she was actively employed towards the end of the Second World War. This vessel is the repair and workshop ship USS *Chourre* (ARV-1). Forward two 40mm twins can be identified, plus the 5in/38 gun aft, and workshop ship USS *Chourre* (ARV-1). Forward two 40mm twins can be identified, plus the 5in/38 gun aft, the raised 40mm quadruple mount, and several 20mm AA guns. The small SG radar antenna is fitted on the mainmast, and there is an antenna on the forward mast which is very probably one of the SA series. *USN official*

ARV/ARV(E)/ARV(A)/ARVH – Aircraft/Helicopter Repair Ships

This group of auxiliary ships was sub-divided into four categories, each of which embraced only one class. The total number of ships concerned was only seven. Three classes were products of the Second World War, while one came out of the Vietnam War.

The ARVs were two 'Liberty' freighters of the Maritime Commission type EC2-S-C1, and hence relatively spacious. By that time the Navy's experience of carrying out repairs in wartime made it clear that a higher degree of specialization was needed. Two tank landing ships (LSTs) were then specialized as ARV(E)s, for repairs to piston engines, and two as ARV(A) for repairs to aircraft airframes, the letters in brackets in the code representing 'engine' and 'airframe' respectively.

The four former LSTs in particular spent a very long time in the reserve fleet after the War.

The only active ARVH served for several years as an advanced repair base for repairing US Army helicopters damaged over Vietnam. As well as the civilian MSTS crew there were workshops with 308 skilled Army personnel.

The four categories/classes included the following ships, with a common code number sequence (with the exception of ARVH-1).

ARV – Chourre Class

USS *Chourre* (ARV-1), ex-USS *Dumaran* (ARG-14)
USS *Webster* (ARV-2), ex-USS *Masbate* (ARG-15)
Reclassification as ARV took effect on 22 February 1944.

ARV(E) – Aventinus Class

USS *Aventinus* (ARV(E)-3), ex-*LST-1092*
USS *Chloris* (ARV(E)-4), ex-*LST-1094*
Reclassification as ARV(E) took effect on 14 December 1944.

ARV(A) – Fabius Class

USS *Fabius* (ARV(A)-5), ex-*LST-1093*
USS *Megara* (ARV(A)-6), ex-*LST-1095*
Reclassification as ARV(A) took effect on 14 December 1944.

ARVH-Corpus Christi Bay

USNS *Corpus Christi Bay* (T-ARVH-1), ex-USS *Albemarle* (AV-5)
Reclassification as ARVH took effect on 27 March 1965. The intended conversion of a second AV, then in reserve, to ARVH-2 was not carried out. ARVH-1 was stricken in 1974.

After completion as a workshop ship USS *Aventinus* (AVR(E)-3) was fitted with the bow door typical of the LST. Note the clearly visible welded seams of the hull and the superstructure which had been added.
USN official

This broadside view shows the second ship of the class USS *Chloris* (ARV(E)-4), taken in the 1950s, with two code numbers of equal size, and the aviation insignia behind the hull number. The side of the ship's hull shows traces of the diesel engine exhaust in the midship area.
USN official

USS *Megara* (ARV(A)-6), showing no obvious differences
from an ARV(E). Featuring the aviation insignia, the ship
was photographed off Toulon on 22 April 1954. The signal
flags are hung out to dry.
Marius Bar

The 1965 conversion of the relatively elegant tender USS
Albemarle (AV-5) to a 'floating aeronautical maintenance
facility' produced a rather ugly vessel in USNS *Corpus
Christi Bay* (T-ARVH). She now had two helicopter
platforms, of which the after one was formed by extending
the former workshop area aft. Note the helicopter flight
control position above the bridge, and the two radar
antennas of the same type. The photo dates from 1966.
USN/MSTS

AV/AVP/AVD Seaplane Tenders

In the period before the Second World War some navies operated seaplane tenders. This term generally covered ships which had several seaplanes (ie float-equipped aircraft) permanently on board. These seaplanes could be used for reconnaissance tasks within Fleet operations. Normally they were launched by the ship's catapult, and hoisted back on board by ship's crane at the end of the mission.

However, in American terminology Seaplane Tenders were support and repair ships, which were so small that at best they were able to hoist one or two aircraft onto a working platform, in order to carry out repairs. Apart from this primary task, the AVs and their variants AVPs and AVDs were used as floating support bases, which had everything on board in the way of supplies, weapons, equipment, replacement parts, fuels etc, required for seaplanes when remote from shore bases. At the same time these ships could offer accommodation and relaxation for aircraft crews after strenuous missions. This was the reason why the larger AVs and the smaller AVPs were used as staff and HQ ships almost until the 1970s, even though seaplanes had long since disappeared from the US Navy – after the P-5M Marlin had been retired.

When the use of seaplanes overseas began to increase, there were no ships available which had been specifically designed and built for this purpose. Hence the Navy 'made do' by reclassifying a few old minesweepers (AM) to AVPs in the mid-1930s, and fitting them out as seaplane tenders. In 1937 the first aircraft carrier of the US Navy, USS *Langley* (CV-1), was reclassified as AV-3, while the Navy began to design the first 'real' AVs and AVPs. These were completed shortly after the USA entered the Second World War, when the need was even greater. Consideration was also given to the large number of four-stack destroyers from the First World War, which were too fragile and poorly armed to undertake destroyer duties with the Fleet, but which were highly suitable for special tasks after relatively minor conversion work. Seven of them were used as AVPs in 1938-39, and were then reclassified as AVDs in 1940, together with a further seven. The increased need for tenders was satisfied by the conversion of seven freighters. Shortly before the Second World War, and also in the period after it, there were the following classes of seaplane tenders:

USS Wright (AV-1)

The first seaplane tender completed for the Navy, she was actually employed as an airship tender until 11 November 1923. She remained a 'one-off', and as a special ship was renamed USS *San Clemente* on 30 December 1944, with the new classification AG-79. The name *Wright* was then used for the Light Aircraft Carrier CVL-49.

USS Jason (AV-2)

The former Navy collier USS *Jason* (AC-12) operated in 1930 as AV-2, but was relieved before the Second World War. She is not mentioned again.

USS *Wright* (AV-1), initially employed as airship tender (AZ-1), was the US Navy's first seaplane tender. *USN official*

USS Langley (AV-3)

USS *Langley* (AV-3, ex-CV-1) ex-USS *Jupiter* (AC-3)

This was the US Navy's first aircraft carrier (see *Aircraft Carriers of the US Navy*), which was first commissioned as the Navy collier USS *Jupiter* (AC-3). Reclassification as AV took place on 21 April 1937. After the outbreak of War, *Langley* was used mainly as an aircraft transport, because of her relative spaciousness. During this activity she was sunk in early 1942 by the Japanese.

USS Patoka (AV-6)

USS *Patoka* (AV-6, ex-AO-9)

The Navy oiler USS *Patoka* (AO-9) operated as an airship tender from 1924, although she never carried the code AZ. For a short period between 1939 and 1940 the ship was reclassified as AV-6, only to be returned to the classification AO-9 before the USA entered the War. This ship is also not mentioned again.

AV-Curtiss Class

USS *Curtiss* (AV-4)

USS *Albemarle* (AV-5)

This was the first class to be planned and designed as seaplane tenders from the keel up. Several features were characteristic of this class and the succeeding *Currituck* class

1) Tall hull and compact superstructure
2) Location of crew acoommodation and other spaces in the forward half of the ship
3) Spacious workshop area forming the after section of the superstructure
4) Spacious working platform on the stern
5) Two heavy standard cranes for hoisting large aircraft
6) Relatively powerful armament—understandable in view of the use of these ships in advanced positions

From the point of view of recognition, the two

USS *Langley* (CV-1), seen here in February 1937, immediately after conversion, but before being reclassified AV-3. After shortening the former flight deck, the bridge, which had been hidden beneath it, became visible, as did two of the four 5in/51 guns.
USN official

ships could be differentiated from the succeeding *Currituck* class by the fact that they had two stacks. Both ships were completed in 1940, and USS *Curtiss* was damaged in the Japanese attack on Pearl Harbor. USS *Albemarle* served in the Atlantic during the Second World War. Both units were decommissioned towards the end of the 1950s, but USS *Albemarle* was converted to an ARVH in 1965 (see under ARVH) and was used during the Vietnam War as a helicopter repair ship.

This photograph shows USS *Curtiss* (AV-4) in 1945, evidently painted the Navy Blue of Measure 21. Note that the ship here carries the old CXAM-1 radar antenna, which had become available when it was replaced by more modern designs on other ships. This antenna was later exchanged again for SK-2. The two heavy standard cranes are an obvious feature here; they were used to hoist seaplanes out of the water and onto the work area. There are numerous life rafts along the sides.
USN official

Above: This picture of USS *Curtiss* was taken between 1951 and 1954. In contrast to its sister ship USS *Albemarle*, the forward superfiring 5in gun is not in an enclosed shield. SPS-6 radar is on the lattice mast.
USN official

Below: Barely a year before being withdrawn from service as an AV, USS *Albemarle* is pictured here in September 1959 near the Azores. There is no lattice radar support now, an SPS-12 radar antenna being fitted on the tripod mast. There are still quadruple 40mm Bofors guns on board.
USN official

Above: USS *Albemarle* (AV-5), seen in January 1958, after completion of the modifications to the after half of the ship, in which one of the cranes was removed. The stern was modified into a short drydock, with a ramp fixed in front of it. This conversion was a preparatory measure for maintenance of the first jet-powered seaplane, the P6M Seamaster, which was then under development. When the Seamaster program was abandoned in 1960, *Albemarle* was withdrawn from service. After being stricken from the official list in 1965, she was once again commissioned as a helicopter repair ship under the name USNS *Corpus Christi Bay* (ARVH-1).
Davis collection

AV-Currituck Class

USS *Currituck* (AV-7)
USS *Norton Sound* (AV-11)
USS *Pine Island* (AV-12)
USS *Salisbury Sound* (AV-13), ex-*Puget Sound*

As their successors, these ships had marked similarity to the *Curtiss* class, although they only had one stack. Their spaciousness made these ships ideal for special duties. USS *Norton Sound* very soon took on the rôle of a guided missile test ship after the War, and the ship continues in this task today, 30 years after completion, and after several conversions. Reclassification from AV-11 to AVM-1 was not carried out until 8 August 1951. By contrast, her three sister ships assumed the rôle of flagship of the 'Commander Fleet Air Western Pacific', who was also the 'Commander Taiwan Patrol Force' in 1967. At an early stage he was also in charge of P5M Marlin seaplanes, but later only of land-based reconnaissance aircraft of the P-2 Neptune and P-3 Orion types.

Right: USS *Currituck* (AV-7) in 1945, with SK radar on the foremast. The two forward 5in mounts were removed to make room for a temporary helicopter platform, but the ship later reverted to its earlier state. No Mk 37 director for the 5in guns can be seen.
Davis collection

Below: February 1954 is the date of this picture of USS *Currituck*, carrying a P5M Marlin flying boat in its first version, with the stabilizer set lower down. There is now SPS-6 radar on the foremast, some 20mm AA guns are still mounted, but there is no Mk 37 director.
USN official

This photo shows USS *Currituck* in her final state in the mid-1960s. All the 20mm and 40mm AA guns have disappeared; the fire control for the 5in guns is now a Mk 37 director with Mk 25 radar. On the forecastle is a radio aerial, while the TACAN homing beacon antenna is fixed to the top of the mast which runs through the center of the top forward standard crane.
USN official

USS *Norton Sound* (AV-11), photographed on 8 February 1945, only a month after commissioning, obviously camouflaged to Measure 32. The foremast carries SK-2 radar, and there is a searchlight on the lattice radar support.
USN official

USS *Norton Sound* on 16 July 1949, in the role of floating guided missile laboratory, but not yet with the code AVM. A temporary helicopter platform replaces the two forward gun turrets. A new king post carries special antennas. The after crane has been removed.
USN official

In 1979 *Norton Sound* was 34 years old but was still in active service as AVM-1*, after several conversions, operating as the experimental ship of the Pacific Missile Range, based a Point Mugu, California. This photograph was taken in March 1975 and shows the ship in her configuration as test ship for the Aegis guided missile program; a combined search and fire control system SPY-1 (above the bridge) and a Mk 26 guided missile launcher (on the stern) are part of this. There is SPS-40 radar on the square lattice mast.
USN official

*More on the various stages of conversion of USS *Norton Sound* (AVM-1) can be found in an article 'Weapons Training and Testing Ships of the US Navy 1930-1976', written by the author of this book, and printed in the June 1976 issue of *Marine Rundschau*.

Note the similarity between these pictures: two stern views of USS *Pine Island* (AV-12), separated by almost a decade. In the top picture, taken in the Panama Canal area on 7 December 1946, two PBM-5 aircraft are on the work area. Note the off-set position of the tub for the 40mm quadruple on the fantail, SK and SG radar on the foremast, and YE on the crane mast. Just visible is the protective net on the right for the helicopter platform erected on the bow.
USN (BfZ collection)

About 10 years later: USS *Pine Island* without 40mm AA gun tub, and one SP-5B (formerly P5M-2) Marlin on the crane hook, belonging to long-range reconnaissance squadron VP-50. Radar antennas SPS-6 and SPS-10 are now fitted on the foremast.
USN official

Above: USS *Salisbury Sound* (AV-13), at full dress ship, seen here on 22 February 1951, still with SK-2 and SG radar antennas. There are two PBM aircraft on the work area.
Davis collection

Right: This photograph of USS *Pine Island* also dates from the mid-1960s, and gives an impression of the asymmetrically placed upper two 5in guns and the crane.
USN official

Below: USS *Salisbury Sound* (AV-13) at the end of her career, photographed in April 1966 as flagship of the 'Commander Patrol Force Seventh Fleet' one year before being withdrawn from service. One SP-5B Marlin is just visible aft of the ship.
USN official

AV – Tangier Class
USS *Tangier* (AV-8), ex-*Sea Arrow*
USS *Pocomoke* (AV-9), ex-*Exchequer*
These ships belonged to the standard C3-Cargo (S) type and were altered to tenders during their construction. They were decommissioned shortly after the end of the War.

Left: USS *Pocomoke* (AV-9), shortly after completion in 1941. The crane post is already fitted, but the crane itself is still absent. Note the king post mast with derricks.
Davis collection

USS *Tangier* (AV-8), the first tender of the standard C3-Cargo (S) type, modified from a merchant ship. The work platform is located between the derricks, between the stack and the after crane.
Davis collection

USS Chandeleur (AV-10)
USS *Chandeleur* (AV-10) was the only AV of the standard C3-S-B1 type. This vessel was also completed as a tender. As in the case of the *Tangier* class, the ship had the heavy standard crane and a reasonably spacious work area for seaplanes needing repair. All the AVs always had one of the larger radar systems on board, and USS *Chandeleur* had SK. Although withdrawn from service in 1947, this ship served for many more years as a station ship, and functioned as HQ ship of the Commander of the Atlantic reserve fleet.

AV – Kenneth Whiting Class

USS *Kenneth Whiting* (AV-14)
USS *Hamlin* (AV-15)
USS *St George* (AV-16)
USS *Cumberland Sound* (AV-17)
USS *Townsend* (AV-18 – not completed)
USS *Calibogue* (AV-19 – not completed)
USS *Hobe Sound* (AV-20 – not completed)

Ships in this class belonged to the standard C3-S Special type, and were conceived and completed as AVs, with similar specifications to the two preceding classes. AV-15 to -17 were withdrawn from service in 1947, but USS *Kenneth Whiting* remained in active service for more than a decade. A long time after being stricken from the official list USS *St George* was removed from the MARAD stand-by fleet and transferred to the Italian Navy in late 1968, where she is still operating as an auxiliary; the last ship of all to carry the SK-2 radar antenna. The construction of AV-18 to 20 was suspended at the end of the War in 1944-45.

USS *Chandeleur* (AV-10) had a very similar layout to USS *Tangier*, and is shown here on 7 November 1945 while transporting troops from the Pacific area on a 'Magic Carpet' operation. The common features of the basic C3 type, to which both ships belonged, are unmistakeable. SK radar is on the mast.
INRO collection

USS *Kenneth Whiting* (AV-14), the name ship of a class of four units of the C3-S Special type, is pictured here off Saipan in August 1944, and obviously camouflaged to Measure 32. The ship has SK and YE radar antennas. There are PBM-5 Mariner aircraft in the water, and one on the ship herself.
USN official

Left: In 1952, when this picture was taken, USS *Kenneth Whiting* still carried the SK antenna. A hose for fuelling seaplanes runs along the hull side.
INRO collection

Above: USS *Kenneth Whiting* was the only ship of the class which stayed in active service until Autumn 1958. The photograph shows the ship on 5 March 1957, 1½ years before being withdrawn from service, off Puget Sound Navy Yard. The second king post now carries an SPS-6 radar antenna.
USN (BfZ collection)

Left: USS *Hamlin* (AV-15) during the Second World War, with the same camouflage as the lead ship of the class.
USN official

Right: Taken on 5 August 1944, USS *St George* (AV-16), also painted to the same camouflage pattern. The photograph gives an idea of the size of the work area. The ship has an SK-2 radar antenna instead of SK and an open 5in gun mount on the quarterdeck.
USN official

Above: 5½ years after being stricken from the official list, USS *St George* was transferred to the Italian Navy, where she operated as an auxiliary ship under the name *Andrea Bafile*. She is still numbered among the reserve ships. This fine photograph dates from 30 March 1971, and shows clearly that SK-2 was still present as well as SPS-6.
A Fraccaroli

Right: This wartime picture of USS *Cumberland Sound* (AV-17) shows that this ship had the same camouflage as its sister ship.
Davis collection

AV – Ashland Class

USS *Ashland* (AV-21, ex-LSD-1)

–(AV-22)

–(AV-23)

At the end of the 1950s the development of the first jet-powered seaplane in the US Navy, the P-7 Seamaster, was in progress, and it became necessary to prepare suitable tenders. In November 1959 it had already been decided that the dock landing ship USS *Ashland* (LSD-1) was to be fitted out as AV-21, and that two sister ships would follow. Eventually the whole Seamaster program was abandoned, and with it the plan to provide further AVs.

Since the retirement of the P5M Marlin in 1967 the US Navy has had no seaplanes, and land-based long-range reconnaissance aircraft have carried out surveillance duties all over the world. They operate from advanced permanent bases in all parts of the world, and there are no longer any active auxiliary ships for their support.

AVP – Lapwing Class

USS *Lapwing* (AVP-1, ex-AM-1)

USS *Heron* (AVP-2, ex-AM-10)

USS *Thrush* (AVP-3, ex-AM-18)

USS *Avocet* (AVP-4, ex-AM-19)

USS *Teal* (AVP-5, ex-AM-23)

USS *Pelican* (AVP-6, ex-AM-37)

USS *Swan* (AVP-7, ex-AM-34)

USS *Gannett* (AVP-8, ex-AM-41)

USS *Sandpiper* (AVP-9, ex-AM-51)

These were the first small seaplane tenders, all of which were classified as AVP on 22 January 1936 after being modified from former minesweepers of the *Bird* class. In contrast to the old destroyers, these ships remained tenders until the end of the War, although they too originated from the time immediately after the First World War. Only USS *Gannett* was lost in action in the War.

USS *Teal* (AVP-5) (*Lapwing* class), shown here with its old AM number 23. The relatively small Keystone PK-1 seaplane could be hoisted on board by the ship's derrick. *Davis collection*

A broadside view of USS *Swan* (AVP-7), with the command flag of a Rear Admiral on the mainmast.
Davis collection

Right: The appearance of a seaplane tender in the early days can be seen from this aerial photo of USS *Pelican* (AVP-6), which also still features the AM number, but already has the aviation insignia next to it.
Davis collection

AVP – Childs Class

USS *Childs* (AVP-14, ex-DD-241)

USS *Williamson* (AVP-15), ex-DD-244)

USS *George E Badger* (AVP-16, ex-DD-196)

USS *Clemson* (AVP-17, ex-DD-186)

USS *Goldsborough* (AVP-18, ex-DD-188)

USS *Hulbert* (AVP-19, ex-DD-342)

USS *William B Preston* (AVP-20, ex-DD-344)

AVP-1 to -9 were old minesweepers, and at that time building numbers 10 to 13 were already reserved for the new *Barnegat* class tenders, and in 1938-39 seven old four-stack destroyers were re-equipped for their rôle as small seaplane tenders, and classified as AVP. The code AVP was retained by these ships for only a short period. On 2 August 1940 these and a further seven ships were reclassified as AVDs.

AVD – Childs Class

USS *Childs* (AVD-1, ex-AVP-14, ex-DD-241)

USS *Williamson* (AVD-2, ex-AVP-15, ex-DD-244)

USS *George E Badger* (AVD-3, ex-AVP-16, ex-DD-196)

USS *Clemson* (AVD-4, ex-AVP-17, ex-DD-186)

USS *Goldsborough* (AVD-5, ex-AVP-18, ex-DD-188)

USS *Hulbert* (AVD-6, ex-AVP-19, ex-DD-342)

USS *William B Preston* (AVD-7, ex-AVP-20, ex-DD-344)

USS *Belknap* (AVD-8, ex-DD-251)

USS *Osmond Ingram* (AVD-9, ex-DD-255)

USS *Ballard* (AVD-10, ex-DD-267)

USS *Thornton* (AVD-11, ex-DD-270)

USS *Gillis* (AVD-12, ex-DD-260)

USS *Greene* (AVD-13, ex-DD-266)

USS *McFarland* (AVD-14, ex-DD-237)

This was certainly an emergency solution, as these relatively small ships could not be very effective. Hence nine AVDs were reclassified again as destroyers at the end of 1943 after the advent of the new *Barnegat* class, while four were scrapped shortly after the end of the War. USS *Thornton* was abandoned in April 1945 after a collision.

Above: The old four-stack destroyers were modified in the course of the Second World War in a variety of ways, and in particular prior to operation as AVD, AVP, APD, DM, DMS or before being loaded to the Royal Navy. The greatest differences lay in the propulsion systems. Depending on the number of boilers retained, the ships had two, three or four stacks, and they carried either no funnel caps or a variety of types. USS *Childs*, shown here as AVD-1, exhibits its modified bridge, with only two funnels and tall caps. *Davis collection*

Left: USS *Gillis* (AVD-12) has all four stacks here, but they are shorter than when the ship was originally completed. Note the shield round the forward gun, and the fuel pipe along the hull side. *Davis collection*

AVP – Barnegat Class

This class is amongst the most interesting of the Navy's aviation auxiliary ships for two reasons: because of the relatively large number of completed units which were employed during the Second World War and long afterwards for a multitude of tasks, and also because of the wide variation in their equipment. Of course, all AVPs were nominally auxiliary ships, but many of the *Barnegat* class were armed as powerfully as destroyers, which is entirely understandable in view of their use in the forward areas, and the fact that they were priority targets for the Japanese Air Force. This class was begun in 1938. Like the large AVs, these first purpose-built small tenders were named after bays. The class was to number 51 units in all, and initially the building numbers AVP-10 to -13 and AVP-21 to -67 were reserved for them. Construction of AVP-42 to -47, and AVP-58 to -67 was suspended in the course of the War, so that in fact only 35 ships were completed between 1941 and 1944. During the War, however, the need for other types of specialist ship also arose, and this class became subject to regrouping and reclassification, as can be seen from the following:

1) AVP-11 was fitted out as a command ship for amphibious forces in 1944, and reclassified as AG-18–later the ship was transferred to the US Coast Guard
2) AVP-27, -28, -56, and -57 were completed as PT boat tenders and were given the codes AGP-7, -6, -8 and -9; in 1951 AGP-6 was transferred to Italy (as the *Pietro Cavezzale*); AGP-8 and -9 were allocated to the US Coast Guard after the War
3) The remainder carried out their intended duties during the War

However, after the War these versatile ships were transferred to a variety of duties. A small number were mothballed, but were given other tasks.

1) In 1948-49, 15 ships were transferred to the US Coast Guard, namely AVP-12, -13, -21 to -26, -29 and -31 to -36. They did excellent service as ocean station ships, thanks to their seaworthiness and their long range
2) AVP-51 was employed as an oceanogrphic research ship (AGOR-1), and later transferred to Greece (as the *Hephaistos*)
3) AVP-30 and -50 became survey ships (AGS) in 1957, but retained their code numbers
4) AVP-39 was transferred to Norway in 1958 (as the *Haakon VII*), and AVP-49 to Ethiopia in 1961 (as the *Ethiopia*)
5) Finally there were three ships which were

fitted out as flagships of the COMMIDEAST-FOR (Commander Middle East Force) in the Persian Gulf

The last-named were USS *Duxbury Bay* (AVP-38), USS *Greenwich Bay* (AVP-41) and USS *Valcour* (AVP-55). The three ships operated on a six months rotation in the Persian Gulf. To reflect the heat of a powerful sun, they were painted white, with black code numbers. Because of the traditional connection with naval aviation, the Aviation insignia was applied next to the code number at first. In mid-1966 AVP-38 and -41 were stricken, and USS *Valcour* remained the only ship with this duty until withdrawn from service in 1972. On 15 December 1965 USS *Valcour* was allocated the new code AGF, and the number changed from 55 to 1. After *Valcour* was stricken on 15 January 1973, the much larger dock landing ship USS *La Salle* (LPD-3) was categorized AGF-3, while retaining her LPD number, and was sent to the Persian Gulf under similar conditions, where she remains in service as a flagship.

At different times during the Second World War and shortly afterwards, these ships differed in the armament carried, and it is worth noting that on long voyages, especially when travelling to and from their operational areas, they were able to operate as escort vessels on anti-submarine duties. They were all equipped with depth-charge racks (DCR) and depth-charge throwers (DCT).

Their capability of assuming the same duties as the large AVs, albeit to a lesser extent, is important. To this end there were supply and crew accommodation spaces, fuel tanks, repair shops for engines and airframes, and above all the standard heavy crane, which was arranged in such a way that it could hoist an aircraft completely out of the water.

As can be seen from the individual ships' notes that follow, 15 AVPs of this class were transferred to the US Coast Guard (USCG) after the end of the Second World War, where they continued to serve as ocean station ships for many more years. As with numerous other ships and boats of the USCG, these were painted white, in order to reflect the sun's radiation. This is also true of three ships of this class which were later reclassified as survey ships (AGS) or hydrographic research ships (AGOR), as also the two ships handed over to Italy and Ethiopia

Left: USS *Humboldt* (AVP-21) (*Barnegat* class), apparently camouflaged to a special design of Measure 32; the picture was taken on 17 November 1944.
Davis collection

Armament of the Barnegat Class

Hull No	Name	Date of armament information	5in/38 (single)	40mm (quad)	40mm (twin)	20mm	MG	Notes
10	*Barnegat*	August 1945	1	1	2	6	—	
(11)	(*Biscayne*)		—	—	—	—	—	October 1944 = AGC-18; August 1946 = WAVP-385
12	*Casco*	August 1945	3	1	2	8	—	April 1949 = WAVP-370
13	*Mackinac*	August 1945	1	1	2	6	—	April 1949 = WAVP-371
21	*Humboldt*	December 1944	1	1	2	6	—	January 1949 = WAVP-372
22	*Matagorda*	December 1944	2	1	2	8	—	March 1949 = WAVP-373
23	*Absecon*	August 1945	2	—	—	4	—	January 1949 = WAVP-374
24	*Chinoteague*	August 1945	2	1	2	8	—	March 1949 = WAVP-375
25	*Coos Bay*	August 1945	4	1	2	8	7	January 1949 = WAVP-376
26	*Half Moon*	August 1945	3	1	2	8	6 (twin)	September 1948 = WAVP-378
(27)	*Mobjack*		—	—	—	—	—	In service as AGP-7
(28)	*Oyster Bay*		—	—	—	—	—	In service as AGP-6; to Italy
29	*Rockaway*	December 1944	1	1	2	6	—	December 1948 = WAVP-377
30	*San Pablo*	August 1945	4	—	—	8	9	1957 AGS-30
31	*Unimak*	August 1945	1	1	2	4 (twin)	—	September 1948 = WAVP-379
32	*Yakutat*	August 1945	3	1	2	8	—	August 1948 = WAVP-380
33	*Barataria*	August 1945	1	1	2	6	—	September 1948 = WAVP-381
34	*Bering Strait*	August 1945	3	1	2	8	6	September 1948 = WAVP-382
35	*Castle Rock*	August 1945	1	1	2	6	—	September 1948 = WAVP-383
36	*Cook Inlet*	August 1945	1	1	2	6	—	September 1948 = WAVP-384
37	*Corson*	August 1945	1	1	2	6	—	
38	*Duxbury Bay*	August 1945	1	1	2	6	—	
39	*Gardiners Bay*	August 1945	1	1	2	6	—	May 1968 to Norway
40	*Floyds Bay*	August 1945	1	1	2	6	—	
41	*Greenwich Bay*	August 1945	1	1	2	6	—	
42-47								Construction suspended 22.4.1943
48	*Onslow*	August 1945	3	1	2	8	—	
49	*Orca*	August 1945	3	1	2	8	—	To Ethiopia 1961
50	*Rehoboth*	August 1945	1	1	2	4 (twin)	—	1957 = AGS-50
51	*San Carlos*	August 1945	3	1	2	8	—	1958 = *J W Gibbs* (AGOR-1)
52	*Shelikof*	August 1945	3	1	2	8	—	
53	*Suisun*	August 1945	1	1	2	6	—	
54	*Timbalier*	September 1946	1	1	2	4 (twin)	—	
55	*Valcour*	September 1946	1	1	2	4 (twin)	—	1965 = AGF-1
(56)	*Wachapreague*							In service as AGP-8; May 1946 = WAVP-386
(57)	*Willoughby*							In service as AGP-9; June 1946 = WAVP-387
(58-67)								Construction suspended 19 October 1942

Above: USS *Matagorda* (AVP-22), pictured off the Boston Navy Yard on 11 May 1942. Both 5in mounts are located forward. The camouflage design is presumably connected with Measure 12. The plating below the bridge superstructure has openings along the top edge.
USN official

Right: USCGC *Absecon* (WHEC-374), formerly AVP-23, pictured in German waters on 2 August 1971. Note the alterations to the ship since she was transferred to the Coast Guard, to be employed as an ocean station ship: only one 5in mount, the plating below the bridge removed, tan-colored stack with a black band, otherwise white paintwork. The after tripod mast carries the air search antenna SPS-29D.
Dr W Noecker

Below: USCGC *Chinoteague* (WHEC-375, ex-AVP-24), photographed in the Mediterranean. She looks similar to *Absecon*, but on the bridge is the slightly larger Mk 56 director, which still carries the gray Navy paint.
C Martinelli

Above: USS *San Pablo*, ex-AVP-30, shown here in the 1950s after reclassification as survey ship with the code AGS-30. Of the original four 5in guns, only the two forward ones remain. Beneath the bridge the side is fully plated in.
USN official

Left: Even when these ships had had nothing to do with naval aviation for a long time, they still carried the aviation insignia next to their hull number to maintain traditional links. This number is black, because the whole ship is painted white to offer better protection against the tropical temperatures of the Persian Gulf. The ship is USS *Duxbury Bay* (AVP-38), one of three ships of this class which served on a rotational basis as flagship of the Commander Middle East Fleet. The photograph dates from 1960, at which time a radar antenna of the SA- series was still carried on the foremast.
INRO collection

Below: Two years later: USS *Duxbury Bay* on 2 May 1962 in the same rôle. By this time SPS-12 radar had been fitted on the mast platform and on the superstructure there was a long range single sideband radio aerial. At this time the armament consisted solely of the forward 40mm Bofors quadruple mounting.
USN (BfZ collection)

Above: USS *Floyds Bay* (AVP-40), one of the ships of its class which only had one 5in gun mount. Note the small hull number, and small aviation insignia, this time *in front* of the hull number.
Ted Stone

Right: USS *Onslow* (AVP-48) had three 5in guns at the end of the War. In this post-war picture only two of them are visible, the one on the quarterdeck being in an open mount.
Davis collection

Below: Ex-USS *Oyster Bay* (AGP-6) was contracted to be built as AVP-28, but was commissioned as a Patrol Torpedo Boat Tender. This ship was photographed in the harbor of Valetta, Malta on 22 July 1967, under the Italian flag, and renamed *Pietro Cavezzale*. She is still active at present. The tripod mast carries SPS-6 radar, and the armament consists of one 3in and two 40mm guns.
Pavia

AVB – Advanced Aviation Base Ships

In the 1950s, US Navy long distance reconnaissance aircraft were stationed in the Western Pacific, in Iceland and in the Mediterranean to support the Seventh, Second and Sixth Fleets, and the need then arose for a support ship to be stationed in the area—especially in the Mediterranean. The aircraft were P-2 Neptunes and later P-3 Orions, operated by VP squadrons (Patrol Squadrons). In the Western Pacific they operated for a time on a rotating basis, and in the Mediterranean they were based at Rota (Spain) and Sigonella (Sicily). These ships

were to carry everything required to allow the VP squadrons to operate in times of crisis away from existing bases and to support them until supplies could be brought from the United States. Between 1957 and 1969 there were only two single ships in the AVB category, both of which had been converted from former tank landing ships (LST): USS *Alameda County* (AVB-1), ex-*LST-32*, and USS *Tallahatchie County* , ex-*LST-1154*. Both ships were stationed in the Mediterranean.

Left: USS *Alameda County* (AVB-1) was transferred to Italy in November 1962, where she continued in service under the name *Anteo*. This photograph was taken on 5 April 1967, when the ship's appearance had not altered since being transferred to Italy. The only change is that the SPS-6 radar on the lattice mast has been replaced by a smaller one.
A Fraccaroli

Below: USS *Tallahatchie County* (AVB-2), photographed on 11 May 1962. It can be seen that the superstructure on the upper deck has provided not only a temporary helicopter delivery platform, but also additional internal space. The bow doors have been retained, as have the rubbing strakes to protect the hull side when using landing craft.
USN official

Two years later: AVB-2 in Valetta harbor on 10 June 1964. Note the derrick, the two LCVP boats on the upper deck, and the long radio aerials.
Pavia

The stern of USS *Tallahatchie County*, photographed on 28 May 1968, about a year before being withdrawn from service; the 5in gun had already been removed from the aft tub. The only radar antenna on the tripod mast is a small navigation unit.
G Gotuzzo

USS Alameda County (AVB-1)

This ship was not converted extensively, and ended her period of service with the US Navy in November 1962 when transferred to the Italian Navy, where she operated for many years as an auxiliary ship under the name *Anteo*.

USS Tallahatchie County (AVB-2)

In contrast, this vessel was extensively converted at a cost of several million dollars. She was fitted with a new, lightweight superstructure of great height, leaving much more deck space than previously. The conversion lasted from December 1960 to February 1962. The ship had all the equipment necessary to erect and maintain a temporary field landing strip for Naval reconnaissance aircraft of the SP-2H Neptune type. The former tank deck now accommodated 'yellow gear' – aircraft tractors, a crash truck, fuel and oil tankers, bulldozers, engine starting vehicles, generator vehicles, auxiliary vehicles with radio direction equipment, and a meteorological station for making weather forecasts. There were also supply, workshop, specialist library and office containers, all of which could be flown to the location where they were required, as AVB-2 also had a helicopter platform. This mobility made it possible to select a site for the landing strip where the long-range reconnaissance aircraft could exploit their full range. A strip of this type could be set up within three hours. The ship also carried a supply of replacement parts for the aircraft, as well as weapons and ordnance. Major and minor repairs to the aircraft could be carried out by the trained crew of mechanics. The crew of 20 officers and 200 men included not only naval and technically trained personnel, but also Navy Construction Battalions (Seabees) and their equipment. In operation the ship was under the command of the COMNAVAIRLANT, and the Captain and Executive Officer were aviators. In addition to the accommodation for the crew, there was extra space for a further 200 men. In her many years of service in the Mediterranean, USS *Tallahatchie County* was based at a large number of ports, visiting some of them a number of times.

AVS – Aviation Supply Ships

During the War and the post-war period this category included only freighters, whose task was to transport all the supplies needed by aircraft squadrons stationed overseas – replacement parts, engines, aircraft, equipment, etc. The category AVS was only introduced in May 1945, and came to an end in 1965 with the deletion of USS *Jupiter* (AVS-8). From this time on the 'Combat Store Ships' (AFS) of the *Mars* class, which were designed by the Navy, took over the transportation of aircraft supplies. The category of AVS embraced a total of four classes.

USS *Fortune* (AVS-2) (*Supply* class). This old, rather inelegant freighter from the 1920s is very high in the water and looks clumsy.
Davis collection

USS *Allioth* (AVS-4) *Grumium* class.
Davis collection

AVS – Supply Class
USS *Supply* (AVS-1, ex-IX-147), ex-*Ward*
USS *Fortune* (AVS-2, ex-IX-146), ex-*City of Elwood*
These were old freighters from the 1920s, which were requisitioned by the Navy in 1944, and initially carried the auxiliary code IX-147 and -146.

AVA – Grumium Class
USS *Grumium* (AVS-3, ex-IX-174, ex-AK-112), ex-*William G McAdoo*
USS *Allioth* (AVS-4, ex-IX-204, ex-AK-109), ex-*James Rowan*
The two ships of this class were new at this time, and were of the standard EC2-S-C1 'Liberty' type.

AVS – Gwinnett Class
USS *Gwinnett* (AVS-5, ex-AG-92, ex-AK-185)
USS *Nicollet* (AVS-6, ex-AG-93, ex-AK-199)
USS *Pontotoc* (AVS-7, ex-AG-94, ex-AK-206)
This class consisted of slightly smaller ships of the standard C1-M-AV1 type. AVS-3 to -7 served as Navy Cargo Ships (AK) until reclassified as AVSs in May 1945.

USS *Pontotoc* (AVS-7) belonged to the *Gwinnett* class, and was one of the smaller C1-M-AV1 merchant ships with diesel engines.
Davis collection

USS Jupiter (AVS-8)
USS *Jupiter* (AVS-8, ex-AK-43), ex-*Santa Catalina*, ex-*Flying Cloud*
Jupiter, the last representative of this category, was of the larger, standard C2-Cargo (S) type, and was reclassified from AK to AVS in May 1945. As the

only ship in this category, USS *Jupiter* featured a helicopter platform aft until being withdrawn from service in the 1960s. She had been permanently homeported in the Western Pacific (Yokosuka).

The US Navy's last AVS: USS *Jupiter* (AVS-8), pictured on 18 July 1960, five years before decommissioning. The C2 freighter had a helicopter platform aft. The tubs contain 3in/50 guns.
USN official

AVT — Auxiliary Aircraft Transports

This category was introduced in 1959 to include a number of aircraft carriers then in reserve which would only be employed as aircraft transports if reactivated. Not one of these ships ever steamed under this code. The following mothballed carriers were classified as AVT for some period until being stricken.

ex-CVL Independence/Saipan Classes
USS *Cowpens* (AVT-1, ex-CVL-25)
USS *Monterey* (AVT-2, ex-CVL-26)
USS *Cabot* (AVT-3, ex-CVL-28)
USS *Bataan* (AVT-4, ex-CVL-29)
USS *San Jacinto* (AVT-5, ex-CVL-30)

USS *Saipan* (AVT-6, ex-CVL-48)
USS *Wright* (AVT-7, ex-CVL-49)

ex-CV Essex type
USS *Franklin* (AVT-8, ex-CVS-13)
USS *Bunker Hill* (AVT-9, ex-CVS-17)
USS *Leyte* (AVT-10, ex-CVS-17) *CVS 3Y*
USS *Philippine Sea* (AVT-11, ex-CVS-47)
USS *Tarawa* (AVT-12, ex-CVS-40)
USS *Lexington* (AVT-16, ex-CVT-16)
Only USS *Tarawa* was reclassified as an AVT on 1 May 1961, AVT-8 to -11 on 15 May 1959, and AVT-16 not until 1978

Appendices

Bibliography

Please refer to the detailed bibliography in *Aircraft Carriers of the US Navy*, page 320. The literature listed there was also used in part for the preparation of this follow-up volume. The additional publications listed below were used for this volume:

Andrade, E, Jr: 'The Ship That Never Was: the Flying-Deck Cruiser', *Military Affairs*, December 1968

Friedman, N: 'US Flight-Deck Cruiser Designs', *Warship*, 13, January 1980

Musgrove, H E: *US Naval Ships Data, arranged by Hull Classification*, Vols I-III, Nautical Books, Stoughton, USA

Poolman, K: *Escort Carriers 1941–45*, Ian Allan, London 1972

Wetterhahn, A: *US-Standard-Fracht-und Passagier-schiffe 1938-1956*. Eckhardt & Messtorf, Hamburg, 1957

Construction Details for British Escort Carriers

Hull No	Name	FY	Builder	Laid Down	Launched	Completed	Returned to USA	Stricken	War Loss
BAVG-1	*Archer*		Sun SB		14.12.39	17.11.41	9. 1.46	26. 2.46	
BAVG-2	*Avenger*		Bethlehem, Staten Is		27.11.40	2. 3.42		16. 5.44	15.11.42
BAVG-3	*Biter*		Atlantic Basin		18.12.40	5. 5.42	9. 4.45*	24. 1.51	
BAVG-5	*Dasher*		Tietjen & Lang		12. 4.41	2. 7.42		2. 6.45	27. 3.43
BAVG-6	*Tracker*		Willamette		7. 3.42	31. 1.43	29.11.46	2.11.46	
CVE-6	*Battler*	1942	Ingalls	P 31.10.42	7. 3.42	31.10.42	12. 2.46	28. 3.46	
CVE-7	*Attacker*	1942	Western Pipe	P 30. 9.42	27. 9.41	30. 9.42	5. 1.46	26. 2.46	
CVE-8	*Hunter*	1942	Ingalls	P 9. 1.43	22. 5.42	9. 1.43	29.12.45	26. 2.46	
CVE-10	*Chaser*	1942	Ingalls	P 9. 4.43	19. 6.42	9. 4.43	12. 5.46	3. 7.46	
CVE-14	*Fencer*	1942	Western Pipe	P 27. 2.43	4. 4.42	25. 3.43	11.12.46	28. 1.47	
CVE-15	*Stalker*	1942	Western Pipe	P 21.12.42	5. 3.42	21.12.42	29.12.45	20. 3.46	
CVE-17	*Pursuer*	1942	Ingalls	P 14. 6.43	18. 7.42	14. 6.43	12. 2.46	28. 3.46	
CVE-19	*Striker*	1942	Western Pipe	P 28. 4.43	7. 5.42	28. 4.43	12. 2.46	28. 3.46	
CVE-22	*Searcher*	1942	Todd, Tacoma	P 27. 7.42	20. 6.42	7. 4.43	29.11.45	7. 2.46	
CVE-24	*Ravager*	1942	Todd, Tacoma	P 1. 5.42	16. 7.42	25. 4.43	27. 2.46	12. 4.46	
CVE-32	*Slinger*	1942	Todd, Tacoma	25. 5.42	19. 9.42	11. 8.43	27. 2.46	12. 4.46	
CVE-33	*Atheling*	1942	Puget Sound N Yd	9. 6.42	7. 9.42	30. 7.43	13.12.46	7. 2.47	
CVE-34	*Emperor*	1942	Todd, Tacoma	23. 6.42	7.10.42	C 31. 5.43	12. 2.46	28. 3.46	
CVE-35	*Ameer*	1942	Todd, Tacoma	18. 7.42	18.10.42	C 28. 6.43	17. 1.46	20. 3.46	
CVE-36	*Begum*	1942	Todd, Tacoma	3. 8.42	11.11.42	C 22. 7.43	4. 1.46	19. 6.46	
CVE-37	*Trumpeter*	1942	Todd, Tacoma	25. 8.42	15.12.42	4. 8.43	6. 4.46	21. 5.46	
CVE-38	*Empress*	1942	Todd, Tacoma	9. 9.42	31.12.42	C 9. 8.43	4. 2.46	28. 3.46	
CVE-39	*Khedive*	1942	Todd, Tacoma	22. 9.42	30. 1.43	25. 8.43	26. 1.46	19. 7.46	
CVE-40	*Speaker*	1942	Todd, Tacoma	9.10.42	20. 2.43	20.11.43	27. 7.46		
CVE-41	*Nabob (RCN)*	1942	Todd, Tacoma	20.10.42	9. 3.43	7. 9.43	16. 3.45	16. 3.45	
CVE-42	*Premier*	1942	Todd, Tacoma	31.10.42	22. 3.43	3.11.43	12. 4.46	21. 5.46	
CVE-43	*Shah*	1942	Todd, Tacoma	13.11.42	21. 4.43	27. 9.43	6.12.45	7. 2.46	
CVE-44	*Patroller*	1942	Todd, Tacoma	27.11.42	6. 5.43	22.10.43	13.12.46	7. 2.47	
CVE-45	*Rajah*	1942	Willamette	17.12.42	18. 5.43	17. 1.44	13.12.46	7. 2.47	
CVE-46	*Ranee*	1942	Todd, Tacoma	5. 1.43	2. 6.43	8.11.43	21.11.46		
CVE-47	*Trouncer*	1942	Commercial Iron Works	1. 2.43	16. 6.43	28. 1.44	3. 3.46	12. 4.46	
CVE-48	*Thane*	1942	Todd, Tacoma	23. 2.43	15. 7.43	19.11.43	5.12.45	16.11.45	
CVE-49	*Queen*	1942	Todd, Tacoma	12. 3.43	2. 8.43	7.12.43	31.10.46		
CVE-50	*Ruler*	1942	Todd, Tacoma	25. 3.43	21. 8.43	20.12.43	29. 1.46	20. 3.46	
CVE-51	*Arbiter*	1942	Todd, Tacoma	26. 4.43	9. 9.43	31.12.43	3. 3.46	12. 4.46	
CVE-52	*Smiter*	1942	Todd, Tacoma	10. 5.43	27. 9.43	20. 1.44	6. 4.46	21. 5.46	
CVE-53	*Puncher*	1942	Todd, Tacoma	21. 5.43	8.11.43	5. 2.44	17. 1.46	12. 3.46	
CVE-54	*Reaper*	1942	Todd, Tacoma	5. 6.43	22.11.43	18. 2.44	20. 5.46	3. 7.46	

'P' = the date the hull was purchased by the Navy. 'C' = the date of Commissioning. *Returned from French service 10.6.66.

Construction Details for US Escort Carriers

Hull No	Name	FY	Builder	Laid Down	Launched	Comm- issioned	Withdrawn from Service	Reactivated	Withdrawn from Service
CVE-1	*Long Island*	—	Sun SB	P 6. 3.41	11. 1.40	2. 6.41	26. 3.46		
CVE-9	*Bogue*	1942	Todd, Tacoma	P 1. 5.42	15. 1.42	26. 9.42	30.11.46		
CVE-11	*Card*	1942	Todd, Tacoma	P 1. 5.42	21. 4.42	8.11.42	13. 5.46	1. 7.58*	10. 3.70
CVE-12	*Copahee*	1942	Todd, Tacoma	P 8. 2.42	21.10.41	15. 6.42	5. 7.46		
CVE-13	*Core*	1942	Todd, Tacoma	P 1. 5.42	15. 5.42	10.12.42	4.10.46	1. 7.58*	25.11.69
CVE-16	*Nassau*	1942	Todd, Tacoma	P 1. 5.42	4. 4.42	20. 8.42	28.10.46		
CVE-18	*Altamaha*	1942	Todd, Tacoma	P 1. 5.42	25. 5.42	15. 9.42	27. 9.46		
CVE-20	*Barnes*	1942	Todd, Tacoma	P 1. 5.42	22. 5.42	20. 2.43	29. 8.46		
CVE-21	*Block Island*	1942	Todd, Tacoma	P 1. 5.42	6. 6.42	8. 3.43			
CVE-23	*Breton*	1942	Todd, Tacoma	P 1. 5.42	27. 6.42	12. 4.43	30. 8.46	1. 7.58	
CVE-25	*Croatan*	1942	Todd, Tacoma	P 1. 5.42	3. 8.42	28. 4.43	20. 5.46	16. 6.58	23.10.69
CVE-26	*Sangamon*	1942	Federal, Kearny	13. 3.39	4.11.39	C.25. 8.42	24.10.45		
CVE-27	*Suwannee*	1942	Federal, Kearny	P 26. 6.41	4. 3.39	C 24. 9.42	28.10.46		
CVE-28	*Chenango*	1942	Sun SB	P 31. 5.41	1. 4.39	20. 6.41	14. 8.46		
CVE-29	*Santee*	1942	Sun SB	P 18.10.40	4. 3.39	30.10.40	21.10.46		
CVE-30	*Charger*	—	Sun SB	P 4.10.41	1. 3.41	3. 3.42	15. 3.46		
CVE-31	*Prince William*	1942	Todd, Tacoma	18. 5.42	23. 8.42	9. 4.43	29. 8.46		
CVE-55	*Casablanca*	1942	Kaiser Vancouver	3.11.42	5. 4.43	8. 7.43	10. 6.46		
CVE-56	*Liscome Bay*	1942	Kaiser, Vancouver	9.12.42	19. 4.43	7. 8.43			
CVE-57	*Anzio*	1942	Kaiser, Vancouver	12.12.42	1. 5.43	27. 8.43	5. 8.46		
CVE-58	*Corregidor*	1942	Kaiser, Vancouver	17.12.42	12. 5.43	31. 8.43	30. 7.46	19. 5.51*	4. 9.58
CVE-59	*Mission Bay*	1942	Kaiser, Vancouver	28.12.42	26. 5.43	13. 9.43	21. 2.47		
CVE-60	*Guadalcanal*	1942	Kaiser, Vancouver	5. 1.43	15. 6.43	25. 9.43	15. 7.46		
CVE-61	*Manila Bay*	1942	Kaiser, Vancouver	15. 1.43	10. 7.43	5.10.43	31. 7.46		
CVE-62	*Natoma Bay*	1942	Kaiser, Vancouver	17. 1.43	20. 7.43	14.10.43	20. 5.46		
CVE-63	*St Lo*	1942	Kaiser, Vancouver	23. 1.43	17. 8.43	23.10.43			
CVE-64	*Tripoli*	1942	Kaiser, Vancouver	1. 2.43	2. 9.43	31.10.43	22. 5.46	5. 1.52	25.11.58
CVE-65	*Wake Island*	1942	Kaiser, Vancouver	6. 2.43	15. 9.43	7.11.43	5. 4.46		
CVE-66	*White Plains*	1942	Kaiser, Vancouver	11. 2.43	27. 9.43	15.11.43	10. 7.46		
CVE-67	*Solomons*	1942	Kaiser, Vancouver	19. 3.43	6.10.43	21.11.43	15. 5.46		
CVE-68	*Kalinin Bay*	1942	Kaiser, Vancouver	26. 4.43	15.10.43	27.11.43	15. 5.46		
CVE-69	*Kasaan Bay*	1942	Kaiser, Vancouver	11. 5.43	24.10.43	4.12.43	6. 7.46		
CVE-70	*Fanshaw Bay*	1942	Kaiser, Vancouver	18. 5.43	1.11.43	9.12.43	14. 8.46		
CVE-71	*Kitkun Bay*	1942	Kaiser, Vancouver	31. 5.43	8.11.43	15.12.43	19. 4.46		
CVE-72	*Tulagi*	1942	Kaiser, Vancouver	7. 6.43	15.11.43	21.12.43	30. 4.46		
CVE-73	*Gambier Bay*	1942	Kaiser, Vancouver	10. 7.43	22.11.43	28.12.43			
CVE-74	*Nehenta Bay*	1972	Kaiser, Vancouver	20. 7.43	28.11.43	3. 1.44	15. 5.46		
CVE-75	*Hoggatt Bay*	1942	Kaiser, Vancouver	17. 8.43	4.12.43	11. 1.44	20. 7.46		
CVE-76	*Kadashan Bay*	1942	Kaiser, Vancouver	2. 9.43	11.12.43	18. 1.44	14. 6.46		
CVE-77	*Marcus Island*	1942	Kaiser, Vancouver	15. 9.43	16.12.43	26. 1.44	12.12.46		
CVE-78	*Savo Island*	1942	Kaiser, Vancouver	27. 9.43	22.12.43	3. 2.44	12.12.46		
CVE-79	*Ommaney Bay*	1942	Kaiser, Vancouver	6.10.43	29.12.43	11. 2.44			
CVE-80	*Petrof Bay*	1942	Kaiser, Vancouver	15.10.43	5. 1.44	18. 2.44	31. 7.46		
CVE-81	*Rudyerd Bay*	1942	Kaiser, Vancouver	24.10.43	12. 1.44	25. 2.44	11. 6.46		
CVE-82	*Saginaw Bay*	1942	Kaiser, Vancouver	1.11.43	19. 1.44	2. 3.44	19. 6.46		
CVE-83	*Sargent Bay*	1942	Kaiser, Vancouver	8.11.43	31. 1.44	9. 3.44	23. 7.46		
CVE-84	*Shamrock Bay*	1942	Kaiser, Vancouver	15.11.43	4. 2.44	15. 3.44	6. 7.46		
CVE-85	*Shipley Bay*	1942	Kaiser, Vancouver	22.11.43	12. 2.44	21. 3.44	28. 6.46		
CVE-86	*Sitkoh Bay*	1942	Kaiser, Vancouver	23.11.43	19. 2.44	28. 3.44	30.11.46	29. 7.50*	27. 7.54
CVE-87	*Steamer Bay*	1942	Kaiser, Vancouver	4.12.43	26. 2.44	4. 4.44	1. 7.46		
CVE-88	*Cape Esperance*	1942	Kaiser, Vancouver	11.12.43	3. 3.44	9. 4.44	22. 8.46	5. 8.50*	15. 1.59
CVE-89	*Takanis Bay*	1942	Kaiser, Vancouver	16.12.43	10. 3.44	15. 4.44	1. 5.46		
CVE-90	*Thetis Bay*	1942	Kaiser, Vancouver	22.12.43	16. 3.44	21. 4.44	7. 8.46	20. 7.56	1. 3.64
CVE-91	*Makassar Strait*	1942	Kaiser, Vancouver	29.12.43	22. 3.44	27. 4.44	9. 8.46		
CVE-92	*Windham Bay*	1942	Kaiser, Vancouver	5. 1.44	29. 3.44	3. 5.44	1.47	31.10.51*	1959
CVE-93	*Makin Island*	1942	Kaiser, Vancouver	12. 1.44	5. 4.44	9. 5.44	19. 4.46		
CVE-94	*Lunga Point*	1942	Kaiser, Vancouver	19. 1.44	11. 4.44	14. 5.44	24.10.46		
CVE-95	*Bismarck Sea*	1942	Kaiser, Vancouver	31. 1.44	17. 4.44	20. 5.44			
CVE-96	*Salamaua*	1942	Kaiser, Vancouver	4. 2.44	22. 4.44	26. 5.44	9. 5.46		
CVE-97	*Hollandia*	1942	Kaiser, Vancouver	12. 2.44	28. 4.44	1. 6.44	17. 1.47		
CVE-98	*Kwajalein*	1942	Kaiser, Vancouver	19. 2.44	4. 5.44	7. 6.44	16. 8.46		
CVE-99	*Admiralty Islands*	1942	Kaiser, Vancouver	26. 2.44	10. 5.44	13. 6.44	26. 4.46		
CVE-100	*Bougainville*	1942	Kaiser, Vancouver	3. 3.44	16. 5.44	18. 6.44	3.11.46		

Reclassification Details

Stricken	Fate	ACV	CVE	CVHE	CVU	LPH	AKV	Notes
12. 4.46	Merchant ship 1949	20. 8.42	15. 7.43					
1.3.59	BU 1960	20. 8.42	15. 7.43	12. 6.55				
15. 9.70	BU 1971	20. 8.42	15. 7.43	12. 6.55	1. 7.58		7. 5.59	*As T-CVU-11
1. 3.59	BU 1961	20. 8.42	15. 7.43	12. 6.55				
15. 9.70	BU 1971	20. 8.42	15. 7.43	12. 6.55	1. 7.58		7. 5.59	*As T-CVU-13
1. 3.59	BU 1961	20. 8.42	15. 7.43	12. 6.55				
1. 3.59	BU 1961	20. 8.42	15. 7.43	12. 6.55				
1. 3.59	BU 1959	20. 8.42	15. 7.43	12. 6.55				
28. 6.44	Sunk 29.5.44	20. 8.42	15. 7.43					
6. 8.71	BU 1972	20. 8.42	15. 7.43	12. 6.55			7. 5.59	
15. 9.70	BU 1971	20. 8.42	15. 7.43	12. 6.55	1. 7.58		7. 5.59	
24 10 45	BU 1948	20. 8.42	15. 7.43					
1. 3.59	BU 1962	20. 8.42	15. 7.43	12. 6.55				
1. 3.59	BU 1962	20. 8.42	15. 7.43	12. 6.55				
1. 3.59	BU 1960	20. 8.42	15. 7.43	12. 6.55				
28. 3.46	Merchant ship 1947	20. 8.42	15. 7.43					
1. 3.59	BU 1961	20. 8.42	15. 7.43	12. 6.55				
3. 7.46	BU 1947	20. 8.42	15. 7.43					
6.12.43	Sunk 24.11.43	20. 8.42	15. 7.43					
1. 3.59	BU 1960	20. 8.42	15. 7.43	12. 6.55				
1.10.58	BU 1960	20. 8.42	15. 7.43	12. 6.55				*As T-CVE-58
1. 9.58	BU 1960	20. 8.42	15. 7.43		12. 6.55			
27. 5.58	BU 1960	20. 8.42	15. 7.43		12. 6.55			
27. 5.58	BU 1960	20. 8.42	15. 7.43		12. 6.55			
1. 9.58	BU 1960	20. 8.42	15. 7.43		12. 6.55			
27.11.44	Sunk 25.10.44	20. 8.42	15. 7.43					
1. 2.59	BU 1960	20. 8.42	15. 7.43		12. 6.55			
17. 4.46	BU 1947	20. 8.42	15. 7.43					
27. 6.58	BU 1959	20. 8.42	15. 7.43		12. 6.55			
5. 6.46	BU 1947	20. 8.42	15. 7.43					
5. 6.46	BU 1947	20. 8.42	15. 7.43					
1. 3.59	BU 1960	20. 8.42	15. 7.43	12. 6.55				
1. 3.59	BU 1959	20. 8.42	15. 7.43	12. 6.55				
8. 5.46	BU 1947	20. 8.42	15. 7.43					
8. 5.46	BU 1947	20. 8.42	15. 7.43					
27.11.44	Sunk 25.10.44	20. 8.42	15. 7.43					
1. 8.59	BU 1960	20. 8.42	15. 7.43		12. 6.55		7. 5.59	
1. 9.59	BU 1960	20. 8.42	15. 7.43	12. 6.55			7. 5.59	
1. 8.59	BU 1960	20. 8.42	15. 7.43		12. 6.55		7. 5.59	
1. 9.59	BU 1960	20. 8.42	15. 7.43	12. 6.55			7. 5.59	
1. 9.59	BU 1960	20. 8.42	15. 7.43	12. 6.55			7. 5.59	
23. 2.45	Sunk 4.1.45	20. 8.42	15. 7.43					
27. 6.58	BU 1959	20. 8.42	15. 7.43		12. 6.55			
1. 8.59	BU 1960	20. 8.42	15. 7.43		12. 6.55		7. 5.59	
1. 3.59	BU 1960	20. 8.42	15. 7.43	12. 6.55				
27. 6.58	BU 1959	20. 8.42	15. 7.43		12. 6.55			
27. 6.58	BU 1959	20. 8.42	15. 7.43		12. 6.55			
1. 3.59	BU 1961	20. 8.52	15. 7.43		12. 6.55			
1. 4.60	BU 1961	20. 8.42	15. 7.43		12. 6.55		7. 5.59	* As T-CVE-86
1. 3.59	BU 1959	20. 8.42	15. 7.43	12. 6.55				
1. 3.59	BU 1961	20. 8.42	15. 7.43		12. 6.55			* As T-CVE-88
1. 8.59	BU 1960	20. 8.42	15. 7.43		12. 6.55		7. 5.59	
1. 3.64	BU 1966	20. 8.42	15. 7.43			28. 5.59		Reclassified as CVHA 1.7.55
1. 9.58	Target 1958	20. 8.42	15. 7.43		12. 6.55			
1. 2.59	BU 1961	20. 8.42	15. 7.43		12. 6.55			* As T-CVE-92
1. 7.46	BU 1947	20. 8.42	15. 7.43					
1. 4.60	BU 1966	20. 8.42	15. 7.43		12. 6.55		7. 5.59	
30. 3.45	Sunk 21. 2.45	20. 8.42	15. 7.43					
1. 9.46	BU 1947	20. 8.42	15. 7.43					
1. 4.60	BU 1960	20. 8.42	15. 7.43		12. 6.55		7. 5.59	
1. 4.60	BU 1961	20. 8.42	15. 7.43		12. 6.55		7. 5.59	
8. 5.46	BU 1947	20. 8.42	15. 7.43					
1. 6.60	BU 1960	20. 8.42	15. 7.43		12. 6.55		7. 5.59	

Hull No	Name	FY	Builder	Laid Down	Launched	Comm-issioned	Withdrawn from Service	Reactivated	Withdrawn from Service
CVE-101	Matanikau	1942	Kaiser, Vancouver	10. 3.44	22. 5.44	24. 6.44	11.10.46		
CVE-102	Attu	1942	Kaiser, Vancouver	16. 3.44	27. 5.44	30. 6.44	8. 6.46		
CVE-103	Roi	1942	Kaiser, Vancouver	22. 3.44	2. 6.44	6. 7.44	9. 5.46		
CVE-104	Munda	1942	Kaiser, Vancouver	29. 3.44	27. 5.44	8. 7.44	13. 9.46		
CVE-105	Commencement Bay	1943	Todd, Tacoma	23. 9.43	9. 5.44	27.11.44	30.11.46		
CVE-106	Block Island	1943	Todd, Tacoma	25.10.43	10. 6.44	30.12.44	28. 5.46	28. 4.51	27. 8.54
CVE-107	Gilbert Island/ Annapolis	1943	Todd, Tacoma	29.11.43	20. 7.44	5. 2.45	21. 5.46	7. 9.51*	15. 1.55**
CVE-108	Kula Gulf	1943	Todd, Tacoma	16.12.43	15. 8.44	12. 5.45	3. 7.46	15. 2.51*	15.12.55**
CVE-109	Cape Gloucester	1943	Todd, Tacoma	10. 1.44	12. 9.44	5. 3.45	5.11.46		
CVE-110	Salerno Bay	1943	Todd, Tacoma	7. 2.44	26. 9.44	19. 5.45	4.10.47	20. 6.51	16. 2.54
CVE-111	Vella Gulf	1943	Todd, Tacoma	7. 3.44	19.10.44	9. 4.45	9. 8.46		
CVE-112	Siboney	1943	Todd, Tacoma	1. 4.44	9.11.44	14. 5.45	11.47*	22. 1.50	3. 7.56
CVE-113	Puget Sound	1943	Todd, Tacoma	12. 5.44	30.11.44	18. 6.45	18.10.46		
CVE-114	Rendova	1943	Todd, Tacoma	15. 6.44	28.12.44	22.10.45	27. 1.50	3. 1.51	30. 6.55
CVE-115	Bairoko	1943	Todd, Tacoma	25. 7.44	25. 1.45	16. 7.45	14. 4.50	12. 9.50	18. 2.55
CVE-116	Badoeng Strait	1943	Todd, Tacoma	18. 8.44	15. 2.45	14.11.45	20. 4.46	6. 1.47	17. 5.57
CVE-117	Saidor	1943	Todd, Tacoma	29. 9.44	19. 3.45	4. 9.45	12. 9.47		
CVE-118	Sicily	1943	Todd, Tacoma	23.10.44	14. 4.45	27. 2.46	5. 7.54		
CVE-119	Point Cruz	1943	Todd, Tacoma	4.12.44	18. 5.45	16.10.45	30. 6.47	26. 7.51*	31. 8.56**
CVE-120	Mindoro	1944	Todd, Tacoma	2. 1.45	27. 6.45	4.12.45	4. 8.55		
CVE-121	Rabaul	1944	Todd, Tacoma	29. 1.45	14. 7.45	C 30. 8.46			
CVE-122	Palau	1944	Todd, Tacoma	19. 2.45	6. 8.45	15. 1.46	15. 6.54		
CVE-123	Tinian	1944	Todd, Tacoma	20. 3.45	5. 9.45	C 30. 7.46			
CVE-124	Bastogne	1944	Todd, Tacoma	2. 4.45		S 12. 8.45			
CVE-125	Eniwetok	1944	Todd, Tacoma	20. 4.45		S 12. 8.45			
CVE-126	Lingayen	1944	Todd, Tacoma	1. 5.45		S 12. 8.45			
CVE-127	Okinawa	1944	Todd, Tacoma	22. 5.45		S 12. 8.45			

'P' = the date the hull was purchased by the Navy. 'C' = the completion date, and 'S' = the date construction was suspended.

Stricken	Fate	ACV	CVE	CVHE	CVU	LPH	AKV	Notes
1. 4.60	BU 1960	20. 8.42	15. 7.43	12. 6.55			7. 5.59	
3. 7.46	BU 1949	20. 8.42	15. 7.43					
21. 5.46	BU 1947	20. 8.42	15. 7.43					
1. 9.58	BU 1960	20. 8.42	15. 7.43		12. 6.55			
1. 4.71		*	*	12. 6.55			7. 5.59	* Begun as CVE
1. 7.59	BU 1960		17. 2.59*			22.12.57	7. 5.59	* Classified as CVE for second time
1. 6.61							7. 5.59	Reclassified as AGMR 1.6.63
15.10.76								* In service as AGMR-1 7.3.64
								** Withdrawn from service as AGMR-1 20.12.69
15. 9.70	BU 1971						7. 5.59	* Second reactivation 30.6.65
								** Third deactivation 6.10.69
1. 6.60*				12. 6.55			7. 5.59	* 1.7.60 re-entered on official list
1. 4.71								
1. 6.61	BU 1962						7. 5.59	
1. 6.60*	BU 1971			12. 6.55			7. 5.59	* 1.11.60 re-entered on official list
1.12.70								
1. 6.70	BU 1971						7. 5.59	* Evidently not completely deactivated. Formerly a station ship for a period
1. 6.60	BU 1962			12. 6.55			7. 5.59	
1. 4.71	BU 1971						7. 5.59	
1. 4.60	BU 1961						7. 5.59	
1.12.70	BU 1972						7. 5.59	
1.12.70	BU 1971			12. 6.55			7. 5.59	
1. 7.60	BU 1961						7. 5.59	
15. 9.70	BU 1971						7. 5.59	* Second reactivation 23.8.65
								** Third deactivation 16.10.69
1. 12.59	BU 1960						7. 5.59	
1. 9.71	BU 1972			12. 6.55			7. 5.59	
1. 4.60	BU 1960						7. 5.59	
1. 6.70	BU 1971			12. 6.55			7. 5.59	
								BU on building ways
								BU on building ways
								BU on building ways
								BU on building ways

Construction Details for Aviation Support Ships

Hull No	Name	Builder	Laid Down	Launched	Comm-issioned	Withdrawn from Service	Stricken	Notes
AKV-1	*Kitty Hawk*	Sun SB	21. 2.32 P 25. 6.41	14. 9.32	26.11.41	24. 1.46		Returned to owners 1946
AKV-2	*Hammondsport*	Sun SB	24. 2.32 P 2. 7.41	26. 9.32	11.12.41	7. 3.46		Returned to owners 1946
AKV-3	*Lt James E Robinson*	Oregon SB	25.11.43 P 1. 3.50	20. 2.44	1. 3.50		7.5.59	AK-274
AKV-4	*Pvt Joseph E Merrell*	California SB	27. 5.45 P 1. 3.50	17. 7.44	1. 3.50		31. 1.74	AK-275
AKV-5	*Sgt Jack J Pendleton*	Oregon SB	15. 4.44 P 1. 3.50	26. 5.44	1. 3.50		15. 2.74	AK-276
AKV-6	*Albert M Boe*	New England SB	26. 5.45 P 1. 3.50	11. 7.45	1. 3.50	1.12.53	11. 3.54	
AKV-7	*Cardinal O'Connell*	New England SB	11. 6.45 P 1. 3.50	31. 8.45	1. 3.50	1.54	11. 3.54	
AKV-8 to -43		See under US Escort Carriers						

Hull No	Name	Builder	Laid Down	Launched	Comm-issioned	Withdrawn from Service	Stricken	Notes
APV-1	*Kitty Hawk*	See under AKV						
APV-2	*Hammondsport*	See under AKV						
APV-3	*Lakehurst*	Sun SB	1939	26. 3.40	13.10.42	2. 8.43*		* To Army as APM-1 3.12.42
ARV-1	*Chourre*	Bethlehem, Baltimore	20. 4.44 P 31. 5.44	22. 5.44	7.12.44	13. 9.55	1961	ARG-14 until 22.2.44
ARV-2	*Webster*	Bethlehem, Baltimore	1. 7.44 P 26. 8.44	5. 8.44	17. 3.45	28. 6.46	1962	ARG-15 until 22.2.44
ARV(E)-3	*Aventinus*	American Bridge	8. 1.45	24. 3.45	19. 5.45	4. 4.52	1. 6.73	
ARV(E)-4	*Chloris*	American Bridge	17. 1.45	21. 4.45	19. 6.45	9.12.55	1. 6.73	8.63 to Chile
ARV(A)-5	*Fabius*	American Bridge	12. 1.45	11. 4.45	31. 5.45	4. 4.52	1. 6.73	
ARV(A)-6	*Megara*	American Bridge	22. 1.45	25. 4.45	27. 6.45	16. 1.56	1. 6.73	To Mexico
ARVH-1	*Corpus Christi Bay*	Conversion Charleston N Yd	See AV-5 *Albemarle*			1973	31.12.74	Conversion began 8.64
AV-1	*Wright*	American Int SB	1919	28. 4.20	16.12.21			30.12.44 = *San Clemente* (AG-79)
AV-3	*Langley*	Conversion to AV Mare Island N Yd	18.10.11	24. 8.12	C 26. 2.37		8. 5.43	Sunk 27.2.42
AV-4	*Curtiss*	New York SB	25. 3.38	20. 4.40	15.11.40	24. 9.57	1. 7.63	BU 1972
AV-5	*Albemarle*	New York SB	12. 6.39	13. 7.40	20.12.40	1960	1. 9.62	27.3.65 = *Corpus Christi Bay* (ARVH-1)
AV-7	*Currituck*	New York SB	14.12.42	11. 9.43	26. 6.44	31.10.67	1. 4.71	
AV-11	*Norton Sound*	Los Angeles SB	7. 9.42	28.11.43	8. 1.45			8.8.51 = AVM-1
AV-12	*Pine Island*	Los Angeles SB	16.11.42	26. 2.44	26. 4.45	17. 6.67	1. 2.71	
AV-13	*Salisbury Sound*	Los Angeles SB	10. 4.43	18. 6.44	26.11.45	31. 3.67		
AV-8	*Tangier*	Moore DD	13. 3.39 P 8. 7.40	15. 9.39	25. 8.41	5.10.46	1. 6.61	
AV-9	*Pocomoke*	Ingalls	14. 8.39 P 16.10.40	8. 6.40	18. 7.41	10. 7.46	1. 6.61	
AV-10	*Chandeleur*	Western Pipe	29. 5.41 P 19.11.42	29.11.41	19.11.42	12. 2.47	1. 4.71	
AV-14	*Kenneth Whiting*	Todd, Pacific	19. 6.43	15.12.43	8. 5.44	30. 9.58	1. 7.61	
AV-15	*Hamlin*	Todd, Pacific	19. 7.43	11. 1.44	26. 6.44	15. 1.47	1. 7.63	
AV-16	*St George*	Todd, Pacific	4. 8.43	14. 2.44	24. 7.44	10. 4.47	1. 7.63	10.12.68 to Italy
AV-17	*Cumberland Sound*	Todd, Pacific	25. 8.43	11. 1.44	21. 8.44	27. 5.47	1. 7.61	
AVD-1	*Childs*	New York SB	19. 3.19	15. 9.20	22.10.20	10.12.45	3. 1.46	
AVD-2	*Willamson*	New York SB	27. 3.19	16.10.19	29.10.20			1.12.43 = DD-244
AVD-3	*George E Badger*	Newport News SB	24. 9.18	6. 3.20	28. 7.20			4.11.43 = DD-196
AVD-4	*Clemson*	Newport News SB	11. 5.18	5. 9.18	29.12.19			1.12.43 = DD-186
AVD-5	*Goldsborough*	Newport News SB	8. 6.18	20.11.18	26. 1.20			1.12.43 = DD-188
AVD-6	*Hulbert*	Norfolk N Yd	18.11.18	28. 6.19	27.10.20			1.12.43 = DD-342
AVD-7	*William B Preston*	Norfolk N Yd	18.11.18	9. 8.19	23. 8.20	7.12.45	3. 1.46	
AVD-8	*Belknap*	Bethlehem, Quincy	3. 9.18	14. 1.19	28. 4.19			14.11.43 = DD-251
AVD-9	*Osmond Ingram*	Bethlehem, Quincy	15.10.18	28. 2.19	28. 6.19			14.11.43 = DD-255
AVD-10	*Ballard*	Bethlehem, Squantum	3. 6.18	7.12.18	5. 6.19	5.12.45	1946	
AVD-11	*Thornton*	Bethlehem, Squantum	3. 6.18	23. 3.19	15. 7.19		13. 8.45	Sunk in collision 5.4.45
AVD-12	*Gillis*	Bethlehem, Quincy	27.12.18	29. 5.19	3. 9.19	15.10.45	1.11.45	
AVD-13	*Greene*	Bethlehem, Squantum	3. 6.18	2.11.18	9. 5.19	23.11.45	5.12.45	
AVD-14	*McFarland*	New York SB	31. 7.18	30. 3.20	30. 9.20			1.12.43 = DD-237
AVP-1	*Lapwing*	Todd, NY	25.10.17	14. 3.18	12. 6.18	29.11.45	1946	
AVP-2	*Heron*	Standard SB New York	26. 8.17	18. 5.18	30.10.18	12. 2.46	1946	
AVP-3	*Thrush*	Pusey & Jones	27. 5.18	15. 9.18	25. 4.19	23.11.45	1946	
AVP-4	*Avocet*	Baltimore SB	13. 9.17	9. 3.18	17. 9.18	10.12.45	1946	
AVP-5	*Teal*	Sun SB	8.10.17	25. 5.18	20. 8.18	25. 8.45	1947	
AVP-6	*Pelican*	Gas Engine	10.11.17	15. 6.18	10.10.18	30.11.45	19.12.45	

Hull No	Name	Builder	Laid Down	Launched	Comm-issioned	Withdrawn from Service	Stricken	Notes
AVP-7	Swan	Alabama SB	10.12.17	4. 7.18	31. 1.19	7.12.45	1946	
AVP-8	Gannett	Todd, NY	1.10.18	19. 3.19	10. 7.19		24. 6.42	Sunk 7.6.42
AVP-9	Sandpiper	Philadelphia N Yd	15.11.18	28. 4.19	9.10.19	18.12.45	1946	
AVP-10	Barnegat	Puget Sound N Yd	26.10.39	23. 5.41	3. 7.41	17. 5.46	23.5.58	
AVP-12	Casco	Puget Sound N Yd	30. 5.40	15.11.41	27.12.41	10. 4.47		
AVP-13	Mackinac	Puget Sound N Yd	29. 5.40	15.11.41	24. 1.42	1.47		
AVP-21	Humboldt	Boston N Yd	6. 9.40	17. 3.41	7.10.41	17. 3.47		
AVP-22	Matagorda	Boston N Yd	6. 9.40	18. 3.41	16.12.41	10. 2.46		
AVP-23	Absecon	Lake Washington	23. 7.41	8. 3.42	28. 1.43	7. 1.47		
AVP-24	Chinoteague	Lake Washington	23. 7.41	15. 4.42	12. 4.43	21.12.46		
AVP-25	Coos Bay	Lake Washington	15. 8.41	15. 5.42	15. 5.43	30. 4.46		
AVP-26	Half Moon	Lake Washington	15. 8.41	12. 7.42	15. 6.43	4. 9.46		
AVP-29	Rockaway	Associated	30. 6.41	14. 2.42	6. 1.43	21. 3.46		
AVP-30	San Pablo	Associated	2. 7.41	31. 3.42	15. 3.43		1. 6.69 as AGS	25.8.49 = AGS-30
AVP-31	Unimak	Associated	15. 2.42	27. 5.42	31.12.43	25. 1.46		
AVP-32	Yakutat	Associated	1. 4.42	2. 7.42	31. 3.44	17. 4.46		
AVP-33	Barataria	Lake Washington	19. 4.43	2.10.43	13. 8.44	24. 7.46		
AVP-34	Bering Strait	Lake Washington	7. 6.43	15. 1.44	19. 7.44	21. 6.46		
AVP-35	Castle Rock	Lake Washington	12. 7.43	11. 3.43	10. 8.44	6. 8.46		
AVP-36	Cook Inlet	Lake Washington	23. 8.43	13. 5.44	5.11.44	31. 3.46		
AVP-37	Corson	Lake Washington	5.10.43	15. 7.44	3.12.44	9. 3.56	1. 4.66	
AVP-38	Duxbury Bay	Lake Washington	17. 1.44	2.10.44	31.12.44	30. 4.66	1. 5.66	
AVP-39	Gardiners Bay	Lake Washington	14. 3.44	2.12.44	11. 2.45	1. 2.58	1. 5.58	17. 5.58 to Norway
AVP-40	Floyds Bay	Lake Washington	16. 5.44	28. 1.45	25. 3.45	26. 2.60	1. 3.60	
AVP-41	Greenwich Bay	Lake Washington	18. 7.44	18. 3.45	20. 5.45		1. 7.66	
AVP-48	Onslow	Lake Washington	18. 5.42	20. 9.42	22.12.43	22. 4.60	1. 6.60	
AVP-49	Orca	Lake Washington	13. 7.42	4.10.42	23. 1.44	3.60		1.62 to Ethiopia
AVP-50	Rehoboth	Lake Washington	3. 8.42	8.11.42	23. 2.44		15. 4.70 as AGS	1.11.49 = AGS-50
AVP-51	San Carlos	Lake Washington	17. 9.42	20.12.42	21. 3.44	30. 6.47		15.12.58 = AGOR-1
AVP-52	Shelikof	Lake Washington	20. 9.42	31. 3.43	17. 4.44	18. 7.54	5.60	
AVP-53	Suisun	Lake Washington	4.10.42	14. 3.43	13. 9.44	24. 5.55	1. 4.66	
AVP-54	Timbalier	Lake Washington	9.11.42	18. 4.43	24. 5.46	15. 8.54	5.60	
AVP-55	Valcour	Lake Washington	21.12.42	5. 6.43	5. 7.46		15. 6.73 as AGF	15.12.66 = AGF-1
AVP-14	Childs	See under AVD						
AVP-15	Williamson	See under AVD						
AVP-16	George E Badger	See under AVD						
AVP-17	Clemson	See under AVD						
AVP-18	Goldsborough	See under AVD						
AVP-19	Hulbert	See under AVD						
AVP-20	William B Preston	See under AVD						
AVB-1	Alameda County	Dravo	17. 2.43	22. 5.43	12. 7.43	15. 6.62	1. 7.62	11.62 to Italy
AVB-2	Tallahatchie County	Boston N Yd	4. 8.45	19. 7.46	24. 5.49	1969	15. 1.70	
AVS-1	Supply	Doullut & Williams	1921 P 5. 2.44	1921	8. 2.44			
AVS-2	Fortune	Dollut & Williams	1921 P 16. 2.44	1921	19. 2.44	18.10.45		
AVS-3	Grumium	Permanente Metals	12.11.42 P 5.10.43	20.12.42	20.10.43	20.12.45		
AVS-4	Allioth	Permanente Metals	1943 P 3.10.43	25. 7.43	25.10.43	18. 5.46		
AVS-5	Gwinnett	W Butler SB	21.12.43 P 24. 2.45	14. 5.44	10. 4.45	11.12.46	7.46	
AVS-6	Nicollet	Globe SB	9. 2.44 P 4. 4.45	31. 7.44	27. 4.45	17. 6.46	3. 7.46	
AVS-7	Pontotoc	L D Smith SB	15. 1.44 P 28. 2.45	2. 7.44	22. 3.45	26. 4.46	8. 5.46	
AVS-8	Jupiter	Federal SB	16. 3.39 P 19. 6.41	30. 9.39	22. 8.41		1. 8.65	
AVT-1 to -7		See CVL Independence and Saipan classes in previous volume						
ATV-8 to -12 and -16*		See CVS Essex class in previous volume						*Lexington (CVT-16) reclassified AVT-16 in 1978

'P' = the date acquired for the US Navy 'C' 3 the date the conversion to auxiliary was completed

Dimensions of Escort Carrier Classes

Hull No CVE-	Class	No in Class	Standard Displacement (tons)	Full Load Displacement (tons)	Length (oa) (ft-in)	Breadth (wl) (ft-in)	Breadth (flight deck) (ft-in)	Draft (ft-in)	Height (flight deck) (ft-in)	Height (bridge) (ft-in)	Height (mast) (ft-in)
1 (BAVG-1-3,5,6)	Long Island	1(5)	7886	14,055	492-0	69-6	102-0	25-6	58-0		69-0
9,11-13, 16,18,20 (33),21,23, 25,(6-8,10, 14,15,17, 19,22,24, 32-54)	Bogue/Prince William	10(33)	8390	13,890	495-8	69-6	111-6	23-3	54-0	73-0	90-0
26-29	Sangamon	4	10,500	23,875	553-6	75-0	105-2	30-7	42-0	59-0	108-0
30	Charger	1	11,800	15,126	492-0	69-6	111-2	25-2	52-0	69-0	87-0
55-104	Casablanca	50	8200	10,900	512-3	65-2	108-1	20-9	41-0	60-0	113-0*
105-122	Commencement Bay	19	11,373†	24,275†	557-1	75-0	105-2	32-2†			

Figures in brackets refer to ships transferred to the Royal Navy. *Includes topmast. †Postwar figures

Dimensions of Aviation Support Ships

Hull No	Class (and Type)	No in Class	Full Load Displacement (tons)	Length (oa) (ft-in)	Breadth (ft-in)	Draft (max) (ft-in)
AKV-1, -2	Kitty Hawk	2	16,480	478-4	63-8	22-3
AKV-3 to -5	Lt James E Robinson (VC2-S-AP3)	3	15,200	455-5	62-0	28-10
AKV-6, -7	Albert M Boe (Z-EC2-S-C5)	2	14,245	441-7	56-9	26-7
AKV-8 to -43	Kula Gulf	36	See under CVE			
APV-1 to -3	Kitty Hawk	3	See under AKV			
ARV-1, -2	Chourre (EC2-S-C1)	2	14,350	441-11	56-1	22-0
ARV(E)-3, -4	Aventinus	2	3960	328-0	50-2	11-2
ARV(A)-5, -6	Fabius	2	3960	328-0	50-2	11-2
ARVH-1	Corpus Christi Bay	1	15,300	527-4	69-3	19-0
AV-1	Wright	1	11,500	448-2	58-5	27-3
AV-3	Langley	1	14,500	542-4	65-7	27-11
AV-4, -5	Curtiss	2	T 12,053	527-4	69-3	21-4
AV-7, -11 to -13	Currituck	4	T 14,300	540-5	69-3	22-3
AV-8, -9	Tangier (C3-Cargo(S))	2	T 11,760	492-0	69-6	22-3
AV-10	Chandeleur (C3-S1-B1)	1	13,700	492-0	69-6	23-9
AV-14 to -17	Kenneth Whiting (C3-Special)	4	12,610	492-0	69-6	23-9
AVD-1 to -14	Childs	14	1900	314-8	31-10	12-2
AVP-1 to -9	Lapwing	9	1400	187-4	35-5	13-5
AVP-10, -12, -13, -21 to -26, -29 to -41, 48 to -55	Barnegat	30	2411 to 2619	310-9 to 312-0	41-11	11-2 to 12-5
AVP-14 to -20	Childs	7	1900	314-8	31-10	12-2
AVB-1	Alameda County	1	4080	328-0	50-2	14-5
AVB-2	Tallahatchie County	1	6000	382-3	54-2	17-0
AVS-1, -2	Supply	2	13,250	412-0	55-1	27-3
AVS-3, -4	Grumium (EC2-S-C1)	2	14,550	441-11	56-1	28-3
AVS-5 to -7	Gwinnett (C1-M-AV1)	3	7450	338-11	50-6	21-0
AVS-8	Jupiter (C2-Cargo(S))	1	14,230	459-4	63-0	26-7
AVT-1 to -7	Cowpens	7	See previous volume, under Independence class			
AVT-8 to -12, -16	Franklin	6	See previous volume, under Essex class			

T = trials displacement

Machinery of Escort Carrier Classes

Class	No in Class	Machinery	hp	Shafts	Speed (kts)	Fuel (tons)	Range (nm/at speed in kts)
Long Island	1(5)	Diesel	8500	1	16	1429	
Bogue/Prince William	10(33)	Geared turbines, 2 boilers	8500	1	18	3420 max	22,500/17 26,300/15
Sangamon	4	Geared turbines, 4 boilers	13,500	2	18	4780★	20,000/17 23,900/15
Charger	1	Diesel	8500	1	17	1295	
Casablanca	50	Reciprocating, 4 boilers	9000	2	19	2279	7200/19 10,200/15
Commencement Bay	19	Geared turbines, 4 boilers	16,000	2	19	3134★	

Figures in brackets refer to ships transferred to the Royal Navy. ★Both the *Sangamon*s, which were ex-oilers, and the *Commencement Bay*s which were based on the *Sangamon*s, retained huge oil cargo capacity, which could be used for additional fuel. The above figures are for the normal ships' bunkers alone.

Machinery of Aviation Support Ships

Hull No	Class (and Type)	No in Class	Machinery	hp	Shafts	Speed (kts)	Fuel (tons)
AKV-1, -2	*Kitty Hawk*	2	Geared turbines, 3 boilers	8000	1	17	2385
AKV-3 to -5	*Lt James E Robinson* (VC2-S-AP3)	3	Geared turbines, 2 boilers	8500	1	17	
AKV-6, -7	*Albert M Boe* (Z-EC2-S-C5)	2	Reciprocating, 2 boilers	2500	1	11	
AKV-8 to -43	*Kula Gulf*	36	See under CVE				
APV-1 to -3	*Kitty Hawk*	3	See under AKV				
ARV-1, -2	*Chourre* (EC2-S-C1)	2	Reciprocating, 2 boilers	2500	1	11	1130
ARV(E)-3, -4	*Aventinus*	2	Diesel	1800	2	11.5	
ARV(A)-5, -6	*Fabius*	2	Diesel	1800	2	11.5	
ARVH-1	*Corpus Christi Bay*	1	Geared turbines, 4 boilers	12,000	2	18	
AV-1	*Wright*	1	Geared turbines, 6 boilers	6000	1	15	
AV-3	*Langley*	1	Turbo-electric, 3 boilers	7152	2	15	
AV-4, -5	*Curtiss*	2	Geared turbines, 4 boilers	12,000	2	18	2164
AV-7, -11 to -13	*Currituck*	4	Geared turbines, 4 boilers	12,000	2	19.2	2324
AV-8, -9	*Tangier* (C3-Cargo(S))	2	Geared turbines, 2 boilers	8500	1	16.5	1309
AV-10	*Chandeleur* (C3-S1-B1)	1	Geared turbines, 2 boilers	9350	1	17	1313
AV-14 to -17	*Kenneth Whiting* (C3-Special)	4	Geared turbines, 2 boilers	8500	1	16.5	1556
AVD-1 to -14	*Childs*	14	Geared turbines, 2 boilers	27,000★	2	27.5	360
AVP-1 to -9	*Lapwing*	9	Reciprocating, 2 boilers	1400	1	14	230
AVP-10,-12, -13,-21 to -26, -29 to -41,-48 to -55	*Barnegat*	30	Diesel	6080	2	18.3	260
AVP-14 to -20	*Childs*	7	See under AVD				
AVB-1	*Alameda County*	1	Diesel	1700	2	11.5	
AVB-2	*Tallahatchie County*	1	Geared turbines, 2 boilers	6000	2	14	
AVS-1,-2	*Supply*	2	Diesel	3500	1	11	
AVS-3,-4	*Grumium* (EC2-S-C1)	2	Reciprocating, 2 boilers	2500	1	11	
AVS-5 to -7	*Gwinnett* (C1-M-AV1)	3	Diesel	1700	1	11	857
AVS-8	*Jupiter* (C2-Cargo(S))	1	Geared turbines, 2 boilers	6000	1	16.5	
AVT-1 to -7	*Cowpens*		See previous volume under *Independence* class				
AVT-8 to -12, -16	*Franklin*		See previous volume under *Essex* class				

★Some ex-destroyers of this class were reduced to 26,000shp and 25kts

Armament of Escort Carrier Classes

Class	Armament	Catapults	Aircraft	Complement
Long Island	1-5in/51, 2-3in/50, 20-20mm (1945)	1	21	970
Bogue/Prince William	2-5in/38, 20*-40mm(twin), 27-20mm (1945)	2	28	890
Sangamon	2-5in/38, 8**-40mm(quad), 14-40mm(twin), 21-20mm	1	30	1080
Charger	1-5in/51, 2-3in/50, 10-20mm	1	21	856
Casablanca	1-5in/38, 16-40mm(twin), 20-20mm (1945)	1	28	860
Commencement Bay	2-5in/38, 12-40mm(quad), 24-40mm(twin), 20-20mm(1945)	2	34	1066

*CVE-18 and -20 had only 8 instead of 10 twin 40mm mounts and CVE-11 had only 21-20mm. **CVE-29 had a total of 28-40mm and 19-20mm in 1945.

Armament of Aviation Support Ships

Hull No	Class	Armament	Complement
AKV-1, -2	*Kitty Hawk*	1-5in/38, 4-3in/50, 4-40mm(twin), 16-20mm	17/238
AKV-3 to -5	*Lt James E Robinson*	None	14/35**
AKV-6, -7	*Albert M Boe*	None	11/28**
AKV-8 to -43	*Kula Gulf*	See under CVE	
APV-1 to -3	*Kitty Hawk*	See under AKV	
ARV-1 to -3	*Chourre*	1-5in/38, 4-40mm(quad), 4-40mm(twin), 14-20mm	71/507
ARV(E)-3, -4	*Aventinus*	8-40mm(quad), 6-20mm	20/225
ARV(A)-5, -6	*Fabius*	8-40mm(quad), 6-20mm	20/225
ARVH-1	*Corpus Christi Bay*	None	**
AV-1	*Wright*	2-5in/51, 2-3in/50	27/284
AV-3	*Langley*	4-5in/51	66/648
AV-4, -5	*Curtiss*	4-5in/38, 12-40mm(quad), 4-40mm(twin), 12-20mm	160/1035
AV-7, -11 to -13	*Currituck*	4-5in/38, 12-40mm(quad), 8-40mm(twin), 20-20mm	162/1085
AV-8, -9	*Tangier*	1-5in/38, 4-3in/50, 8-40mm(twin), 15-20mm (1945)	120/955
AV-10	*Chandeleur*	1-5in/38, 4-3in/50, 8-40mm(twin), 15-20mm (1945)	120/955
AV-14 to -17	*Kenneth Whiting*	2-5in/38, 8-40mm(quad), 4-40mm(twin), 16-20mm	113/964
AVD-1 to -14	*Childs*	2-3in/50, 7 or 8-20mm, 2 DCT	34/145
AVP-1 to -9	*Lapwing*	2-3in/50, 4-20mm, MG, 2 DCT	15/170
AVP-10, -12, -13, -21 to -26, -29 to -41, -48 to 55	*Barnegat*	Various. See table under class entry	73/294
AVP-14 to -20	*Childs*	See under AVD	
AVB-1	*Alameda County*	4-40mm(quad), 4-40mm(single)	13/106
AVB-2	*Tallahatchie County*	2-5in/38, 4-40mm(twin)	14/255
AVS-1, -2	*Supply*	1-4in/50(1-5in/51 in AVS-2), 1-3in/50, 8-20mm	15/153 (13/150 in AVS-2)
AVS-3, -4	*Grumium*	1-5in/38, 1-3in/50, 8-20mm	
AVS-5 to -7	*Gwinnett*	1-3in/50, 6-20mm	9/96
AVS-8	*Jupiter*	1-5in/38, 4-3in/50, 8-20mm	20/194
AVT-1 to -7	*Cowpens*	See previous volume under *Independence* class	
AVT-8 to -12, -16	*Franklin*	See previous volume under *Essex* class	

*Civilian MSTS crew. **Civilian MSTS crew, plus 308 military workshop personnel

Escort Carrier Air Groups

Air Group	Formed	Disbanded	Originally Formed	Reclassified	Known Operations Carrier/Date	Squadrons
1	15.11.46	1. 9.48	26. 3.45 as CVEG-41	1. 9.48 as VC-21		
2	15.11.46	1. 9.48	19. 7.45 as CVEG-42			
24					3-7.45	VF-24, VT-24
25	28. 8.44	20. 9.45	15. 2.43 as CVLG-25		CVE-28/3-7.45	VF-25, VT-26
26	4. 5.42	13.11.45			CVE-26/7.43	VF-26, VC-26
					CVE-29/10.44	VF-26, VT-26
					CVE-29/7-8.45	
27					CVE-27/7.43	VF-27, VT-27
28					CVE-28/7.43	VF-28, VC-28
33	15. 5.44	19.11.45			CVE-28/8.45	
35	15. 7.43	19.11.45			CVE-28/11.43-2.44	VF-35, VC-35
					CVE-28/7-8.45	As previously
					CVE-28/10.45	As previously
36	15. 5.44	28. 1.46			CVE-112/9.45	VF-36, VT-36
37	15. 7.43	20.12.45			CVE-26/1-2.44	VF-37, VC-37
					CVE-26/7-8.44	As previously
					CVE-26/10.44	As previously
38	15. 8.44	31. 1.46	16. 6.43 as CVLG-38			
39	15. 3.45	27. 7.45		27. 7.45 as CVLG-39		
40	15. 6.43	19.11.45			CVE-27/3-4.45	
41	26. 3.45	15.11.46		15.11.46 as CVEG-1		
42	19. 7.45	15.11.46		15.11.46 as CVEG-2		
43	9. 8.45	17. 6.46				
49	10. 8.44	2. 1.45		2. 1.45 as CVLG-49		
50	1.10.44	29.10.45	10. 8.43 as CVLG-50			
60	15. 7.43	19.11.45			CVE-27/1-2.44	VF-60, VC-60
					CVE-27/7-8.44	VF-60, VT-60
					CVE-27/10.44	As previously
63(N)					CVE-108/1945	
66	1. 1.45	6. 7.45				

Escort Carrier Squadrons

Sqn	Formed	Disbanded	Originally Formed	Reclassified	Known Operations Carrier/Date	Notes
1(A)	1. 3.43	1. 4.44	5. 4.41 as VS-201 1. 4.42 as VGS-1		CVE-1/7.41 CVE-11/7-9.43 CVE-77/4.45	This sqn was commissioned twice as VC-1
1(B)	1. 8.45	17. 9.45	15.12.43 as VOF-1 18.12.44 as VOC-1		CVE-65/1-4.45 CVE-77/4-7.45	Carrier service as VOC-1
2(A)	1. 3.43	15. 9.43		15. 9.43 as VC-25		This sqn was commissioned twice as VC-2
2(B)	20. 8.45	13. 9.45	1. 3.44 as VOF-2 13.12.44 as VOC-2		CVE-70/3-8.45	Carrier service as VOC-2
3	26. 8.43	28.10.45			CVE-27/4-5.44 CVE-57/7-8.44 CVE-68/4-10.44 CVE-78/8-9.45	
4	2. 9.43	16.10.45			CVE-70/3.44 CVE-66/6-10.44	
5	16. 9.43	1.10.45			CVE-71/5-11.44	
6	1. 9.43	5.10.45	1. 1.43 as VGS-25 1. 3.43 as VC-25		CVE-21/2-3.44 CVE-64/8-10.44	
7	1. 9.43	1.10.45	24. 2.43 as VGS-31 1. 3.43 as VC-31		CVE-61/1-7.44	
8	9. 9.43	9.10.45			CVE-59/12.43 CVE-60/5-6.44 CVE-70/2-3.45 CVE-74/4-9.45	
9	1. 3.43	19. 9.45	6. 8.42 as VGS-9		CVE-9/3-7.43 CVE-11/9-11.43 CVE-67/3-6.44 CVE-62/3-7.45	
10	23. 9.43	25.10.45			CVE-73/3-10.44 CVE-70/8-9.45	
11(A)	1. 3.43	16. 5.43	5. 8.42 as VGS-11	16. 5.43 as VF-21		This sqn was commissioned twice as VC-11
11(B)	30. 9.43	10.10.45			CVE-74/6.44-2.45	
12(A)	1. 3.43	16. 5.43	28. 5.42 as VGS-12	16. 5.43 as VT-21	CVE-12/11.42	This sqn was commissioned twice as VC-12
12(B)	6.10.43	7. 6.45			CVE-69/3.44 CVE-11/7.44 CVE-13/4-5.45	
13	1. 3.43	24. 9.45	5. 8.42 as VGS-13		CVE-13/6-11.43 CVE-64/3.44 CVE-57/3-8.45	
14	12.10.43	1.10.45			CVE-75/5-12.44	
15	18.10.43	14. 6.45			CVE-72/3.44	
16	1. 3.43	15.11.45	8. 8.42 as VGS-16	15.11.45 as VF-33	CVE-23/7.43 CVE-23/3.44	
17	1. 5.43	15. 9.43		15. 9.43 as VC-31		
18	1. 3.43	15. 8.43	15.10.42 as VGS-18	15. 8.43 as VF-36	CVE-16/7.43	
19	1. 3.43	14. 6.45	1. 1.43 as VGS-23		CVE-25/7.43 CVE-9/9-12.43 CVE-9/2-4.44 CVE-9/4-5.45	
20(A)	1. 3.43	15. 6.43	6. 8.42 as VGS-20		CVE-76/8.44-2.45	This sqn was commissioned twice as VC-20
20(B)	24.10.43	1.10.45				
21(A)	1. 3.43	16. 6.43	15.10.42 as VGS-21			This sqn was commissioned twice as VC-21
21(B)	30.10.43	15. 9.45			CVE-16/4.43 CVE-77/8.44-2.45	
22	1. 3.43	15.12.43	16.11.42 as VS-22	15.12.43 as VT-22		
23	1. 3.43	15.11.43	16.11.42 as VS-23	15.11.43 as VT-23		
24	1. 3.43	15.12.43	31.12.42 as VS-24	15.12.43 as VB-98		
25(A)	15. 9.43	15.12.43	15. 2.43 as VS-25	15.12.43 as VT-25	CVE-28/3-4.45	Operated on CVE-28 as VT-25
25(B)	1. 3.43	1. 9.43	1. 3.43 as VC-2		CVE-21/7.43	
26	1. 3.43	15.11.43	5. 5.42 as VGS-26	15.11.43 as VT-26	CVE-26/11.42 CVE-26/11-12.43 CVE-29/10.44	

Sqn	Formed	Disbanded	Originally Formed	Reclassified	Known Operations Carrier/Date	Notes
27	5.11.43	11. 9.45			CVE-27/11.42 CVE-27/12.42 CVE-27/11.43 CVE-78/8.44-2.45	
28	1. 3.43	20. 1.44	4. 5.42 as VGS-28	20. 1.44 as VT-28	CVE-27/11.42 CVE-28/11.43	
29	1. 3.43	15.12.43	20. 7.42 as VGS-29	15.12.43 as VT-29	CVE-29/6-8.43	
30	1. 4.43	15.12.43		15.12.43 as VT-30		
31(A)	1. 3.43	1. 9.43	24. 2.43 as VGS-31	1. 9.45 as VC-7	CVE-61/7.43	
31(B)	15. 9.43	1.11.43	1. 5.43 as VC-17	1.11.43 as VT-31		
32	1. 6.43	1.11.43		1.11.43 as VT-32		
33	1. 3.43	16.11.45	22. 1.43 as VGS-33		CVE-57/7.43 CVE-57/11-12.43 CVE-57/1-2.44 CVE-26/3-4.45 CVE-83/7-8.45	
34	1. 3.43	15. 8.43	24. 2.43 as VGS-34	15. 8.43 as VF-34	CVE-20/7.43 CVE-20/3.44	On board as VC-34 On board as VF-34
35	1. 3.43	10. 3.44	28. 1.43 as VGS-35	10. 3.43 as VT-35	CVE-28/1-2.44 CVE-28/7-8.44	
36	1. 3.43	30. 7.45	21. 2.43 as VGS-36		CVE-60/7.43 CVE-59/9-10.44	
37	1. 3.43	10. 3.44	22. 1.43 as VGS-37	10. 3.44 as VT-37	CVE-26/1-2.44 CVE-26/7-8.44 CVE-26/10.44	
38	16. 1.42	11. 5.44		11. 5.44 as VT-38		
39	1. 4.43	15.12.43			CVE-56/7-11.43	
40	15. 6.43	1. 6.44		1.6.44 as VT-40		
41	5. 5.43	16.11.45			CVE-58/7.43 CVE-58/3.44 CVE-58/7-8.44	
42	15. 4.43	5. 7.45			CVE-63/7.43 CVE-25/4-5.44 CVE-9/8-9.44 CVE-84/11.44 CVE-58/1-5.45	
43	1. 8.43	8.11.43				
44					CVE-58/11.43-2.44	
50	10. 8.43	8.11.43		8.11.43 as VT-50		
51	22. 9.43	8.11.43		8.11.43 as VT-51		
52	1. 9.43	8.11.43				
55	1. 3.43	21. 6.45	16. 1.43 as VGS-55		CVE-62/7.43 CVE-11/11.43-1.44 CVE-21/5.44 CVE-21/3-4.45	
58	1. 3.43	8. 6.45	24. 2.43 as VGS-58		CVE-59/7.43 CVE-21/12.43-2.44 CVE-21/12.43-2.44 CVE-21/4-5.44 CVE-60/3-4.44	
60	1. 3.43	10. 3.44	24. 2.43 as VGS-60		CVE-65/6-8.44	
63	20. 5.43	23.10.43			CVE-65/7.43 CVE-62/1-2.44 CVE-71/5-9.45	
64	1. 6.43	15. 8.43		15. 8.43 as VF-39	CVE-31/7.43	
65	10. 6.43	8.10.45			CVE-67/7.43 CVE-63/3-10.44	
66	21. 6.43	12.10.45			CVE-64/7.43 CVE-16/1-3.44 CVE-18/3-4.44 9-11.45 CVE-57/8-9.45	
68	1. 7.43	1.10.45			CVE-66/7.43 CVE-66/3.44 CVE-70/6-8.44	

Sqn	Formed	Disbanded	Originally Formed	Reclassified	Known Operations Carrier/Date	Notes
69	1. 7.43	22. 6.45			CVE-69/7.43 CVE-9/5-7.44	
70	5. 8.44	6.10.45			CVE-96/5-9.45	
71	20. 8.44	6.10.45			CVE-61/6-9.45	
72	1. 9.44	1.10.45			CVE-69/6-9.45	
75	11.11.43	21. 9.45			CVE-79/8.44-1.45	
76	17.11.43	11. 9.45			CVE-80/8.44-3.45	
77	23.11.43	17. 9.45			CVE-81/3-8.44	
78	29.11.43	21. 9.45			CVE-82/3.44-3.45	
79	6.12.43	11. 9.45			CVE-83/3.44-2.45	
80	16.12.43	11. 9.45			CVE-84/3.44 CVE-61/10.44 CVE-61/1.45	
81	22.12.43	20. 9.45			CVE-81/3.44 CVE-62/10.44 CVE-62/1-2.45 CVE-95/2.45	
82	28.12.43	18. 9.45			CVE-57/8.45 CVE-86/3.44 CVE-20/2-7.45	
83	3. 1.44	17. 9.45			CVE-87/3.44 CVE-58/11-12.44 CVE-83/3-7.45	
84	6. 1.44	17. 9.45			CVE-88/3.44 CVE-93/11.44-4.45	
85	12. 1.44	15. 9.45			CVE-89/3.44 CVE-94/11.44-4.45	
86	18. 1.44	7. 6.45			CVE-90/3.44 CVE-95/1-2.45	
87	24. 1.44	12. 6.45			CVE-91/3.44 CVE-96/11.44-2.45 CVE-77/2-4.45	
88	29. 1.44	3. 7.45			CVE-92/3.44 CVE-75/12.44-2.45 CVE-82/3-5.45	
89	3. 1.44	1. 4.44				
90	3. 2.44	18. 9.45			CVE-93/3.44 CVE-87/12.44-5.45 CVE-80/5-7.45	
91	11. 2.44	22. 9.45			CVE-94/3.44 CVE-71/11.44-2.45 CVE-78/2-5.45 CVE-93/6.45	
92	17. 2.44	18. 9.45			CVE-95/3.44 CVE-72/12.44-7.45	
93	23. 2.44	11. 8.45			CVE-96/3.44 CVE-101/10.44 CVE-80/3-4.45	
94	29. 2.44	27. 7.45			CVE-97/3.44 CVE-84/3-5.45	
95	1. 2.44	28. 6.45			CVE-25/6.44 CVE-59/3-4.45	
96	1. 3.44	28. 7.45			CVE-98/3.44 CVE-81/3-7.45 CVE-84/5.45	
97	8. 3.44	24. 7.45			CVE-99/3.44 CVE-91/2-5.45 CVE-85/5-7.45	
98	15. 3.44	11.10.45			CVE-100/3.44 CVE-94/6-9.45	
99	22.3.44	30.10.45			CVE-101/3.44 CVE-75/4-9.45	

Ship Names Index

Name printed in *italics* are those under which the ships concerned operated during their service in the US Navy. All other names appear in standard type. The names of those ships which were loaned to the Royal Navy are preceded by 'HMS' or 'HMCS'. Names with an asterisk(*) indicate the names of the lead ships of a class.

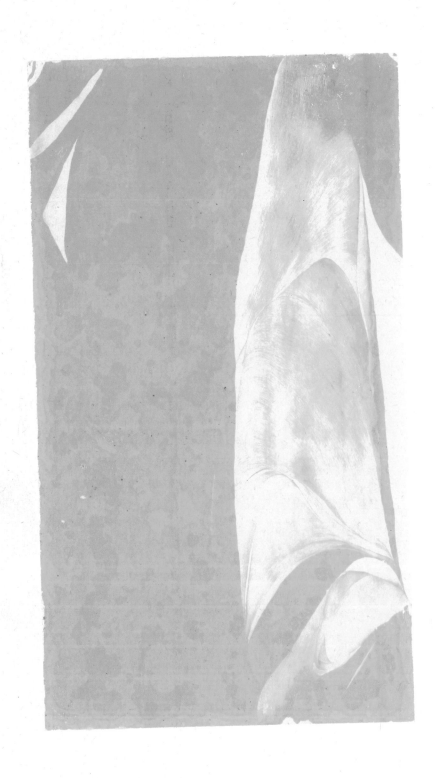